The Hitler Conspiracies

The Hitler Conspiracies

RICHARD J. EVANS

OXFORD
UNIVERSITY PRESS

OXFORD
UNIVERSITY PRESS

Oxford University Press is a department of the University of Oxford.
It furthers the University's objective of excellence in research, scholarship,
and education by publishing worldwide. Oxford is a registered trade mark of
Oxford University Press in the UK and certain other countries.

Published in the United States of America by Oxford University Press
198 Madison Avenue, New York, NY 10016, United States of America.

Library of Congress Control Number: 2020941402

ISBN 978-0-19-008305-2

1 3 5 7 9 10 8 6 4 2

Printed by Sheridan Books, United States of America

Contents

For the 'Conspiracy and Democracy' Team

Introduction

The idea that nothing happens by chance in history, that nothing is quite what it seems to be at first sight, that everything that occurs is the result of the secret machinations of malign groups of people manipulating everything from behind the scenes, is as old as history itself. But conspiracy theories seem to many to be growing more popular and more widespread in the twenty-first century, powered by the rise of the Internet and social media, enabled by the declining influence of traditional gatekeepers of opinion such as newspaper editors and book publishers, and encouraged by the spread of the uncertainty about truth and falsehood encapsulated in the perverse concept of 'alternative facts'.[1]

Many years ago, the American liberal intellectual Richard Hofstadter drew attention to conspiracy theories in his celebrated article 'The Paranoid Style in American Politics', first published in *Harper's Magazine* in its November issue for 1964. Hofstadter was clear that he was not calling conspiracy theorists clinically deranged. Rather, he wrote: 'I call it the paranoid style simply because no other word adequately evokes the sense of heated exaggeration, suspiciousness, and conspiratorial fantasy that I have in mind.' It was, of course, he noted, nothing new: it could be traced back to writing about groups such as the Freemasons or the Illuminati in the eighteenth century. But it had re-emerged in the twentieth, in particular in the form of McCarthyism after the Second World War. Senator McCarthy's warped vision of clandestine Communists in every corner of American society was a classic example of the paranoid style, envisioning a malign, concealed enemy manipulating events in order to undermine the social and political order. Hofstadter continued:

Unlike the rest of us, the enemy is not caught in the toils of the vast mechanism of history, himself a victim of his past, his desires, his limitations. He wills, indeed he manufactures, the mechanism of history, or tries to deflect the normal course of history in an evil way. He makes crises, starts runs on banks, causes depressions, manufactures disasters, and then enjoys and profits from the misery he has produced. The paranoid's interpretation of history is distinctly personal: decisive events are not taken as part of the stream of history, but as the consequences of someone's will.

Paranoid writing displayed, he noted, a surprisingly high level of pedantry and pseudo-scholarship. 'One of the impressive things about paranoid literature,' he wrote, 'is the contrast between its fantasied conclusions and the almost touching concern with factuality it invariably shows. It produces heroic strivings for evidence to prove that the unbelievable is the only thing that can be believed.'

Since Hofstadter wrote, and particularly since the turn of the century, the assumption on which his essay was based – that public discourse in general and political rhetoric in particular rested on a shared set of liberal values embodying rationality and rejecting the idea that hidden forces lay behind every major political event – has come to seem to many commentators to have been overtaken by events. As Joseph Uscinski, a leading contemporary scholar in the field, has observed, conspiracy theories

have become a marker of the early twenty-first century. Conspiracy theories have dominated elite discourse in many parts of the world and have become the rallying cry of major political movements . . . The Internet, once touted as an instrument of democracy, has been used to manipulate the masses – for profit or power – with fake news consisting mainly of conspiracy theories constructed out of whole cloth . . . Our culture is awash in conspiracy theories.[2]

Nowhere has the spread of conspiracy theories and 'alternative facts' become more obvious than in revisionist accounts of the history of the Third Reich. Long-discredited conspiracy theories have taken on a new lease of life, given credence by claims of freshly discovered evidence and novel angles of investigation. At the centre of this world of conspiracy theories lies the figure of Adolf Hitler. 'Anyone who loves a good conspiracy theory will have heard a shed load about Hitler,' as a student journalist recently noted.[3] Hitler, indeed, is rarely absent from online discussions about almost anything. Already in 1990 the American writer Mike Godwin propounded what has become known as 'Godwin's Law', namely that the longer an Internet discussion goes on, the more likely it is to mention Hitler, at which point it usually though not always comes to an end. By 2012 the term had even entered into the sacred linguistic halls of the *Oxford English Dictionary*. Comparisons with Hitler are everywhere, especially of course in the world of politics, where it is almost *de rigueur* to compare anybody of whom one disapproves to the Nazi dictator, from Donald Trump downwards. Why Hitler? As Alec Ryrie has written in his history of atheism and agnosticism:

> The most potent moral figure in Western culture is Adolf Hitler. It is as monstrous to praise him as it would once have been to disparage Jesus. He has become the fixed reference point by which we define evil . . . Nazism, almost alone in our relativistic culture, is an absolute standard: a point where argument ends, because whether it is good or evil is not up for debate . . . Nazism has crossed the barrier separating historical events from timeless truths.[4]

A key aspect of conspiracy theories is often said to be a strong tendency to divide the world into good and evil, and who could be more evil than Hitler?

But these considerations need a certain amount of qualification. In practice, the beliefs described by Ryrie are not quite universal. There are some who, in spite of everything that is known about the Nazi leader, retain a strong admiration for him, and such people are more than likely to support conspiracy theories, including Holocaust denial (which involves believing that the 'truth' about the Holocaust – that it did not happen – has been systematically suppressed by the world's academics and journalists since the 1940s, as the result of a global conspiracy of Jewish elites). Other conspiracists, as we shall see, from those who believe that the world has been, and continues to be, visited by aliens from outer space, to those who believe that human history has been governed by occult, supernatural forces, sometimes look to the involvement of Hitler in their theories to lend them interest for non-believers, or to bolster their claims by associating them with this most notorious of historical figures. The sharp opposition between good and evil that some have posited as characteristic of conspiracy theories often turns out to be more complex and more ambivalent than first appears.

Conspiracy theories, as these examples begin to suggest, are not all the same. Students of the genre have divided them into different types. There are two principal variants. First, there is the *systemic conspiracy theory*, in which a single conspiratorial entity carries out a wide variety of activities with the aim of taking control of a country, a region, or even the whole world. Often, according to the theory, the conspiracy is hatched over a long period of time, even centuries, and spreads over a very wide geographical area, in some instances virtually the entire globe, propagated and perpetuated by some kind of universal organization like the Illuminati, the Freemasons or the Communists, or a racial or religious group such as the Jews. Then there is the *event conspiracy theory*, in which a secret organized group stands behind a single event such as the assassination of US President John F. Kennedy, or the faked landing of humans on the moon. The conspiracies imagined in this case are usually short-term, plotted over just a few weeks or months or, at the most, a couple of years. The two types of conspiracy may, in the minds of some conspiracists, be linked – that is, an *event conspiracy* may be thought of as one expression of a *systemic conspiracy* – but this is not necessarily the case.[5] What is important is the fact that both types of conspiracy theory imagine a hidden hand behind historical (and, in many cases, current) events. Common to both is also the idea that what conspiracy theorists describe as the 'official' or, in other words, generally accepted version of a process, or event, or series of events, is false. Indeed, the very use of the term 'official' implies that state governments or powerful elites have coerced, or misled, historians, academics, journalists and others into telling stories designed to conceal the truth in the interests of maintaining the status quo and keeping them in power. This in turn provides an assurance to conspiracy theorists that they alone are privy to the real truth.

Real conspiracies exist, of course, and not every conspiracy theory is wrong. The obvious example is Watergate, in which US President Richard M. Nixon, the Republican candidate in the Presidential elections of 1972, organized the burglary of the rival Democratic Party's campaign headquarters at the Watergate hotel in Washington, DC, with the aim of planting concealed wiretapping devices. There have been numerous other genuine conspiracies over the centuries. What they all have in common is, first, the fact that they involve a very small number of people. Since a conspiracy has perforce to be carried out in secret, if it is not to be discovered and stopped by those at whom it is aimed, it follows that the more people there are involved, the greater is the danger that the conspiracy will be betrayed and come to naught. Second, they are all to a greater or lesser extent time-limited. That is because they have a specific object in mind, and come to an end when they achieve it, or (in most cases) before they get that far, when they are uncovered. At the same time, not everything that has been called a conspiracy theory has actually involved allegations of a plot. A conspiracy theory is not the same as an example of 'fake news', the distortion or manipulation of the truth, or the positing of 'alternative facts' to explain, deny, or explain away, an event of some kind. A genuine conspiracy theory must posit a group of people plotting in secret to undertake an illicit action. The group has to intend a certain outcome to its actions, a view corresponding to the central belief of conspiracy theorists that no major event in history happens by chance, is the product of coincidence, or is undertaken by a lone, maverick individual.

In Nazi Germany, the vast state-run propaganda apparatus controlled by Joseph Goebbels pumped out huge quantities of 'fake news' – or, in other words, lies – and Hitler consistently tried to mislead people both inside and outside Germany about his real purposes, assuring Britain, France and other European countries of his peaceful intentions even as he rearmed and carried out acts of international aggression. But little of this propaganda output involved conspiracy theories; nor did Hitler's and Goebbels's concealment of the truth about what they were doing amount to a conspiracy. Unlike Stalin, who saw conspiracies all round him, and launched a long series of purges and show trials against many of his subordinates based on fantastic allegations of plotting against the Soviet regime, Hitler himself was not much of a conspiracy theorist. While Stalin had fought his way to the top of the Soviet hierarchy against rivals who were, initially at least, better known and better liked than he was, and so felt in the end he had to eliminate any possibility of their turning against him, Hitler was carried to the top by his immediate underlings almost from the very beginning and so remained loyal to them almost to the very end. True, in the 'Night of the Long Knives' in 1934, he ordered the murder of the stormtrooper leadership and a number of conservative politicians against whom he had a grudge, but their opposition had been public, not carried on behind the scenes. Hitler's own actions, prepared in secret and executed without prior warning, bore many of the hallmarks of a conspiracy, but his allegation of an attempted putsch by Ernst Röhm and the advocates of a 'second revolution' following the Nazi seizure of power the year before was some distance away from embodying a conspiracy theory, for everything Röhm said and did, he said and did openly.

There was of course a real conspiracy to overthrow Hitler, prepared in secret by a group of army officers and their associates during the war and culminating in the failed attempt to kill him with the bomb planted by Claus von Stauffenberg on 20 July 1944. Through a series of chances, Hitler survived; the plotters committed suicide, were shot, or were arrested, put on trial and executed. In his radio address after the failure of the bomb plot, Hitler ascribed the attempt on his life to 'a really small clique of ambitious, conscienceless and at the same time criminally stupid officers'. The police investigation that followed took as its starting point this assumption that only a very few people were involved. It was, in other words, a classic, tightly organized conspiracy. The participants were exclusively military men. Their aims were reactionary through and through. But while the Nazis continued to adhere to this line, repeated it endlessly in their public pronouncements on the plot, and insisted on it in their selection of participants to stand trial, the inquiries undertaken behind closed doors by the Gestapo revealed a much larger number of people to have been involved to one degree or another. They included civilians as well as military, and politicians from the left and centre as well as from the conservative right. Rather than viewing the plot as a classic conspiracy, it makes more sense to see it in terms of a set of overlapping networks, some more central than others.

There is no doubt that Stauffenberg and the fellow-officers who actually prepared and attempted to carry out both the assassination attempt and the planned military putsch stood at the very centre of these networks. But there were many more individuals who occupied a variety of positions further away from it, for example the men whom the plotters envisaged forming a civilian government after Hitler had been killed. Diplomats, lawyers, industrialists, landowners, trade unionists, Social Democrats, theologians, higher civil servants and many others were involved in one way or another. In the end, of course, only the military men who plotted and executed the planned assassination were in a position to carry it out, but to see it exclusively as a military operation would be to underestimate its breadth and depth. What united the plotters, however, was the fact that almost all of them were above suspicion; they could only succeed because they were not under close surveillance by the Gestapo as real or potential opponents of the regime – and even so, the conspiracy had become so large by the time the bomb was planted in Hitler's headquarters that several of its members had already been arrested and the Gestapo was closing the net on many others.[6] There were other clandestine opposition movements, for example the 'Red Orchestra' Soviet spy network, but these were not really conspiracies in the classic sense, since they were not working towards a single, definable object. The 1944 bomb plot remained more or less unique, a very rare instance of Hitler actually accusing people of being involved in a conspiracy against him.

Still, conspiracies, real or imagined, were not entirely alien to the world of the Nazis. Historians have identified some they think influenced Hitler, some they think he masterminded, and some he actively engaged in himself. This book is not about real conspiracies, however.[7] It is about how the paranoid imagination is related to Hitler and the Nazis. It examines five different alleged conspiracies, each of which has hitherto been treated in isolation, both by serious historians and by conspiracy theorists of one kind and another. By viewing them all through the same lens of recent, general work on conspiracy theory, it is possible to see them in a different light, and reveal some perhaps surprising things they have in common. The first of them is the notorious antisemitic forgery *The Protocols of the Elders of Zion*: where did this tract originate, why was it so widely distributed, and was it really a 'warrant for genocide', providing the impulse that drove Hitler to launch the Holocaust? Does it provide a classic example of the dangers of conspiracy theories if they are left to proliferate and spread across the world? What kind of conspiracy theory does it embody? At first sight, the *Protocols* appear to fit neatly into the category of *systemic conspiracy theories* and, certainly, the document's contents were vague and generalized in the extreme. The *Protocols* are often seen as the most important conspiracist text of antisemitism, raising the question of how far antisemitism itself is a conspiracy theory. Beyond this, the *Protocols* point to a further, often overlooked issue: to what extent, and in what way, antisemitism was, and is, different from other kinds of racism. Viewing them in the light of current debates on conspiracy theories can provide some unexpected answers to these questions.

The second chapter examines the stab-in-the-back legend, according to which Germany's defeat in the First World War was the outcome of a plot to undermine the German armed forces through preparing and carrying out a revolution on the home front. Unlike the *Protocols*, this can be understood as an *event conspiracy theory*, though it is still relatively vague and generalized in some crucial respects. Three levels exist. First, there was the very general claim that Germany lost the war because of an increasingly desperate supply situation, leading to shortages of munitions for the battlefront and of food and domestic necessities for the home front. This caused in turn a crisis in the will to fight, expressed in growing support for the idea of a compromise peace. A collapse in morale at home stabbed the armed forces in the back and made it impossible for them to continue the struggle against a better-resourced enemy. Second, there was the more specific allegation that socialists undermined the troops' morale by fomenting discontent at home and then in the armed forces themselves, in order to bring about the democratic revolution which overthrew the Kaiser on 9 November 1918 and thereby ended what could have been a real possibility of Germany carrying on fighting. Third, and finally, on the ultra right of the political spectrum, socialism and revolution were both seen as expressions of Jewish subversion, raising both the question of how far Hitler and the Nazi Party, on their way to power in the aftermath of the war's end, used the stab-in-the-back legend as a propaganda weapon and, more broadly, how far the legend was a factor in bringing millions of Germans to vote for the Nazis in the final years of the Weimar Republic. Disturbingly, the stab-in-the-back legend, at least in its milder forms, has undergone something of a revival recently, and this chapter asks whether the new claims about Germany's defeat in November 1918 stand up to closer examination.

The third chapter revisits the burning down of the Reichstag, the German national parliament, on 27/8 February 1933, a few weeks after Hitler's appointment as Reich Chancellor. The arson provided the pretext for the Hitler government's suspension of civil liberties, marking the first, crucial step towards the creation of the Nazi dictatorship. The Nazi leader's own claim that it was committed by the Communists as the first stage in a planned *coup d'état* was easily discredited; here was a conspiracy theory that even the Third Reich's own judges were unable to confirm. It was clear, however, who benefited from the fire. The Communists were quick to claim on their side that it had been deliberately planned in advance and carried out by the Nazis themselves as a 'false flag' operation, a pretext for introducing the quasi-legal basis of a dictatorship, legitimating the arrest of thousands of Communists and their imprisonment in the newly founded concentration camps. Here, therefore, was an event that formed the subject of two diametrically opposed conspiracy theories. Unlike the Nazis' own theory, the Communist version has been put forward again many times, despite detailed evidence presented since the 1960s showing that the fire was the work of a single arsonist, the young Dutchman Marinus van der Lubbe. In recent years, indeed, this *event conspiracy theory* has been revived yet again. How plausible are these new arguments, and is there any convincing new evidence to support the theory? And how well do they stand up to critical assessment when viewed in the wider context of our understanding of conspiracy theories and how they work?

Debates have also swirled around the sudden, unheralded flight of the deputy leader of the Nazi Party, Rudolf Hess, to Scotland on 10 May 1941. The large literature about this topic, much of it recent, has put forward a variety of theories and led to many historians regarding Hess's flight as an unsolved mystery. Was Hess the bearer of an offer by Hitler for a separate peace, was he encouraged by a significant group of British politicians to make it, and was there another conspiracy by Churchill and the war party in Whitehall to reject it and suppress the truth about the flight? Or was there a conspiracy hatched by the British security and intelligence services to lure Hess to Britain and, if so, what was its aim? Many years later, in 1987, when Hess was found dead in his prison cell at Spandau, was this the final outcome of the British conspiracy to suppress the inconvenient truths that the former leading Nazi was about to reveal? This was clearly another *event conspiracy theory*, but how convincing is the evidence adduced to back it up?

Finally, the book asks why the persistent rumours of Hitler's escape from the bunker in Berlin in 1945, to live out his days in Argentina, have become more widespread in the media over the last few years. Where did they originate, are they in any way convincing, and why have they refused to die in the face of repeated attempts to discredit them? Along with many of the other fantasies discussed in the following chapters, the claim that Hitler was still alive in the 1950s and even later has recently undergone a revival in the media. Of all the *event conspiracy theories* examined in this book, this is undoubtedly the wildest and most fantastical: its transformations in the age of the Internet and social media have a great deal to tell us about how conspiracy theories work and, in particular, what kinds of people propagate them and believe in them.

This is a book about fantasies and fictions, fabrications and falsifications. The conscious exploitation of myths and lies for a political purpose is not merely the creation of the twenty-first century. Some of those who have espoused conspiracy theories about Hitler, or the Jews, or the Nazi Party have clearly believed what they were saying. Others have equally clearly manipulated stories they have known to be false. On occasion, they have cynically distorted the facts or invented complete lies for political purposes. Sometimes they have merely fostered sensational claims in order to line their own pockets. In some cases, they have said that it doesn't matter in the end whether their actual claims are true or false; what matters is that, even if, like the *Protocols*, they are clearly based on forged or falsified evidence, they reveal an underlying truth and so are true in some broader sense than the merely empirical. A claim such as this raises profound questions about the nature of truth itself, laying down a challenge that people who believe in the careful and impartial elucidation of the evidence in order to arrive at tenable and sustainable conclusions have often been slow to meet. This is a history book, but it is a history book for the age of 'post-truth' and 'alternative facts', a book for our own troubled times.

Protokolle
der Weisen von
Zion
die grösste
Fälschung des
Jahrhunderts!

I

Were the *Protocols* a 'warrant for genocide'?

I

The Protocols of the Elders of Zion, a short tract that first made its appearance in the early twentieth century, is perhaps one of the most notorious publications of all time. It remains 'to this day', according to Michael Butter, a leading student of conspiracy theories, 'the most important text on the Jewish world conspiracy' because it 'helped create an atmosphere in which it came in the end to the genocide of the European Jews'.[1] In his classic work on the origins and influence of the tract, Norman Cohn argued that it had provided the ostensible justification for the Nazi extermination of the Jews: to quote the title of Cohn's book, it was a 'Warrant for Genocide'. In Cohn's view, the document was 'the supreme expression and vehicle of the myth of the Jewish world-conspiracy'. It 'took possession of Hitler's mind and became the ideology of his most fanatical followers at home and abroad – and so helped to prepare the way for the near-extermination of European Jews'.[2] In similar fashion, a more recent study of the *Protocols*, by Alex Grobman, is entitled *License to Murder*.[3] A leading historian of antisemitism, Robert Wistrich, also identified a direct line of causality from the *Protocols* to the Holocaust. The tract's importance was also affirmed by the philosopher Hannah Arendt. In her influential book *The Origins of Totalitarianism*, published in 1951, Arendt described the *Protocols* as the central text of Nazism, and said the Nazis used them as a 'textbook'.[4] This view goes back even to Hitler's own day, when Alexander Stein, a Menshevik of Baltic-German origin, described the *Protocols* as 'the Bible of National Socialism' in a book entitled *Adolf Hitler – Pupil of* the 'Wise Men of Zion'.[5] Hitler, the German-Jewish historian Walter Laqueur asserted, realized the enormous propagandist potential of the basic ideas of the *Protocols*. He refers to them in *Mein Kampf*; 'much of what he says in his *magnum opus* is based on this book.'[6] 'The *Protocols*,' another historian has asserted, '. . . became a key element in Hitler's conspiratorial thinking.'[7] Klaus Fischer has put this view forward in detail in his textbook *Nazi Germany: A New History*. Hitler, he argues,

> believed in the existence of a Jewish world conspiracy, as foretold in *The Protocols of the Elders of Zion*. In his lengthy survey of the secret machinations of the Jews over the ages, Hitler revealed that he passionately believed in a conspiratorial view of history according to which the Jews are the real causal forces behind events . . . Thus, every destructive event is unmasked by Hitler's paranoid mind as being plotted by a scheming Jew.[8]

As a consequence, Fischer adds, Hitler thought he was carrying out a deed of world-historical importance in launching the extermination of Europe's Jews during the Second World War. By this time, the *Protocols* had become, according to the social psychologist Jovan Byford, 'the cornerstone of Nazi propaganda'.[9] The *Protocols* were widely considered a document of such significance that the writer Umberto Eco devoted his second-last novel, *The Prague Cemetery*, to a fictionalized account of their origin and composition: the penultimate chapter is entitled 'The Final Solution', echoing the Nazi euphemism of 'the final solution of the Jewish problem in Europe' to denote the Holocaust.[10] The historian Wolfgang Wippermann, in a study of conspiracy theories published in 2007, has described the *Protocols* as 'the best-known, and to the present day the most effective conspiracy theory', with an 'immense influence', whose 'enthusiastic readers' included among many others the Nazi leader, Adolf Hitler.[11] A literary scholar, Svetlana Boym, has claimed that the *Protocols* 'inspired and justified pogroms in Russia and the Ukraine and Nazi policies of extermination'.[12] Stephen Bronner has declared of the document that Hitler 'sought to implement its practical implications'.[13] It has even been claimed that 'Hitler used the *Protocols* as a manual in his war to exterminate the Jews.'[14]

Given this widespread view that the *Protocols* constituted the most influential of all statements of the theory that Jews were engaged in a worldwide conspiracy to overthrow society and its institutions, a theory leading directly to the Holocaust, not least through its influence on Adolf Hitler, it is not surprising that a great deal of research has been carried out on them by historians and textual scholars. In addition, we now have far more complete documentation of Hitler's views than was available when Cohn was writing, both directly, through editions of Hitler's works, and indirectly, through new publications such as the Goebbels diaries. All of this raises the question of whether Hitler was indeed a follower of the *Protocols*. Are they really the most dangerous and influential of all conspiracy theories? To answer these questions requires us to go back to the beginning and examine the actual contents of the *Protocols* themselves. Who put them together, how, and for what purpose? The answers to these questions turn out in many respects to be rather surprising.

II

The document known generally as *The Protocols of the Elders of Zion* actually bears the heading 'From the Reports of the "Wise Men of Zion" on the Meetings held at the First Zionist Congress held in Basel in 1897' – 'protocols' here, essentially means 'minutes'. The Congress was a real event but, the document implies, it supposedly provided the occasion for some very secret meetings held behind the scenes. Zionism at this very early stage of its history was a tiny fledgling movement, barely familiar even to Jewish circles. Even in the 1920s it was still not widely known to the general public. Its aim was to encourage Jews to resettle in Palestine, at that time a fiefdom of the Ottoman Empire. To many readers, the 'First Zionist Congress' could easily be made to appear like a general assembly of the world Jewish community, though no such thing in fact existed.[15]

The 'minutes' record twenty-four sessions in all, summarized in a lengthy series of very short paragraphs. Everywhere, it begins, the evil outnumber the good, and force and money rule the world. 'We' – that is, the Jews – control the world's money and so we control the world. Might is right, and rule over the blind masses can only be exercised without moral restraint. Terror and deceit are our methods, and in order to grasp power we will destroy the privileges of the nobility and replace them with the rule of our own bankers and intellectuals. Our control over the press will enable us to undermine the beliefs that ensure social stability; indeed, we have already succeeded in propagating the pernicious doctrines of Marx, Darwin and Nietzsche. In a similar manner, our newspapers and pamphlets divide society by sowing discord, undermining confidence in the government by enrolling the masses in subversive movements such as anarchism, communism and socialism. At the same time, by fomenting a damaging economic struggle of all against all in the free market, we are leading the Gentiles' attention away from the real masters of the economy, namely ourselves. We will exert our influence to destroy industry by creating our own monopolies, by encouraging overspending and unwise speculation, and by causing inflation. We will create an arms race and bring about destructive wars. In the end, the Gentiles will be impoverished and ripe for takeover.[16]

Universal suffrage will bring the masses to power, the supposed minutes continue, and we, the Jews, control the masses. 'The Gentiles are a flock of sheep, and we Jews are the wolves.' We have undermined the moral order by spreading immoral publications. We shall rise up in revolution all over the world at the appointed hour, and pitilessly execute all who stand in our way. Once we have attained power, we will censor the press and publishers so strictly that no criticism will be possible. The people's awareness of the realities of the situation will be dulled by mass sports, entertainments and the provision of brothels. We will not allow any religion except Judaism. All non-Jewish Freemasons will be executed, and Jewish lodges will spread across the globe. Old judges will be replaced by younger ones who are willing to bend to the rule of the stronger. The teaching of law, political science, all humanistic disciplines will be removed from the universities. 'We shall remove from humanity's memories all the facts of history that we find uncomfortable, and only leave those that cast a particularly unfavourable light on the errors of non-Jewish governments.' Education will concentrate on practical skills. Teachers will be forced to make propaganda for us. Lawyers will no longer be independent but will have to serve the interests of our state. The Pope will be replaced by a new Jewish king. Property taxes will be increased step by step. Speculation will be made impossible. Unemployment and alcoholism will vanish as modern, mass-production industry is curbed and small-scale artisan craft production reinstated.[17]

Rambling, chaotic and unstructured, the document is hardly an example of rabble-rousing antisemitic rhetoric. It is couched in abstract language, it is extremely repetitive, and it is full of contradictions, most notably perhaps in the constant reference in the subsection headings to Freemasonry, where often there is no mention of Freemasonry in the text. At some places there is talk of a general world revolution, at others the document proceeds on the assumption that the revolution will take place within a single state only. Among the text's eccentricities is a claim that the Jews will fill with explosives the underground railways being constructed beneath many of the world's major cities at the time and blow them all up if they should ever feel endangered.[18] The dystopia that it is alleged the Jews would create once they had achieved supreme power is in many ways an oddly positive one: who, for example, could object to a world with full employment or a world from which alcoholism had been banished?[19]

It is noticeable that many of the core ideas of antisemitic ideology are missing from the document. Among the traditional claims of religious antisemitism, the supposed Jewish conspirators do not say that the Jews have killed Christ, desecrated the Communion Host, poisoned wells or ritually murdered Christian boys.[20] Nor can we find in the document modern, racist antisemitic images; nowhere do the 'Elders of Zion' talk, for example, of Jewish racial characteristics such as the antisemitic author of the tract might have imagined them, rail against the supposed identifying marks of other races, or exhibit a desire to subvert the social order through racial intermixing (one of Hitler's most potent obsessions). As Stephen Bronner has noted, 'the document lacked the primitive biological and pseudoscientific foundations so admired by more modern bigots like Adolf Hitler'.[21] The context of the composition of the *Protocols* around the turn of the nineteenth and twentieth centuries is indicated rather by their obsession with the teachings of the universities, the irresponsibility of the press and the manipulations of the financial world.[22] Beyond this, their talk of an arms race, the reinstatement of domestic production, the advent of mass enfranchisement and political democracy, or the threat of anarchism, further point to their origin in the decade and a half before the outbreak of the First World War. There is also, obviously, no mention of the threat of Bolshevik subversion and revolution, whose identification as part of an imaginary Jewish world conspiracy became a central element in the rabid antisemitic fantasies of the years following the European revolutions of 1917–18. The document represented, in its strange amalgam of often bizarre ideas, and its numerous omissions, neither traditional nor modern antisemitism: it was very much *sui generis*.

A few general principles can be extracted from it, not without difficulty in some cases: (1) the idea that there was, and is, an organized group of Jewish 'Elders' conspiring on a global scale to bring about the systematic undermining of society and its replacement by a Jewish dictatorship; (2) that this is being achieved by the proliferation of divisive ideologies, namely liberalism, republicanism, socialism and anarchism; (3) that these organized Jews control the press and the economy and are using their power to impoverish society and undermine its core values; (4) that beneath the surface of everyday life, political institutions and economic structures as we perceive them lies a hidden, malignant power; (5) that what we think of as progressive and democratic, whether it is the extension of voting rights or the spread of liberal institutions, is in fact just another tactic by the Jewish world conspiracy to gain power over the non-Jewish world; (6) that wars are brought about not by the clash of aims and beliefs between different countries but, once more, by the machinations of the 'Elders of Zion'; (7) and finally, implicitly, that seemingly deep-rooted antagonisms, for example between socialists and capitalists, are also caused by a Jewish conspiracy that seeks to undermine non-Jewish society by dividing it against itself.[23] These principles, however, are neither exclusive to the *Protocols* nor originated by them; they already existed by the early twentieth century, and what the *Protocols* offered was an apparent confirmation of their accuracy from within the supposed conspiracy itself.

On the face of it, this is a text cast in the classic mould of conspiracy theories, promising to the reader who accepts it a revelation of truths hidden from the vast majority of people, including scientists, scholars, governments and politicians: it boosts the self-esteem of believers by sharing with them secrets that the world of 'official knowledge' and the millions deceived by it do not possess; and it provides a key to understanding seemingly incomprehensible, complex events and processes, from wars and revolutions to stock exchange crashes and economic crises, by bringing them all together through one grand, paranoid explanation: they can all be boiled down to the activities of a single, tightly organized set of malign individuals.[24] It is misleading, however, to portray the document as 'marking the dividing-line between medieval–early-modern anti-judaism and modern antisemitism', in which 'the focus lay now less on the Jews as religious enemies of Christians; they were seen, rather, through the lens of racial theory as a particular race of people with their own attributes'.[25] On the contrary, although they were undoubtedly used as 'evidence' of Jewish racial characteristics by antisemites after the First World War, they were not in fact themselves influenced at all by racial theory: evidence, perhaps, of how they were too often not read carefully but simply cited in support of beliefs which they did not themselves represent.

What gave the *Protocols* currency was above all their claim to provide authentic evidence of the Jewish world conspiracy emanating from an organizational centre of the international Jewish community itself. And yet, the *Protocols* were anything but authentic. A great deal of scholarly time and energy has gone over the years into tracing their origins. It is now clear that the idea of a subversive conspiracy to undermine the social and political order began in the wake of the French Revolution of 1789. Eight years after the Revolution, and five years after the Terror, a French Jesuit, the Abbé Barruel, in a sprawling, five-volume work on Jacobinism, ascribed the outbreak of the Revolution and the execution of Louis XVI to the machinations of Enlightenment thinkers and secret societies, especially the *philosophes*, the Bavarian Illuminati and the Freemasons, influenced by the older tradition of the Templars.[26] Of course, the Illuminati and the Freemasons, for all their ambitions to transform society, were far less influential than Barruel claimed, and the Templars had been definitively destroyed in the Middle Ages and not revived since. Barruel was driven to seek out culprits for the suppression of the Jesuit order by Enlightenment regimes in a number of countries in the late eighteenth century, and for the Revolution's secularization programme, its confiscation of Church lands and its destruction of churches. His work was paralleled by a similar tract by the Scottish mathematician John Robison, *Proofs of a Conspiracy against All the Religions and Governments of Europe, Carried on in the Secret Meetings of Freemasons, Illuminati and Reading Societies* (1797).[27]

Neither author mentioned the Jews, but on 20 August 1806 Barruel received a letter from a Piedmontese army officer called Giovanni Battista Simonini, who told him that in reality the Jews were behind all these plots and, granted civil equality by the Revolution in France, and by Napoleon in every land he conquered, were planning to take over the world. The conspiracy theory was given credence by Napoleon's convocation of an assembly of Jewish rabbis and scholars in France in 1806, with the aim of ensuring that the Jewish community was on his side. By calling it 'the Great Sanhedrin', the name of the Jewish supreme court in the ancient world, the emperor sparked in some of his arch-conservative opponents the idea that a Jewish pseudo-government had existed in secret down the centuries and was exercising a malign influence over human affairs in the present. Barruel, however, was only partially won over by these arguments, and right up to his death in 1820 remained convinced that the main blame for the outbreak of the Revolution lay with the Freemasons. The Jews might have exerted an influence on them, but the key to understanding the Revolution in his mind was the Freemasons' operation of an elaborate system of lodges and a parallel secret framework of interconnections which he considered that the Jews did not possess. Barruel decided, indeed, not to publish Simonini's letter, or anything deriving from it, since he feared it might provoke pogroms against the Jews, and it remained unpublished until 1878. After its publication it enjoyed a life of its own, however, and was reprinted in a variety of early-twentieth-century antisemitic tracts.[28]

Throughout the nineteenth century, a number of reactionary writers articulated antisemitic prejudices in their rejection of the proposal, which was advocated by liberal reformers across the Continent, that the religious minority of the Jews should be granted full and equal civil rights with the Christian population. For the proponents of a restoration of the pre-Revolutionary order, Europe and all its constituent states and nations had to be grounded on the principles of a renewed and watchful Christianity if disorder, war and the dissolution of society were to be avoided. It was all too easy for them to progress from arguing that the emancipation of the Jews, the only significant non-Christian community in most of Europe, would undermine the hegemony of these principles, to declaring that the Jews were engaged in a deliberate campaign to do so.

It was hardly surprising, therefore, that such theories emerged again in the wake of a fresh outbreak of revolutions that swept across the Continent in 1848–9, which a few ultra-conservative commentators, above all in Germany, ascribed yet again, though with no more justification than had been evident in the allegations of Simonini, to the machinations of the Freemasons. One of the principal acts of virtually all the mostly short-lived revolutionary governments in 1848–9, after all, was the emancipation of the Jews. Two decades after the outbreak of the revolution a novel appeared under the title *Biarritz*, casting these theories in the form of a conspiracy theory. The author featuring on the title page was 'Sir John Retcliffe', but, contrary to appearances, he was not an Englishman but a German, Hermann Goedsche, writing under a pseudonym. Author of a number of highly successful Romantic novels in the style of Sir Walter Scott, Goedsche had also been employed by the Prussian political police, working in the postal service forging letters incriminating German democrats, though he had been caught out and tried in 1849 and had to abandon this activity. Following this, he worked as a journalist for the arch-conservative *Kreuzzeitung* newspaper.

About forty pages of his novel describe a scene in a Prague cemetery, where once every century the representatives of the twelve tribes of Israel gather with a representative of the diaspora to plot the take-over of the world. Among their chosen means are driving the aristocracy into bankruptcy, provoking revolutions, taking over the stock exchanges, abolishing laws preventing profiteering, dominating the press, driving countries to war with each other, encouraging industry and impoverishing the workers, spreading free thought and undermining the Church, emancipating the Jews (who were still at the time denied full civil rights in many parts of Europe), and more besides. In a distorted and negatively interpreted form, Goedsche presented virtually the entire programme of mid-century German liberalism as the expression of a Jewish plot to destroy state and society.[29]

The cemetery scene, which owes a great deal to an episode in the novel *Joseph Balsamo* by Alexandre Dumas *père* in which the conspiracist Alessandro Cagliostro and his accomplices plot the discrediting of Queen Marie Antoinette in the 'affair of the diamond necklace', was a typical invention of Gothic fiction. Among other things, it describes how the thirteen representatives, clad in flowing white robes, approach a grave one by one and kneel down in front of it: as the last of the thirteen kneels, a blue flame suddenly appears and lights up the scene and a hollow voice is heard saying, 'I greet you, heads of the twelve tribes of Israel,' to which they all chant in reply, 'We greet you, son of the accursed.' There is further Gothic flummery of this sort. It is hard to imagine anyone taking it very seriously, let alone viewing it as a true description of real events.

But the passage took on a life of its own, quite separate from the rest of the novel. This bizarre transformation began in Russia, when it was printed as a pamphlet in 1872 with the remark that, while it was fiction, it was based on fact (a characteristic of many conspiracy theories, which frequently elide the distinction between fact and fiction, claiming that in the end it does not matter if the details of a narrative are false so long as they express the fundamental truth that lies beneath them). Other editions of the pamphlet appeared in Russia in the following years, and in 1881 the text was published in French, the speeches now merged into a single address, supposedly delivered in the cemetery by a chief rabbi; the source was given as a book by an English diplomat, 'Sir John Readclif'. *The Rabbi's Speech*, as it was known, was itself reprinted by antisemites in a number of languages, including Russian. In Germany it was publicized by the radical antisemitic propagandist Theodor Fritsch in his *Handbook of the Jewish Question* (1907). It became a standard component in the paranoid imagination of antisemites across Europe.[30]

Long before Fritsch produced his encyclopedia, the idea of a Jewish world conspiracy, inspired by Satan and propagated through the institutions of Freemasonry, had thus become a standard weapon in the armoury of French antisemitism, among others. In the 1870s and 1880s, following France's defeat by Prussia and the fall of Napoleon III, the new Third Republic had launched a determined attack on the privileges of the Roman Catholic Church, which was still largely monarchist in its sympathies. Freemasons, secular and republican (though, in very few cases, Jewish), were strong supporters of the new liberal political order, and clerical and arch-conservative writers launched a series of publications condemning the Republic as the creature of a conspiracy of Jews and Freemasons, just as, in their fevered imaginations, the Revolution of 1789 had been. Some, indeed, began to claim that there was a secret Jewish world government that was manipulating not only the French republicans but also governments and politicians across the entire world, through its control of international finance and the organs of the press. These claims found an outlet in the real political world in the fervently Catholic and ferociously antisemitic atmosphere of the Dreyfus affair during the 1890s, when the Jewish army officer Alfred Dreyfus was wrongly convicted of spying for the Germans.[31]

It was in Russia, however, that the ideas that went into the *Protocols* found their final synthesis. Russia's five million or so Jews were subject to numerous legal restrictions, including the obligation to live in an area on the western side of the Tsar's domains known as the Pale of Settlement. As a number of Jews, angered by these restrictions, joined the growing revolutionary movement, the supporters of the Tsarist autocracy and the Orthodox Church unleashed a swelling wave of extreme and violent antisemitism. It was in this atmosphere of mounting political tension that the *Protocols* came into the public domain. They were first published, though without the final section, in the autumn of 1903 in a newspaper edited by Pavel Aleksandrovich Krushevan, a noted antisemite who had recently organized a pogrom in Kishinev, in his native province of Bessarabia, in which forty-five Jews had been killed and over a thousand Jewish homes and shops destroyed.[32] In 1905 a revised version was published by Sergei Nilus, a minor landowner and former civil servant who blamed the Jews for the failure of his estate. A religious rather than a racist antisemite, obsessed with visions of the coming Apocalypse, Nilus procured a wider distribution for the document, improved the quality of the language and added material bringing the *Protocols* into a bogus relationship with the Basel Zionist Congress. Significant portions of the text took up features of *The Rabbi's Speech*, putting them into a new form and context.[33]

But these did not form the main part of the text. In presenting it to the public, Krushevan mentioned that the document was at least in part translated from the French, and indeed sections of it were extensively lifted from a tract published in 1864 by a French writer, Maurice Joly. This was anything but an antisemitic document. It was in fact an attack from the left on the manipulative and dictatorial regime of the Emperor Napoleon III, cast in the form of an imaginary dialogue between Montesquieu, who speaks in favour of liberalism, and Machiavelli, who expounds many of the cynical justifications for dictatorship that can be found in the *Protocols* and which Joly attributed to the Emperor Napoleon III. Not surprisingly, it is Machiavelli's arguments that mostly feature in the antisemitic tract, transmuted into justifications for the political aims and methods of the supposed Jewish world conspiracy.[34] It was most probably in 1902 that the *Protocols* were actually put together in southern Russia (the language used in early editions bears strong traces of Ukrainian). The unknown compiler assembled parts of *The Rabbi's Speech* and the satire by Joly (which made its way from France to Russia in the mid-1890s and was translated into Russian) with a concoction of the supposed decisions of the Zionist Congress in Basel to form the final text of the *Protocols*.[35] The hybrid origins of the tract were also revealed by their obsession with finance, especially the Gold Standard, in which they gave a distorted version of some of the policies that the Russian Finance Minister Sergei Yulyevich Witte was trying to introduce in order to modernize the Russian economy, bitterly opposed by conservative elements among the Russian elites.

In their final form, therefore, the *Protocols* were a hastily assembled mishmash of French, German and Russian sources, and their confused and chaotic nature bears witness to the slapdash and careless manner in with which they were composed.[36] Cohn's hypothesis that they already existed in full, in French, in 1897 or 1898, has no foundation in the documentary record: the pre-Nilus assembly was definitely carried out in Russia. Unfortunately, it is still unclear precisely who produced this final version: although Pavel Krushevan may well have played a role in putting them together, there is no hard evidence to back up this suspicion, and the identity of the compiler remains for the moment at least a mystery.[37]

Russian antisemitism found violent expression before 1914 in the shape of the counter-revolutionary 'Black Hundreds', gangs who roamed the country in the wake of the failed 1905 Revolution murdering Jews, whom they identified as the malign agents of the upheaval. Antisemitic violence re-emerged in the wake of the Revolution of 1917, above all in the 'White' counter-revolutionary movement against the Bolsheviks, who came to power in 1917 and imprisoned and subsequently murdered Tsar Nicholas II, along with his family. As civil war spread across Russia in the autumn of 1918, two 'White' officers, Pyotr Nikolaevich Schabelsky-Bork and Fyodor Viktorovich Vinberg, both fanatical antisemites, escaped to the West on a train provided by the Germans, who were evacuating the areas they had continued to occupy in Ukraine during the First World War until the Armistice of 11 November. Arriving as Germany itself was in the throes of revolution, following the enforced abdication of the Kaiser, the two men lost no time in publicizing their view that both the Russian and the German revolutions, as well as the world war itself, were the work of the 'Elders of Zion'. They brought a copy of the *Protocols* with them, and in the third issue of their yearbook *Luch Sveta* (*Ray of Light*) they printed the complete text of Nilus's final, 1911 version of the document.[38]

They also gave a copy to a man called Ludwig Müller von Hausen, founder of an obscure ultra-right organization established in Germany shortly before the war called the Association against the Presumption of the Jews. Subsidized by a group of aristocratic patrons, including most probably members of the deposed German royal family, the pamphlet was translated into German and published by Müller von Hausen in January 1920. In the violent post-revolutionary atmosphere of the times, when the former Imperial Establishment, along with many of its middle-class supporters and beneficiaries, was raging against the German revolution and the democratic Weimar Republic founded in its wake, the tract was an instant success in circles of the far right. It was reprinted five times before the end of 1920 and sold over 120,000 copies within a few months. By 1933 it had gone through thirty-three editions, many of them decked out with freshly composed appendices and specially drawn illustrations.[39] 'With the publication in German of *The Protocols of the Elders of Zion*,' Hitler's most recent biographer Volker Ullrich has concluded, '. . . conspiracy theory had become a stock element of ethnic-chauvinistic German propaganda.'[40] For extreme right-wing antisemites, Germany's defeat in 1918, the fall of the Kaiser's regime and the coming of democracy in the Weimar Republic were all proof of the accuracy of the *Protocols*. The Jews had triumphed, and so they no longer needed to keep the document secret, as they had allegedly done up to then.[41]

One of the first to read the book in German was General Erich Ludendorff, who had been in effect the military leader of Germany during the latter part of the First World War and took a leading part in two violent but unsuccessful attempts to overthrow the Weimar Republic, including the Kapp Putsch of 1920, when Berlin was briefly taken over in an ultra-right military coup, and the Nazi 'beer-hall putsch' in Munich in 1923. By the time he got hold of a copy, he had already written his account of the war, but he was still able to insert an extra footnote recommending the *Protocols* to his readers and declaring that in the light of their revelations, modern and especially contemporary history would need to be completely rewritten. Ludendorff went on to note that the document 'has been strongly attacked by the opposing side and characterized as historically inaccurate'. But this did not really matter. The fact was that he had already formulated his views, and the *Protocols* did not in the end have a great deal of influence on them.[42]

However, the document clearly did influence a secret, conspiratorial collection of young far-right extremists in the early years of the Weimar Republic known as the *Organisation Consul*. The group was among other things responsible for the assassination of Walther Rathenau, a wealthy businessman, intellectual and politician who had been a key figure in the management of the economy during the war. In 1922 Rathenau was appointed German Foreign Minister. He quickly concluded a treaty with the Soviet Union in which Germany and Russia, the two pariahs of the international order, renounced territorial and financial claims on each other. It was an important step towards bringing Germany back into the diplomatic arena. But for the extreme right, it was an act of treachery to conclude any kind of agreement with the Bolsheviks, let alone one renouncing all claims on Soviet territory. For the *Organisation Consul* in particular, it was a product of the international Jewish conspiracy described in the *Protocols*. For Rathenau was a Jew, and in 1909 he had been incautious enough to complain in a newspaper article that 'three hundred men, all of whom know one another, guide the economic destinies of the Continent and seek their successors among their followers'. His purpose was to advocate a broadening out of the economic elites of Germany, France and other European countries, and he made no mention of Jews anywhere in the article, but for the young fanatics of the *Organisation Consul*, encouraged by Ludendorff, the claim could only have one meaning: Rathenau, as Ernst Techow, one of the members of the organization, alleged, 'was one of the three hundred Elders of Zion, whose purpose and aim was to bring the whole world under Jewish influence, as the example of Bolshevist Russia already showed'. Questioned by the judge at the assassins' trial, Techow said that he had got the idea of the 'three hundred Elders' from 'a pamphlet', namely the *Protocols*, and in his summing-up the judge drew the attention of the courts and the media to 'that vulgar libel, the *Protocols of the Elders of Zion*', which 'sows in confused and immature minds the urge to murder'.[43]

The *Protocols* did not impact on these young murderers in an ideological vacuum. For the thinking of the ultra right in Germany already before the war was permeated by a heady brew of ideas derived from the French monarchist Artur de Gobineau, who in the mid-nineteenth century invented the concept of an 'Aryan master race'; the Social Darwinist concept of history as a struggle between races for the 'survival of the fittest'; and the identification of socialism as the product of a Jewish plot to destroy European civilization. Such ideas were propagated in a number of publications, most notably the *Foundations of the Nineteenth Century* (1899) by the antisemitic composer Richard Wagner's son-in-law, the even more antisemitic Houston Stewart Chamberlain. Similar works, such as Theodor Fritsch's *Handbook of the Jewish Question* or Adolf Wahrmund's *The Law of the Nomad and Today's Jewish Domination* (1887), also advanced the claim that the Jews were the hidden force behind many events and tendencies their authors regarded as malign.[44] Ultra-right nationalist newspapers, magazines, tracts and pamphlets propagated the idea of the Jews as a hidden influence behind everything they hated in modern life, from feminism and socialism to atonal music and abstract art, well before the First World War.[45] In the wake of Germany's defeat in the First World War, and the febrile atmosphere of revolution and counter-revolution that followed it, antisemitism became a central part of far-right ideology.

In post-revolutionary Bavaria in particular, a number of tiny counter-revolutionary political groupings fulminated against the Jews, who, they claimed, both prompted revolutionary subversion and engaged in war profiteering. Such propaganda of course grossly exaggerated the role of Jews both in the Socialist and Communist parties and in the world of banking and high finance. The obvious objection to such claims, namely that capitalists and Communists spent much of their time and energy fighting each other, was met with the paranoid response that this only showed how the Jews were acting as hidden puppet-masters, dividing society against itself from behind the scenes. It was from this milieu, rather than directly from the *Protocols*, that Adolf Hitler gained the antisemitic beliefs that were so central to his world-view.[46]

Hitler first mentioned the *Protocols* in notes he compiled for a meeting held on 12 August 1921; a report of a speech he delivered in the south Bavarian town of Rosenheim on 19 August 1921 noted that 'Hitler shows from the book *The Elders of Zion*, drawn up at the Zionist Congress in Basel in 1897, that establishing their rule, by whatever means, has always been and will always be the Semites' goal.'[47] However, Hitler's private library, which eventually contained more than 16,000 volumes, did not contain a copy of the *Protocols*. Even if it had, that would not have proved that he had read the document; almost all of the volumes in the collection were clearly unread. Like many people, he learned about the *Protocols* indirectly.

Leaving aside the probability that he was informed of their content, or at least their import, through conversations with his friends, notably his early mentor Dietrich Eckart, after the end of the First World War the vehicle seems to have been a series of newspaper articles ghost-written for the American motor manufacturer Henry Ford and published in 1920 in a collected, bound edition under the title *The International Jew: The World's Foremost Problem*, and translated into German in 1922. A copy was included in Hitler's library. A large part of the book, beginning with Chapter 10, is devoted to an exposition of the *Protocols*, illustrated by copious quotations from the text.[48] It was from this book that Hitler's later propaganda chief Joseph Goebbels also learned about the *Protocols* in 1924, prompting him to seek out the actual document so that he could gain a proper understanding of the 'Jewish question', as he put it.[49]

By 1923, as hyperinflation was destroying economic life and social stability in Germany, Hitler was referring to the *Protocols* in his speeches. Among other things, he declared: 'According to the Zionist Protocols the intention is to make the masses submit through hunger to a second revolution [after that of 1918] under the Star of David.'[50] Not long after this, Hitler attempted to seize power in Munich in a violent armed coup and was arrested, tried and sentenced to a brief period of 'fortress confinement' by a lenient nationalist judge. He used his enforced leisure to compose his lengthy political and autobiographical tract *Mein Kampf* (*My Struggle*), and here, too, he made reference to the *Protocols*.

III

However, by this time, the *Protocols* had become widely known as a blatant forgery.[51] On 13 July 1921 the Istanbul correspondent of *The Times*, Philip Graves, excitedly informed his editor in London, Henry Wickham Steed: 'A very curious discovery has been made by a Russian (Orthodox) here ... It is that the "Protocols of the Learned Elders" is largely a plagiarism of a book published at Geneva ... [in] 1864. The book is a series of dialogues between Montesquieu and Machiavelli ... A great many of the resemblances are extraordinary.'

Graves supplied a number of examples of textual passages plagiarized from this book by the author of the *Protocols*. 'There are <u>scores</u> of other resemblances: "The Protocols" in many parts is a mere paraphrase. There seem to me to be the elements of a scoop in this,' he told Steed.[52] The day before, he went on, the Russian who had made the discovery, Mikhail Mikhailovich Raslovlev, who was related by marriage to the *Times* correspondent in St Petersburg, had contacted him and offered to sell him the copy of Joly's book, which had originally been published in Geneva. 'Mr Raslovleff,' Graves reported, 'got the Geneva Book from a Russian ex-colonel of the Okhrana [Tsarist secret police] who attached no importance to it.' Raslovlev was himself an antisemite ('He thinks the Jewish peril lies in the materialism of the Jew rather than in his revolutionary idealism,' Graves reported), and belonged to a group of Russian monarchists exiled by the Bolshevik Revolution in 1917. He was down on his luck, and needed money, after losing his estates and his property to the Bolsheviks.

However, money was not his only motive, otherwise, he said, he would have offered the book to a Jewish purchaser, who would undoubtedly have paid more for it. 'I would not like to give a weapon of any kind to the Jews,' he told Graves, 'whose special friend I never have been. I kept for a long time the secret of my discovery (for <u>it is</u> a discovery!) in the hope of using it one day or other as a proof of impartiality of the political group to which I belong. And it is only a very urgent need of money that persuaded me now to change my mind.' He did not want to sell the book outright, however: believing that the ongoing civil war and famine in Russia would soon bring the Bolshevik regime to an end, Raslovlev asked only for a loan of £300, repayable after five years; in return, *The Times* would have exclusive rights over the material until the money was repaid. A contract was quickly drawn up and signed on 1 August 1921. 'I feel this may be a very big scoop for the *Times*,' Graves told his Foreign Editor in London, 'so have taken the step mentioned above so as <u>to have a hold on the discoverer</u>.' There was a danger otherwise that Raslovlev might try to sell the secret to someone else, or that the plagiarism might be independently discovered. Graves agreed, however, to keep the name of his informant anonymous, in order to protect relatives of Raslovlev who had remained in Russia.[53]

His decision to expose the document was motivated not least by the fact that London newspapers including the *Morning Post* and the *Illustrated Sunday Herald* had produced an English translation of the *Protocols* the year before, eliciting interest in the political world and winning favourable comments from none other than Winston Churchill, among many others. There was pressure from some Conservative MPs for an official inquiry into the Jewish conspiracy supposedly uncovered in the document. Under its editor, the High Tory H. A. Gwynne, the *Morning Post* was at the time strongly anti-Bolshevik and had many far-right connections, particularly with Tsarist exiles. The exposure of the *Protocols* by *The Times* would therefore strike a serious blow to the rival newspaper's credibility.[54] But even before this, a German author, Otto Friedrich, had drawn attention, in a book entitled *Die Weisen von Zion: Das Buch von Fälschungen* (*The Wise Men of Zion: The Book of Falsifications*), published in 1920, to *The Rabbi's Speech* in the *Protocols*.[55] Another journalist, Lucien Wolf, had also exposed the *Protocols* as plagiarized from *The Rabbi's Speech* in 1920.[56] In the USA, the Russian-born Jewish activist and journalist Herman Bernstein published a similar denunciation the following year.[57] The evidence that the *Protocols* were a falsification was accumulating rapidly. But Raslovlev's exposure of the extensive plagiarism of Joly's text was entirely new, and constituted a revelation of a much more devastating kind.

Graves quickly wrote it up into three articles for *The Times*. 'I think publication should take place as soon as possible,' he told his Foreign Editor back home. This was not easy, however. He needed to entrust the articles and the books to a reliable British subject travelling home from Constantinople. 'The trouble is,' he told his Foreign Editor on 25 July 1921, 'that the people travelling just now are people whom [*sic*] I know are slapdash sort of fellows who might quite conceivably stop two or three times "pour faire la noce" on the way home at Venice or Paris & increase risks of loss.' Eventually he found a 'trusty messenger who will leave by the Orient Express ... He will stop nowhere en route, as he had intended, & will hand over a packet to the Foreign Editor on the night of his arrival.' The journey on the luxurious train took five days. The Foreign Department of *The Times* duly noted on 9 August 1921 that 'The secret parcel from Constantinople arrived by special messenger tonight.' Graves's articles appeared on 16, 17 and 18 August 1921 and were quickly reprinted as a pamphlet, which was so widely demanded that it was reprinted in a new edition of 5,000 copies on 22 August. Foreign translations were rapidly negotiated with continental European newspapers and publishing houses. Only in Paris did the agent acting for *The Times* meet with failure. 'The subject, somehow or other,' he reported, 'does not seem to be of interest – the French are a funny lot!'[58]

The charge of falsification appeared in detail in German in 1924 and was given widespread publicity.[59] Hitler must certainly have read about the allegations in the German press. But the exposure did not deter him. The fact that 'the *Protocols of the Elders of Zion*', he declared, were hated by the Jews, led to claims that they were

> based on a 'forgery'; which is the surest proof that they are genuine. What many Jews do perhaps unconsciously is here consciously exposed. But that is what matters. It is a matter of indifference which Jewish brain produced these revelations. What matters is that they uncover, with really horrifying reliability, the nature and activity of the Jewish people, and expose them in their inner logic and their final aims. But reality provides the best commentary. Anyone who examines the historical development of the last hundred years from the standpoint of this book will at once understand why the Jewish press makes such an uproar.[60]

This was, however, the only reference he made to the document in the many hundreds of pages of *Mein Kampf*.

Similarly, Joseph Goebbels, two days after he had decided to inform himself of the document's contents, confided to his diary:

> I believe that *The Protocols of the Elders of Zion* is a forgery. That is not because the worldview of Jewish aspirations expressed therein are too utopian or fantastic – one sees today how one point after the other of *The Protocols* is being realized – but rather because I do not think the Jews are so completely stupid as not to keep such important protocols secret. I believe in the inner, but not the factual, truth of *The Protocols*.[61]

Far more enthusiastic about the *Protocols* was the self-appointed Nazi philosopher and ideologue Alfred Rosenberg, a Baltic German who had fled the Revolution in Russia and was convinced it had been the outcome of a Jewish plot. He saw the machinations of the Jews everywhere and, once he had arrived in Germany, churned out a seemingly unending stream of radically antisemitic tracts. Rosenberg produced a commentary on the *Protocols* as early as 1923, in which he claimed that 'the Jew' had triumphed in Germany with the creation of the Weimar Republic, but warned his 'fall into the abyss' would soon come, after which 'there will be no place for the Jew in Europe or America'. Ten years later, when the Nazis had come to power, he proclaimed that this moment had finally arrived: 'May the new edition of this book reveal yet again to the German people in what delusion they were imprisoned, before the great German movement shattered it . . . and how deeply this understanding was rooted amongst the leaders of National Socialism from the very beginning of the movement.'[62] When Propaganda Minister Joseph Goebbels ordered a nationwide boycott of Jewish shops on 1 April 1933, supposedly in retaliation for a boycott of German goods advocated by Jewish groups in the USA – in itself a sign of the Nazi belief in 'world Jewry' – the Nazi Party boss in Franconia and editor of the antisemitic Nazi paper *Der Stürmer* (*The Stormer*), Julius Streicher, described the boycott as a 'defensive action against the Jewish world-criminals' and their 'plan of Basel' (which was where the meeting supposedly minuted in the Protocols had allegedly taken place). Streicher's newspaper made frequent mention of the *Protocols* and did as much as it could to keep them in the public eye. The Nazi Party itself published the *Protocols* in a cheap and widely available edition and urged 'every German to study the terrifying avowal of the Elders of Zion, and to compare them with the boundless misery of our people, and then to draw the necessary conclusions and to see to it that this book comes into the hands of every German'.[63]

In the mid-1930s however, the claims of the *Protocols* to authenticity, such as they were, met with two further blows. In July 1934, during a trial in Grahamstown of three South African 'Grey Shirt' fascist leaders, Nahum Sokolow, President of the World Zionist Organization, testified that the *Protocols* which the defendants were accused

he had relatives by marriage living in Munich who, he feared, might be subject to reprisals by the Nazis, but he did provide a written statement confirming the conclusions reached in his articles of 1921. By now, however, he had lost the support of his newspaper. The new editor of *The Times*, Geoffrey Dawson, a strong advocate of Appeasement, regretted his newspaper's exposure of the *Protocols*, as Graves reminded him subsequently:

> Some time ago I remember that you told me that you regarded the discovery by T.[he] T.[imes] of the forgery as in some respects unfortunate. I quite see that in the present state of feeling in a great part of the Continent, <u>The Times</u> might wish to be dissociated from this publication in the future, not on account of any sympathy whatever with the prevailing anti-Semitism, but because the connexion of The Times with the exposure makes it hard to persuade many important people in Germany and elsewhere that The Times is not 'Jewish influenced' or 'Jewish run'.[67]

On the very eve of the war, the assistant manager of *The Times* told Graves that if his pamphlet was reprinted, 'it might be wise for us not to give it too much, or perhaps any, publicity in the columns of THE TIMES, in view of the possibility of reprisals against us in Germany'.[68]

The verdict of the Bern trial was one of a number of factors that influenced officials in Goebbels's Propaganda Ministry to decide against making much use of the *Protocols* in their public pronouncements. At his daily press briefings, where the Propaganda Ministry laid down the lines German newspapers and magazines had to follow on major, and sometimes not so major, issues of current interest, one Nazi paper, the *Deutsche Zeitung*, came in for sharp criticism for claiming that the exposure given to the *Protocols* at the Bern trial would alert the German public once more to the threat posed by Jewish machinations across the world. 'The experts in the Propaganda Ministry are in no way of the same opinion,' it was reported. 'The German press is asked not to turn the Bern trial ... into a major antisemitic action.' Accordingly, the newspapers played down the trial, presenting it in the main as an internal Swiss affair. They interpreted the court's verdict as based on the niceties of Swiss law, rather than a condemnation of the *Protocols'* claims to authenticity. The prosecution itself was evidence in the eyes of the Nazi press of the continuing international Jewish effort to 'spread poison about Germany'. It was not only Nazi officials' awareness of public knowledge of the fraudulent nature of the *Protocols*, however, but also, most likely, their consciousness of the limitations of the document's contents that led to the Nazis' continuing reluctance to use them as a tool of antisemitic propaganda. Only the most extreme of antisemites, notably Streicher, cited them with any frequency. As far as antisemitic indoctrination in general was concerned, there were far more important and widely distributed documents to hand, notably Nazi handbooks on antisemitism of one kind and another. As the most thorough and judicious investigation of the subject has concluded, 'the evidence . . . suggests that the Nazi propaganda leadership knew that *The Protocols* was not what it purported to be. But that seems not to have troubled them much. Whatever *The Protocols* was, it made for useful propaganda as long as one did not go into excessive detail.' But as a central plank in the Nazi regime's antisemitic platform, the document was of limited importance.[69]

Nevertheless, while it seldom made direct reference to the *Protocols*, the Nazis' antisemitic rhetoric was permeated all the way up to the end of the war by direct and indirect references to 'the Jewish world conspiracy'. The Jew, Goebbels declared at the 1937 Nazi Party rally, was 'the world's enemy, the destroyer of civilizations, the parasite among the peoples, the son of Chaos, the incarnation of evil, the ferment of decomposition, the demon who brings about the degeneration of mankind'.[70] On the sixth anniversary of his appointment as Reich Chancellor in 1933, Hitler declared, to the thunderous applause of the serried ranks of Nazi officials gathered in the Reichstag, that 'if the international Jewish financiers in and outside Europe should succeed in plunging the nations once more into a world war, then the result will not be the Bolshevising of the earth, and thus the victory of Jewry, but the annihilation of the Jewish race in Europe!'[71] By 'world war' he meant essentially the involvement of the United States in a war against Germany, and it is no coincidence that when this happened, in the summer of 1941, the full-scale extermination of the Jews began. As Goebbels said in November 1941, 'All Jews by virtue of their birth and race belong to an international conspiracy against National Socialist Germany.'[72] The idea that all Jews, everywhere, were dedicated to the complete destruction of Germany and the Germans was endlessly repeated by Goebbels's propaganda apparatus throughout the rest of the war, gaining in vehemence and intensity as the military tide began to turn in the Allies' favour. 'Just as the potato beetle destroys potato fields, indeed has to destroy them,' Goebbels told an enthusiastic crowd in the Berlin Sportpalast on 15 June 1943, 'so the Jews destroy states and nations. For that there is only one remedy: radical removal of the threat.'[73] The Propaganda Ministry continued with this line even in defeat. 'If it were possible to checkmate the 300 secret Jewish kings who rule the world,' the Ministry informed the press to report on 29 December 1944, in an extrapolation of the figure originally applied to Germany, without mention of the Jews, by Rathenau many years before, 'the people of this earth would at last find peace.'[74] Nevertheless, Nazi propaganda seldom if ever mentioned the *Protocols* directly when referring to the alleged global Jewish conspiracy. It is a mistake to think that every such reference was also a reference to the *Protocols*, as some historians have done.[75] The idea of a Jewish world conspiracy was spread by other publications as well; it was a commonplace of antisemitic ideology, and the *Protocols* were really only one illustration among many.[76]

IV

On the face of it, the idea of a Jewish world conspiracy is unrealistic in the extreme. To imagine that millions of individuals are all being centrally directed by a small, secret conspiratorial group, whether it consists of thirteen men or three hundred, is to indulge in the politics of fantasy to an extraordinary degree. To work at all, a conspiracy has to be tightly knit. The secret of its operation has to be jealously guarded. It has to involve as few people as possible. Conspiracies involving thirteen people are feasible enough, but three hundred is already coming up against the limits of possibility. The more people there are in a conspiracy, the greater the likelihood of its being betrayed. However many members there are, they also need to be in constant communication with one another as they bring their plans to maturity and put them into action. And yet the *Protocols* invariably mention only the meetings at the 1897 World Zionist Congress; there is no mention of any other meetings except in one of the document's precursors, where it is claimed the encounters in the Prague cemetery took place once every hundred years. Surely over the years one, or most likely many more, of the conspirators would have betrayed their secrets? One would imagine, too, that the supposed intended victims of the conspiracy would have taken up arms to defend themselves against subversion on this scale; yet nowhere in the *Protocols* is there any mention of precautions the 'Elders' supposedly took to protect themselves from retribution.

And then there is the question of how the Elders' instructions were transmitted to the millions of people who formed the Jewish community across the globe. No evidence, not even forged 'evidence', was ever brought to light that contained even the slightest hint that Jews anywhere were in receipt of any instructions issued by the alleged masters of the conspiracy. In fact, as the former Higher SS and Police Leader in Central Russia, Erich von dem Bach-Zelewski, a ruthless mass murderer of the region's many Jews, admitted after the war:

> Contrary to the opinion of the National Socialists that the Jews were a highly organized group, the appalling fact was that they had no organization whatsoever . . . It gives the lie to the old slogan that the Jews are conspiring to dominate the world and that they are so highly organized . . . If they had had some sort of organization, these people could have been saved by the millions; but instead they were taken completely by surprise. They did not know at all what to do; they had no directives or slogans as to how they should act . . . In reality they had no organization of their own at all, not even an information service.[77]

As Norman Cohn commented, the myth of the Jewish world conspiracy 'reached its most coherent and deadly formulation at the very time when Jews were in reality more divided than ever before – between orthodox and reformed, practising and indifferent, believing and agnostic, assimilationist and zionist', not to mention divisions of class, politics and national allegiance. The *Protocols* and the myth of a worldwide Jewish conspiracy in the end had 'very little to do with real people and real situations and real conflicts in the modern world', a fact evident, at least after the event, even to a hardened Nazi mass murderer like Bach-Zelewski.[78]

As we have seen, the kind of conspiracy theory represented by the *Protocols* bore little resemblance to traditional expressions of antisemitism. Ancient and medieval antisemitism was religious in character: an unconverted, alien body in Christendom, blamed by the Church for bringing about the death of Christ, the Jews, practitioners of a different religion from that of the vast majority of Europeans, were easily imagined as engaged in nefarious activities, poisoning wells used by Christians, or killing Christian boys in order to use their unsullied blood for sacrificial purposes. These legends always, however, focused on specific incidents in specific places at specific times and involved named individuals. The systemic conspiracy theory exemplified by the *Protocols* and their antecedents right back to the decades after the Revolution of 1789 was entirely different. It never named any of the individuals the *Protocols* claimed were behind the destructive conspiracies of the Freemasons, nor did it identify any of the Jews who were supposedly engaged in the subversion of the foundational principles of the traditional Christian social order. In the vagueness of these allegations, indeed, lay much of their power: to a degree, the *Protocols* were an 'open' text, allowing a variety of different readings.[79] Such conspiracy theories were designed, whether consciously or not, to create fear and suspicion through the suggestion of unseen and unknown forces at work.[80] And the proof that was supplied was almost always historical, referring to a conspiratorial meeting that had taken place in the recent or in some cases the distant past, involving a secret group or organization that had been working subversively behind the scenes for decades or even centuries.[81]

An early critical essay on the *Protocols* by the historian John Gwyer, published in 1938, generalized from these points with unusual clarity. Dedicating it ironically to 'all believers in the Hidden Hand', Gwyer remarked that such people become believers, members of that unfortunate crew who can see a plot in anything. They can no longer open their newspapers, or read a book, or go to the cinema without observing the Hidden Hand at work, either involving them in subtle propaganda, or attempting to make them pawns in an elaborate scheme of sabotage ... [Yet] the Hidden Hand had done far too much to be true. It had engineered the French Revolution, the troubles in Ireland, and the Great War ... It had organized the Bolshevik revolution, while remaining persistently at the back of High Finance ... There was, in fact, no end to its activities. But its plots (I would object) were nearly all contradictory; it appeared to organize with one hand what it was at pains to overthrow with the other.[82]

Gwyer went on to remark that the literature of what he called 'the Hidden Hand', or what we would call conspiracy theories, encompassed so many events and processes of world history that 'I cannot but feel proud of our civilization's power to withstand attack'. The paranoid belief in the Hidden Hand must on the face of it 'surely be as disquieting and uncomfortable as any other form of persecution-mania'. But in fact, he considered, it was convenient. 'It saves so much thinking to think like this, to survey the world and know that all its disorders are due to the malignity of a single group of mysterious plotters.'[83] Perhaps, he mused, such beliefs were harmless enough provided they were not allowed to impinge on real life. But in the case of belief in a Jewish Hidden Hand, this was regrettably not the case: it had led to repeated acts of violence against the Jews by antisemites, many of whom in recent years had used the *Protocols* as justification for their 'startlingly savage' acts, including 'murders, persecutions, evictions, and massacres'. Hence his decision to devote a short book to demonstrating their fraudulence.[84]

'One is reluctant to think,' Gwyer wrote in the conclusion to his short book, 'that the average intelligence of mankind is really so low that it cannot distinguish between plain truth and fantastic falsehood.'[85] But this seemed to be the case with the adherents of the *Protocols*. The exposure of their fraudulence had not prevented thousands from continuing to read them, treating them as if they were indeed genuine. And in fact, conspiracy theories such as those purveyed by the *Protocols* do operate in a number of ways that are outside the normal practice of rational discourse. To begin with, they are self-sealing: that is, criticism, all the way up to their exposure as plagiarized and falsified, generally meets with the response that the critics are themselves part of the conspiracy, either Jewish or tools of the Jews. No advocate of the *Protocols* has ever attempted to defend them by advancing proofs that they are genuine, or providing evidence in support of their authenticity. Instead, in a vindicatory procedure typical of conspiracy theorists, the proponents of the *Protocols* focus their attention on the motives, or the character, or the racial background, or the politics of the document's critics. But of course the question of who advances an argument, of why they do so, or what their motivation might be, has nothing at all to do with the actual validity or otherwise of the argument itself, which has to be tackled on its own terms.

And then, some at least of those who have made use of the *Protocols* have been fully aware of the fact that they are a crude fabrication. They have frequently been employed as a kind of 'pious falsehood', a low and disreputable means to what those who have exploited them have presented as high and honourable ends. As Hitler himself said, the proof of their intrinsic truth lay not so much in the document itself as in the history of the past two centuries of Jewish plotting and conspiracy. In similar terms, Alfred Rosenberg admitted that the document's origins were obscure, but felt it was genuine because it corresponded to his intuition.[86] The fact that the *Protocols* were a forgery was thus more or less irrelevant, just as the French antisemites who insisted so stubbornly that the Jewish officer Alfred Dreyfus was guilty of spying for the Germans in the 1890s did not care that the documents that incriminated him were forged: forged or not, for them, the documents testified to a higher truth, namely that all Jews were traitors, either actually or potentially, because the Jews in their eyes had no allegiance to any one country – a belief, as this shows, that was widespread in antisemitic circles even before the composition of the *Protocols*.[87]

As Jovan Byford has remarked, the exposure of the *Protocols* as a falsification by Philip Graves and again by the Bern trial did not seem to undermine the book's cult status among millions of readers around the world who fell under its spell. Many of the book's admirers simply dismissed the evidence against it as a campaign by Jews to undermine the 'leaked' document which exposes so clearly their sinister secret. On the other hand, there were those, among them the Nazi ideologue Alfred Rosenberg, who were aware from the outset that the *Protocols* are not genuine, but for whom this simply did not matter.[88]

For these conspiracy theorists, even if the *Protocols* themselves were a forgery, they nevertheless testified to a reality of which they were already conscious. Henry Ford concluded that they 'fit with what is going on', a statement strikingly similar to Hitler's in *Mein Kampf*. In the same way, the antisemitic conspiracy theorist Nesta Webster, writing in 1924, concluded that *'whether genuine or not'* (my italics), 'the Protocols represent the programme of a world revolution'.[89] As Byford concludes, 'for the antisemitic conspiracy theorist the *Protocols* function like the Bible: they are an ahistorical document that "invites incantation, not critical interpretation" '.[90] Like many if not most conspiracy theorists, Hitler and other Nazi antisemites lived in a hermetically sealed ideological cocoon which could not be penetrated by any rational criticism.[91]

Reinforcing the tendency of those who used the *Protocols* as a means of 'proving' that the Jews were engaged in a worldwide conspiracy to subvert the existing order was the probability that very few of them had actually troubled to read the document. The document was, to be sure, printed and reprinted in the hundreds of thousands, but few people could have made sense of its contents, and what it needed in any case was for the eighteenth- and nineteenth-century conspiratorial fantasies it contained to be translated into terms that were relevant to a twentieth-century readership. No edition appeared without an explanatory foreword, and many contained copious explanatory notes, usually linking the *Protocols* to issues of the day.[92] Not infrequently they printed additional documents, most of which were also falsified or invented. Alfred Rosenberg's edition was full of notes and additional examples designed to show, as he put it, that 'today's politics correspond exactly and in detail to the intentions and plans that were discussed and committed to paper 35 years ago in the *Protocols'*. The Foreword, indeed, was usually the most readable part of every edition. Most of the document itself was, as one commentator has noted, 'stupendously boring', but the marginalia that appeared from Nilus's edition onwards and were incorporated into the document as subheadings for the different sections were often dramatic and sensational. The fact that they often had little to do with the actual contents made no difference.[93] They were what made the *Protocols* so widely read, insofar as they were read at all and not merely cited as an unexamined 'proof': 'Reign of Terror'; 'Removal of the Privileges of Gentile Nobles'; 'Economic Wars as Basis for Jewish Domination'; 'Making the Gentiles Degenerate'; 'The Nobility's Money is Taken Away'; 'Ferment, Disputes, Antagonism throughout the World'; 'The Success of Statecraft through Keeping Its Aims Secret'; 'The Poison of Liberalism'; 'The Spreading of Epidemics and Other Strategies of the Freemasons'; 'Gentiles are Sheep'; 'Serfdom of the Future'; 'The Emasculation of the Universities'; 'The King of the Jews as True Pope and Patriarch of the World Church'; 'Disturbances and Revolts'; and so on.[94] In the end, however, people did not even need to read these: what mattered was that the *Protocols* existed.

V

In his book on the *Protocols*, Norman Cohn sought to analyse the myth of the Jewish world conspiracy in psychoanalytic terms. Most of his arguments lack both plausibility and supporting evidence of any kind, and are little more than unsubstantiated speculations that are difficult to accept unless one is a convinced follower of Sigmund Freud. Moreover, by the time Hitler and the Nazis came to put their own particular version of the myth of the Jewish world conspiracy into operation, it had evolved far beyond the future prognostications of the *Protocols*. Whatever else that document predicts, it is not the extermination of the Gentile world. Nowhere in the *Protocols* do we find any statement of genocidal intent. What is striking about Nazi antisemitism, however, is its apocalyptic vision of a Jewish world conspiracy hell-bent on the absolute and entire elimination of the Gentile world. In this sense, perhaps there is some merit in Cohn's identification of the Nazi version of the myth of a Jewish world conspiracy as a kind of negative projection of the Nazis' own destructive and genocidal instincts. Just as the *Protocols* outlined a future apocalypse in which the Jews would bring about a Nietzschean 'revaluation of all values', and the end of Christian civilization as it had grown and developed over the previous two millennia, so the Nazis portrayed the twentieth century as the apocalyptic culmination of thousands of years of race war, in which 'the eternal Jew, that fomenter of destruction, will celebrate his second triumphal Purim among the ruins of a devastated Europe'.[95] All of this, however, was a world away from the future projected by the *Protocols*, in which the Gentiles would give up their freedom in exchange for a paternalistic and in some ways benevolent world order run by the Jews.

For Hitler, and for the Nazis more generally, the will to conspire and subvert social, political, cultural and economic institutions in Germany in particular, and the civilized world in general, was innate in the Jewish character. It was stamped on it by heredity, just as the supposed virtues of the 'Aryan' race were handed down from generation to generation in the blood. Hence Hitler's revealing statement in *Mein Kampf* that the *Protocols* exposed 'consciously' 'what many Jews do perhaps unconsciously'. In other words, the Jews, in Hitler's mind, were not acting in a conscious kind of conspiracy, they were acting by racially determined instinct. The conspiracy allegedly uncovered in the *Protocols* was just an example of a far wider behavioural tendency. The Jews were not consciously subverting 'Aryan' values and institutions, they probably did not even know that they were doing so. There was no active, clandestine group of 'Elders of Zion' behind all the crises that were besetting the world, in other words. In this respect, too, the *Protocols* were not to be taken literally.

Hitler's understanding of the nature and origins of what he regarded as Jewish subversion through the ages, an understanding shared by leading figures in the Nazi regime, changed little from the 1920s to the end of his life. It was expounded once more, this time at some length, by Joseph Goebbels in his diary for 13 May 1943:

I am studying the Zionist Protocols in detail once again. Up to now I have always been told that they were not suitable for propaganda on the issues of the day. I am concluding as I read that we could make very good use of them. The Zionist Protocols are as modern today as on the day when they were first published. One is astounded by the extraordinary consistency with which the Jewish drive for world domination is characterized here. Even if the Zionist Protocols are not genuine, they were none the less invented by a brilliant critic of the age. At midday I touch on the subject in conversation with the Führer. The Führer takes the view that the Zionist Protocols can make a claim to be absolutely genuine. Nobody can describe the Jewish drive to world domination as the Jews themselves feel it. The Führer takes the view that the Jews don't need at all to work to a fixed programme; they work according to their racial instinct, which will always prompt them to undertake the kind of action shown in the course of their entire history.[96]

As Goebbels himself concluded, 'One can't speak of a conspiracy of the Jewish race in any straightforward meaning of the term; this conspiracy is more a characteristic of the race than a case of intellectual intentions. The Jews will always act as their Jewish instinct tells them.'[97] In this sense, the vague and unspecific contents of the *Protocols* meshed perfectly with the already existing basic tenor of Nazi ideology.[98] During the war years, when the Nazi persecution and genocide of Europe's Jews was reaching its terrible climax, the *Protocols* were not reprinted again in Germany; their message, the Nazis concluded, was no longer necessary; it had been superseded by propaganda that was more powerful and more direct, such as the antisemitic movies *The Eternal Jew* and *Jew Süss*, both released in 1940.[99]

The impact of the *Protocols* on Hitler and the Nazis was thus indirect rather than direct. Tracing parallels between their actions of antisemitic persecution and the nostrums propagated in the *Protocols* does not convince, particularly in the light of the document's contents; and even if there were parallels, this would still not be evidence that the actions resulted from a reading of the document.[100] In fact, far from being a revelation, their existence was taken by the Nazis to confirm what they already knew.

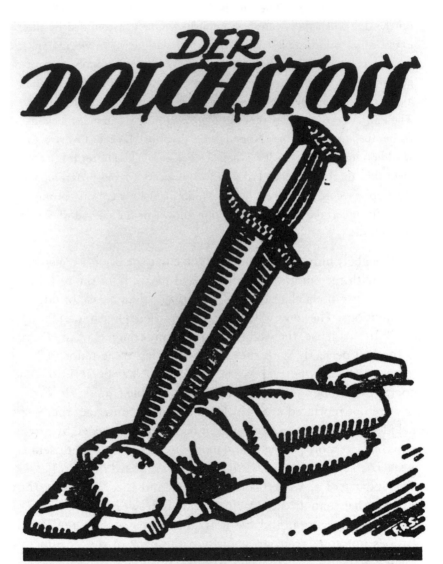

DER DOLCHSTOSS

Süddeutsche Monatshefte G. m. b. H., München
Preis Goldmark 1.10.

2

Was the German army 'stabbed in the back' in 1918?

I

When the First World War ended in 1918, many people hoped that it would be 'the war to end all wars'. The peace settlement signed the following year aimed to put in place a range of measures to stop war ever happening again. They ranged from a ban on secret diplomacy to the creation of a League of Nations to settle differences between states on the basis of arbitration, from the prioritizing of multilateral disarmament to the subjection of foreign and military policy to democratic controls in all countries. Germany, blamed by the victorious Allies for starting the war in 1914, became a democratic republic, and was saddled with peace conditions designed to curb its ambitions and restrict its military capabilities. After the mass death and destruction of the war years, the way seemed open for a better, more peaceful and more rationally ordered world.

And yet a mere two decades later, these worthy ambitions had been utterly confounded. In one nation after another, democracy had given way to dictatorship. The League of Nations had proved totally unable to keep the peace. The world economy had been plunged into the deepest depression of modern times. Former subject nations of the Habsburg Monarchy had fought each other in a series of border disputes. Revolution, civil war and armed conflict had raged across Europe from Poland to Spain. Racism and nationalism had led to harsh discrimination in one nation after another. Germany had rearmed and had invaded first Austria and then Czechoslovakia, subjecting their citizens to brutal and murderous occupation policies. In 1939 Germany invaded Poland, ignoring the objections of Britain and

47

France, and a second world war broke out, leading to even greater destruction than the first.

A fundamental reason for the failure of the First World War to bring peace and stability to Europe and the wider world lay in the Germans' refusal to accept the fact that they had lost. The terms to which they were forced to agree in the peace settlement did not help. But it was not simply the consequences of the war but also the fact of defeat itself that proved to be unacceptable. The defeat sent shock waves through the German population. Far from being repressed or forgotten, as some historians have suggested, it remained a running sore on the German body politic in the following years.[1] Throughout the 1920s and 1930s, when Germans spoke of 'peacetime' they did not mean the time after the war, but the time before it.[2] The war was unfinished business; and when Hitler came to power in 1933, it was above all with the aim of renewing it and bringing it to a successful conclusion.[3]

Why did the vast majority of Germans refuse to accept the reality of defeat in 1918? A major reason lay in the fact that as the war came to an end German troops were still occupying foreign soil, in Belgium and northern France and a large tract of north-eastern Europe, in complete contrast to the situation after the end of the Second World War in 1945, when every inch of German soil had been overrun by enemy troops. German government propaganda had trumpeted the triumphs of German arms almost until the very end of the war in 1918.[4] The expectation of victory was, if anything, reinforced by the military events of the first half of the war's final year. In November 1917, after the rule of Tsar Nicholas II of Russia had disintegrated under the pressure of continual war against Germany and Austria-Hungary, an uprising led by Vladimir Ilyich Lenin and his Bolshevik Party had established a Communist dictatorship. Responding to the overwhelming desire of ordinary citizens for peace, the Bolsheviks negotiated the cessation of hostilities on 3 March 1918 at Brest-Litovsk, leaving the Germans free to transfer huge numbers of troops to begin a massive spring offensive on the Western Front, decided on by their military leadership without any thought of launching a parallel diplomatic campaign; victory on the battlefield, it was felt, would bring its own rewards.[5] For the first time since it had gone on the defensive following the costly Battle of Verdun in 1916, the German army seized the initiative and went on the attack. The long stalemate finally seemed to be over: victory was in sight.

On 21 March 1918 German forces broke through the Allied lines and crossed the River Marne. Paris seemed to be within their grasp. But the reinforcements transferred across from the East were nowhere near strong enough to tip the balance in the West, and German logistics and resources simply could not sustain the rapid advance. The Germans' supply lines were soon stretched to breaking point, and the assault did not bring the expected victory. The all-important momentum of the advance petered out by the end of April. There were further assaults on Allied positions over the following months, and German troops managed to push the front line forward in several places. But the strategic value of this was limited, the ground they won was blasted beyond recognition by years of fighting, and the loss between March and July 1918 of nearly a million men on the German side, particularly of experienced and elite troops, left the army weakened beyond recovery.[6]

The deployment by the Allies of increasing quantities of tanks, able to overrun entrenched defensive positions, helped turn the tide against Germany and Austria (the 'Central Powers', along with Bulgaria and Ottoman Turkey). In early August the German army's de facto supreme commander, Erich Ludendorff, was forced to begin a series of tactical retreats. Ludendorff knew that in 1919 the Allies would be able to deploy thousands of tanks on the Western Front; the Germans only ever managed to manufacture twenty. The war had lasted so long not least because trenches, barbed wire and machine-guns had given defensive tactics the upper hand. The invention and rapid improvement of the tank now began to give the advantage to offensive warfare. Tanks could crush barbed-wire barricades, roll over trenches and ward off machine-gun bullets with their armour. After some initial mistakes, the Allies were learning fast how best to use them, especially in combination with airpower, artillery and massed infantry attacks. In addition, the Allied economic blockade, in force since the beginning of the war, was causing serious shortages, with munitions, equipment, fuel, food and even uniforms in short supply. In the autumn of 1918 desperate German troops began to attack supply trains in search of food, surrender to the Allies en masse, and desert in ever-increasing numbers.[7]

After the failure of the spring offensive, in which so much hope had been invested, morale among the German and Austrian troops crumbled fast, starting with the ordinary soldiers and moving up quickly through the ranks until despair at the prospects of staving off defeat eventually reached the very top. The Supreme Army Command set up a political education division to try to counter this, but the crucial step – promising democratic reforms at home to the politically disfranchised troops – was rejected by the conservative generals, who remained wedded to the authoritarian political system headed by the Kaiser. Continued, pointless and bloody fighting sapped the troops' will to carry on.[8] Mass slaughter on the battlefield reduced average divisional strength from nearly 7,000 men earlier in the war to fewer than 1,000 by the late summer. By July over a million troops had arrived at the front from the United States, which had joined the war in 1917, reinforcing the Allied superiority in armour and tipping the balance decisively against the Germans. Writing in the mid-1920s, Adolf Hitler, who served as a soldier on the Western Front throughout the war, remembered that by August 1918, 'reinforcements coming from the homeland were becoming rapidly lower and lower in quality, so that their arrival meant more a decline than an increase of fighting strength. In particular, the young reinforcements were for the most part worthless.'[9]

A new offensive mounted by the Allies in the late summer of 1918 began to drive back the Germans on the Western Front, breaking the stalemate. On 2 September 1918 Ludendorff informed the civilian politicians in Berlin that the war could not be won, though defensive operations might be continued successfully for some time. Ludendorff decided that in this situation it would be advisable to sue for peace, to cut off the possibility of an Allied advance into Germany and preserve the existing political system. It was agreed on 5 October 1918 that a new civilian government should be formed in Berlin, supported by the democratic parties and led by the liberal Prince Max von Baden. It promised democratic political reforms in the hope that this would make it easier to negotiate peace terms. If these terms turned out to be harsh and therefore unpopular in Germany, Ludendorff, an extreme nationalist and enemy of democracy, calculated that the German liberals and democrats would take the blame. Indeed, he believed that they had already undermined the war effort simply by campaigning for a democratic civilian government to be installed in Berlin instead of the strong military dictatorship which he believed was necessary to bring the war to a successful conclusion. So he said that his intention was 'now to bring those circles to power which we have to thank for coming so far. We will therefore now bring those gentlemen into the ministries. They can now make the peace which has to be made. They can eat the broth which they have prepared for us!'[10]

Crucially, however, Ludendorff did not inform the army command, the politicians or indeed the German public about the rapidly deteriorating military situation. On the contrary, he continued to put out optimistic propaganda for several weeks after he had privately admitted the hopelessness of the army's position. Strict military censorship prevented any hint of the seriousness of the crisis from reaching the general public. Even when the Allied offensive was in full swing in August 1918, German army propaganda spoke of 'defensive victories' and insisted that an Allied triumph over the 'unconquerable' German people was not a possibility. On 1 October 1918, however, Ludendorff warned Max von Baden's government that the situation had deteriorated still further. A decisive Allied breakthrough could occur at 'any moment' and it was possible that one or another division on the front could 'fail at any time'. Hence it was vital to obtain the best peace terms while the front was still intact.[11] Yet Prince Max still insisted, in public at least, that the front remained 'unbroken'. Even in mid-October the German press was virtually unanimous in its failure to admit the seriousness of the military situation.[12] This widespread refusal to recognize reality was to prove a significant factor in the generation of later conspiracy theories about the reasons for Germany's defeat.[13]

Meanwhile, the military situation of the Central Powers underwent an even more drastic deterioration with the defeat of Bulgaria. This small Balkan state was effectively under German control, enforced by a number of army divisions transferred from the Russian front after the peace of Brest-Litovsk. A major Allied offensive in the south began on 15 September 1918 and soon French and British troops had entered the country. Bulgarian military morale was very low by this time.

German food requisitions and a poor harvest had caused starvation conditions in the trenches, the troops were poorly equipped, and Austrian, German and Turkish claims over major agricultural areas of the country had discredited the government. Troops deserted from the front and units began to enter the capital, Sofia, to join forces with socialist revolutionaries to demand the punishment of the government, which was forced to resign. With the army melting away, the Bulgarians had no choice but to surrender. A ceasefire came into effect on 29 September 1918. With Bulgaria out of the way, Allied forces advanced to the Danube, cutting communications between Germany and its ally Ottoman Turkey, and threatening Austria-Hungary, which was being rapidly weakened as troops from its subject nationalities, notably the Czechs, began to desert.[14]

The German Foreign Secretary was forced at the beginning of October 1918 to pass on the bad news to the leadership of the German army in a brief but decisive telegram:

> According to the most recent reports from Bulgaria we must give up the game there. From a political point of view, therefore, there is no point in our keeping our troops there, let alone reinforcing them. On the contrary, it would be politically desirable to evacuate them from Bulgaria itself, so that we do not push the Bulgarian government over to the side of the enemy.[15]

The Germans had no strategy to respond to the situation in the Balkans. The collapse of Bulgaria led directly to a German request to the Allies for an armistice on 6 October. US President Woodrow Wilson was now calling the shots as fresh American forces and resources kept flooding on to the war-weary Western Front. Wilson had previously issued a fourteen-point agenda for peace, reinforcing it in a speech delivered on 27 September 1918. His demands included the evacuation by the Germans of all occupied territory, the ending of secret diplomacy, the right to self-determination of all nations, the formation of an independent Poland from territory taken from Germany, Russia and Austria, and the creation of a League of Nations to regulate international relations in future. The German government did not accept Wilson's agenda outright in its communication of 6 October, but regarded it as the inevitable basis for negotiations.[16]

Meanwhile, the situation of the Central Powers continued to deteriorate. The British and French governments took this as an opportunity to press Wilson into making his terms for an armistice harsher, including the return to France of the provinces of Alsace and Lorraine, annexed by Germany in the Franco-Prussian War of 1870–71. Crucially, in his third note to the German government, on 23 October 1918, Wilson insisted that the armistice terms must make it impossible for the Germans to renew hostilities, and declared he would not negotiate the peace with a 'monarchical autocrat', thus effectively requiring the abdication of Kaiser Wilhelm II. Max von Baden then enforced the resignation of the German military leadership, above all Erich Ludendorff, who was all for rejecting these conditions and fighting on to defend the Fatherland, and began peace negotiations in earnest.

These events helped precipitate another major German ally, Ottoman Turkey, into signing a regional armistice on 30 October. By this point, too, Germany's principal European ally, the Habsburg Empire of Austria-Hungary, was in deep trouble. Increasingly dominated by German military advisers, it had become highly unpopular, particularly after the death of the aged and much-respected Emperor Franz Joseph in 1916. Conditions of life in the Empire had worsened to the point where people were starving, and the Italian front, stable for most of the war, was disintegrating following an Italian victory begun on 24 October at Vittorio Veneto. Bulgaria's collapse threatened the Empire from the south and east as British and French troops advanced on its borders. A final ministerial council in Vienna on 27 October 1918 brought a formal end to the Austrian alliance with Germany. The young Emperor Karl, who had succeeded his grandfather Franz Joseph but could in no way match his prestige, or popularity, told the German Kaiser on the same day that the hopelessness of the military situation compelled him to seek a separate peace in order to concentrate on preserving the Empire.[17] However, one after another, the subject nationalities of the Empire now declared their independence, not least because they could no longer be confident that the Habsburg administration in Vienna would be able to stave off the Bolshevik revolution threatening to spread westwards from Russia.

By the end of October, the Germans were left without allies. Even had this not been the case, the rapidly deteriorating military situation on the Western Front meant that they would have been unable to fight on, especially given their numerical inferiority in tanks, men and equipment. Facing advancing enemies in the west and south, the Germans had no alternative but to accept whatever armistice terms were offered by the Allies. Max von Baden's government sent the moderate conservative Matthias Erzberger, Minister without Portfolio, to Compiègne in northern France on 7 November 1918 to conclude terms. The delegations met in a railway carriage parked in a siding. There was no negotiation. Erzberger and his team were simply presented with the necessary documents and told to sign them. Under pressure from the civilian government and his own military entourage, the Kaiser abdicated on 9 November 1918 and went into exile in the Netherlands, where he remained until his death in 1941.

As news of the imminent end to hostilities spread, German naval officers attempted to order the fleet out from its base in Kiel to go down fighting against the Royal Navy in the North Sea, but the sailors mutinied on 3 November 1918 and stopped this futile sacrifice of their lives before it had even begun. Ad-hoc sailors' councils formed on 4 November arrested and disarmed officers and took charge of the ships. The council movement spread rapidly, reaching Berlin on 9 November 1918 in the form of a Workers' and Soldiers' Council which seized power as the Kaiser's regime melted away. The far left – soon to become the Communist Party of Germany – under the leadership of Karl Liebknecht, proclaimed a socialist republic, but was outmanoeuvred on 9 November by Philipp Scheidemann, a leading figure in the Majority Social Democrats, Germany's largest political party, who proclaimed a democratic republic the same day. The Social Democrats rapidly formed a Council of People's Delegates as a provisional revolutionary government in coalition with the Independent Social Democrats, a coalition of left-wing politicians united only by their opposition to continuing the war. The Majority Social Democrats' leader, Friedrich Ebert, became de facto head of the new republican government and, backed by the titular army chief, Field-Marshal Paul von Hindenburg, instructed Erzberger to accept the terms of the Armistice, which he did under protest shortly after 5 a.m. on 11 November, with effect from eleven o'clock French time.

The terms included the immediate evacuation of all territory still occupied by German forces on the Eastern and Western fronts and the removal of German troops from all territory west of the River Rhine. The Germans had to hand over their combat aircraft and ships, and a large quantity of military resources including weapons and railway locomotives. The Allied naval blockade of Germany continued until a full and formal peace settlement was reached. This took many months. Eventually, at the Paris Peace Settlement on 20 October 1919, the Treaty of Versailles came into effect, imposing harsh terms on Germany, including the cession of 13 per cent of the territory of the Reich to France, Denmark and Poland, and the payment of huge financial reparations, in gold, for the damage caused by the German occupation of northern France, Belgium and Luxemburg. A significant number of conservative nationalist German politicians and former military men urged the rejection of these harsh terms. Some thought that Germans could take up arms against the victorious Allies once more; others thought that even if the country were invaded and occupied it might be possible to preserve the core of the old Prussia in the East, where the beginning of armed conflict between the new state of Poland and the Bolshevik regime in Russia, against the background of a Russian civil war, might provide the opportunity for Germany to carve out its own autonomous territory. Even more apocalyptically, Count Brockdorff-Rantau, who represented Germany at the Paris Peace Conference, speculated that Allied troops ordered to invade Germany might mutiny, outraged at having to carry on fighting after the war was formally over, sparking a revolution at home and undermining Allied attempts to enforce the Treaty. All of this was illusory. The terms of the Treaty were enforced in full.[18]

II

Throughout the war, Germany's military leadership regarded criticism of its conduct of affairs, including the aim of annexing large amounts of enemy territory following a German victory, as little better than treachery. It went to considerable trouble to prevent critics' views being given an airing in public. An elaborate system of military controls, including the censorship of newspapers, books and magazines, and the arrest and imprisonment of leading opponents of the war, was put in place almost immediately and kept there almost to the very last day.[19] Yet it was unable to stop left-wing, liberal and democratic politicians from advocating an end to the fighting on the basis of a compromise peace.[20] 'What we expect from the home front,' General Wilhelm Groener, who had been appointed to lead the army following Ludendorff's dismissal, complained on 1 November 1918, 'is not criticism and polemics but the strengthening and toughening of heart and soul. If a rapid change doesn't occur, the home front will destroy the army.' Even before this, on 20 October 1918, a right-wing Protestant magazine was complaining about 'collapse behind the front, – not collapse of our heroic front'. Such rhetorical attacks on politicians who were demanding a peace without territorial annexations provided the essential background for the emergence of the stab-in-the-back legend after the war.[21] In many ways, this was the result of a progressive polarization of the German political system during the war, which saw an ever more radical nationalist, authoritarian and anti-socialist right confronting an increasingly critical, oppositional and ultimately revolutionary left.[22]

None of this, as yet, amounted to any kind of conspiracy theory. But the rhetoric ratcheted up after the war was over and the peace treaties were signed. Ludendorff blamed the defeat on 'the effect of the poor spirit of the homeland on the army'. Germans had lost their nerve. Appeals by the Kaiser to the home front to pull itself together had been in vain.[23] The general fired off these allegations in part as a measure of self-defence against the widespread, and far more plausible, accusation that it had been he himself who had suffered the loss of nerve after the failure of his ruinously mishandled and costly offensives on the Western Front. Nevertheless, Ludendorff was reflecting a view that had by this time become widespread across the army officer corps that victory and defeat had in the end been a matter of willpower. The army's will had held firm; the civilians' had not – a belief that was, in fact, very far from the truth, as the disintegration of the army's morale following the defeat of the 1918 spring offensive clearly showed.[24]

It was some time before the end of the war that the phrase 'stab in the back' was first used to express this belief (the phrase invoked the episode in the medieval epic the *Nibelungenlied*, later also in Richard Wagner's music-drama *The Twilight of the Gods* in which the villainous Hagen plunges his spear into the back of the courageous hero Siegfried, whom no one, not even a god, can vanquish in a fair fight).[25] The first occasion on which it is known to have been employed was following the passage of a Reichstag resolution by the Social Democrats, Left-Liberals and Catholic Centre Party deputies on 19 June 1917 calling for a negotiated peace, without annexations. General Hans von Seeckt, a senior staff officer who was to become commander-in-chief of the army after the war, had asked angrily: 'What are we still fighting for, really? The home front has fallen on us from behind, and with that, the war is lost.'[26] In similar fashion, the arch-conservative aristocratic politician Elard von Oldenburg-Januschau charged in February 1918 that a fresh resolution passed by the Reichstag in favour of a negotiated peace had 'fallen upon the army from the rear'.[27] The original idea of a 'stab in the back' referred, therefore, merely to Reichstag resolutions that conservatives and leading military men considered undermined the soldiers' will to fight on until they achieved final victory.

Such ideas were shared, perhaps paradoxically, even by some on the left and centre of German politics, although they referred not to peace resolutions but to general economic and social conditions on the home front. At the very beginning of November 1918, the left-wing socialist Kurt Eisner, who was to form a revolutionary government in Munich not long afterwards, warned a meeting in the city that it was important for the home front not to 'break the spine' of the fighting troops, while on the same occasion the left-liberal Reichstag deputy Ernst Müller-Meiningen declared that 'as long as the external front holds, we have the damned duty to keep going at home. We would have to face our children and grandchildren with shame if we fell upon the front from behind and knifed them.'[28] Remarks such as these reflected not only the desire of moderate liberals and Social Democrats to avoid being deemed unpatriotic, but also their ignorance even at this late point of the true state of affairs at the front. Once the war had ended, such views became more widespread. The liberal politician Gustav Stresemann, writing on 17 November

1918, observed for example that the military front had carried on fighting to the end, but the home front had collapsed.[29]

The revolution that broke out on 9 November 1918 led to a dramatic sharpening and radicalization of the idea of a 'stab in the back', as it was focused from now not on the general state of the home front or the effect on the army's fighting spirit of peace resolutions, but on the specific activities of the Social Democrats and their allies on the left who had brought the revolution to power. Already on 10 November 1918, the day following the revolution, before the Armistice had been signed, but after he had been told the nature of the Allies' demands, a senior military commander, Crown Prince Rupprecht of Bavaria, opined that the peace terms would not have been so harsh had the Allies not been convinced by the outbreak of the revolution that the Germans were no longer capable of resisting whatever terms they were offered – a view echoed by the sociologist Max Weber, who declared that the revolution had 'struck the weapons from Germany's hand'. On 11 November 1918 a speech delivered to front-line troops by an army major, Count Friedrich zu Eulenburg-Wicken, who in February 1919 was to form the violent, far-right paramilitary 'Free Corps Eulenburg', claimed that 'traitors in the homeland, led by selfish agitators', were 'exploiting this moment' of Allied advances and German retreats 'to knife us in the back'. They had occupied the bridges across the Rhine, he alleged, in order to cut off supplies to the front. Ludwig Beck, an officer on the General Staff who later rose to head the organization under the Nazis, complained in similar terms on 28 November 1918 that a 'long-prepared' revolution had 'fallen on us from behind at the most critical moment of the war'.[30] This theory was even given credence by the Communists. On 12 November 1918 the Soviet Foreign Minister Georgy Chicherin declared in a message to Allied troops that 'Prussian militarism was crushed not by the guns and tanks of Allied imperialism but by the uprising of German workers and soldiers,' while the German Spartacus League, the forerunner of the Communist Party of Germany, convened an assembly of military deserters on 30 November 1918 to celebrate their flight from the front lines as a revolutionary deed.[31] These claims, of course, like those made by nationalists on the right, ignored the fact that the Allies had already drawn up their non-negotiable terms for an armistice well before the German delegation arrived at Compiègne on 8 November 1918 and so before the outbreak of the revolution on 9 November. But statements such as Chicherin's did a good deal to lend credence to the right's allegations of treachery on the part of the left.

The stab-in-the-back idea was given more widespread currency by an official investigation carried out in 1919. At the end of the war, Allied politicians clamoured for those in Germany they believed had unleashed the conflict to be put on trial. Efforts to bring the Kaiser to justice eventually fizzled out – he was out of reach in his Dutch exile – and legal proceedings against a handful of army officers brought few tangible results. In the meantime, however, the accusations and counter-accusations that flew across the floor of the German National Assembly elected in January 1919 led it to take pre-emptive action by setting up its own committee of investigation into the origins and conduct of the war in August that year. The 'Weimar Coalition' parties – the Social Democrats, Left-Liberals and Catholic Centre Party – dominated the committee. But by calling prominent nationalists and war leaders as witnesses and allowing them to speak at length, they played into the hands of the right. The politician and economic expert Karl Helfferich, of the German-national People's Party, caused a sensation by refusing to answer questions put by the representative of the Independent Social Democrats, Oskar Cohn. 'Herr Cohn,' he said, 'was partly, perhaps primarily, to blame for the collapse of the German front.' He was referring to 'a sum of money the Russian Bolsheviks had given Herr Cohn to support the German revolution'. Cohn denied the allegation, which further radicalized the rhetoric of blaming the revolution at home for the German defeat at the front, adding an extra layer of conspiracism by claiming the Russian Bolsheviks were behind it.[32] Nevertheless, the rhetoric still fell some way short of amounting to a genuine conspiracy theory, which would have required an element of intent. So far, at any rate, nobody seemed to be claiming that the German left had acted with the specific aim of bringing about Germany's defeat in order to hand victory to the revolutionaries.

The biggest sensation at the hearings was caused by the testimony of Field-Marshal von Hindenburg, which was most probably written for him by Helfferich in consultation with Ludendorff.[33] On

18 November 1919, he stood before the committee of investigation, giving his prepared testimony 'like a living corpse', reciting a narrative that 'someone had taught him and which he had learned by heart'. The field-marshal declared: 'We could have carried on the struggle to a successful conclusion if there had been undivided and unified co-operation between the army and the homeland.' But this had not been forthcoming. 'As an English general has very truly said, the German Army was "stabbed in the back".'[34] Who was the English general who said this? The story seems to have originated in an article published in the London *Daily News* by General Sir Frederick Maurice, who had served on the Imperial General Staff until May 1918 and was now a sought-after military analyst. Maurice was already explicitly referred to by a far-right deputy in the German National Assembly, Albrecht von Graefe, on 29 October 1919 as the originator of the stab-in-the-back idea. But it was Hindenburg's testimony that really ensured the English general's identification as the man responsible, thus giving it the appearance of objectivity that German military men and conservative politicians were unable to supply themselves.[35]

In fact, all Maurice was arguing was that the failure of the German spring offensive, definitively halted in June 1918, was decisive in bringing about the end of the war. 'From the time when Germany's failure became clear,' he wrote, 'the moral bond which held her allies together snapped' – in other words, the Allied victories on the Western Front following this 'wore down the enemy's power of resistance and exhausted his reserves' so much that it became impossible for the Kaiser's forces to come to the rescue of Bulgaria and Austria-Hungary when their military strength began to fail. On 17 December 1918 the leading Swiss paper, the *Neue Zürcher Zeitung*, published a report, taking Maurice's article as its starting point, which argued 'that an army cannot fight without having the people behind them. Because the courage of the German people had been worn away, the army and navy both broke down ... As far as the German army is concerned, the common view can be summed up in the phrase: it was stabbed from behind by the civilian population.'[36]

Was this an accurate rendition of Maurice's views? In his book *The Last Four Months*, published in 1919, Maurice stated firmly that:

'There is no question that the German armies were completely and decisively beaten in the field.' The problem was that German government and military propaganda suppressed this fact, and so, Maurice stated, 'the German people ascribed the surrender . . . to the revolution, if they were not in favour of it'. But he was in no way responsible for encouraging this misleading impression.[37] The Swiss newspaper had misinterpreted him. In July 1922 he said as much: 'I have never at any point expressed the opinion that the outcome of the war was the result of the army being stabbed in the back by the German people.' Maurice had his own purpose in declaring that Germany's military defeat had been decisive and complete well before the German revolution had broken out, of course: he was arguing against commentators who had said the Armistice of 11 November was premature and wanted the Allied armies to push on further, even into Germany. This, Maurice thought, was unnecessary and would have incurred further, pointless loss of life. Still, there is no reason to doubt his judgement. As the editor of the Social Democratic daily *Vorwärts!*, Erich Kuttner, declared in 1921: 'Nothing is more characteristic of the stab-in-the-back legend than the fact that its existence is based on a forgery . . . Indeed, the "words" of General Maurice were from A to Z an invention.'[38]

An alternative version of the story was also circulating, involving a completely different English general, the head of the British Military Mission in Berlin, General Sir Neill Malcolm. Ludendorff recalled later that he was dining with Malcolm, who asked him why he thought Germany had lost the war. The German general launched into his familiar tirade about the weakness of the home front and the government and their failure to give proper support to the fighting troops. Malcolm asked him: ' "Are you trying to tell me, General, that you were stabbed in the back?" Ludendorff's prominent blue eyes lit up at the phrase. "That's it!" he shouted triumphantly. "They stabbed me in the back!" '[39] In fact, Ludendorff was either confusing the two men, or inventing the story, which had no corroborating evidence to support it.[40] In the end, as with so many conspiracy theories, the truth did not much matter. 'Whoever invented the phrase "the Stab in the Back," ' the Prussian general Hermann von Kuhl remarked dismissively in the final report of the committee of investigation,

'– whether it comes from the British General Maurice or not – is immaterial.'[41]

The fact that Hindenburg endorsed the stab-in-the-back story in his appearance before the parliamentary investigating committee in 1919 was of immense significance.[42] The committee's proceedings were given national prominence by the press, and Hindenburg's own appearance was accompanied by massive demonstrations against the Republic by his admirers, many of whom thought that he should not have been exposed to the indignity of being summoned by a mere parliamentary committee at all. The damage done to the orderly conduct of the committee's business was such that from this point onwards it decided to hold its proceedings behind closed doors. The nationalist press extracted the maximum capital from Hindenburg's testimony, which he repeated shortly afterwards in his memoirs (also ghost-written), writing that 'our weary front collapsed like Siegfried under Hagen's treacherous spear; it had tried in vain to gain new life from the dried-up spring of the homeland's resources'. It was notable that he conceded that the front – unlike the strapping young hero Siegfried – was 'weary'. Notable also was the vagueness of Hindenburg's accusation, which made it eminently suitable to be used for a variety of purposes.[43] By lending his authority to the myth, Hindenburg not only helped to anchor it in the ideology of the Republic's opponents on the right, but also provided them with a potent weapon for countering attempts to discredit it.[44] The fact that the myth, was also given credibility by ex-Kaiser Wilhelm II himself only added to its influence among people who regretted the disappearance of the monarchy.[45] And it turned Hindenburg into a tragic figure, betrayed by his enemies at home, instead of the failed war leader he really was.

The failure of the home front now became subsumed in a genuine conspiracy theory for the first time. Extreme right-wing militarists like Ludendorff's former aide Colonel Max Bauer, author among other things of a lengthy (if unpublished) diatribe against feminism, now felt justified in proclaiming that 'the war was lost solely and alone because of the failure of those at home'.[46] So far, so vague. But he went on to allege that the rapid depletion in strength of the German armed forces in the summer and autumn of 1918 had been caused by a huge increase in the numbers of men avoiding the draft.

Hermann von Kuhl also claimed that 'shirkers' and 'deserters' had been encouraged by pacifists and socialists who had been pressing vigorously for the war to be brought to an end; their activities had also had a material effect in undermining the will to fight at the battlefront, which of course, he claimed, was exactly the effect they were aiming at. Ultimately, too, 'the possibility of the continuation of the war by Germany . . . was prevented only by the revolution that broke the sword in the commander's hand, subverting all order and discipline in the Army – above all, behind the front – and rendered all further resistance impossible'.[47] Ludendorff alleged in similar fashion that German democrats of all shades of opinion had seized the opportunity to destroy the authoritarian Empire so patiently built up by Bismarck and his successors. At the moment when a strong state was needed, these traitorous pacifist criminals had seized power with the aim of concluding peace just as the army was continuing to fight for the life of the Fatherland at the front. This was the result of years of socialists undermining the people's will to fight. Germany's defeat in 1918 was thus the product of a deliberate campaign by socialists and pacifists to cause Germany's defeat in order to bring about a revolution, in conformity with Lenin's concept of 'revolutionary defeatism'.[48]

Such accusations were by no means confined to the military. Significant groups on the domestic, civilian political right also blamed the home front. Right-wing student associations, for example, backed by some nationalist professors, took the same line, as did elements in the conservative Evangelical Protestant Church. The official state church before the war, it had been closely linked to the monarchy, so that supporters of the Kaiser and proponents of the re-establishment of his regime also seized on the stab-in-the-back myth as a means of discrediting the new democracy.[49] On the radical nationalist right, the Pan-German League, a small but influential organization, declared on 4 March 1919 that the defeat had been the fault of 'traitors' in the homeland who had been allowed 'systematically to undermine the will to victory of our people' by a weak-willed government.[50] There thus emerged the allegation that Germany had been defeated not so much by a general weakness of will and lack of resources on the home front as by a specific conspiracy against the nation by socialists, communists and pacifists that had exercised its deadliest effect in the revolution itself.

III

To the ultra-patriots of the far right, looking back at these events during the 1920s, it seemed obvious that, as Dr Albrecht Philipp, a leading member of the German-national People's Party, opined, 'the army was stabbed in the back by the revolution, after prolonged efforts had been made to subvert it beforehand. The stab-in-the-back legend is no vague and dangerous myth, as has been claimed. It is a clear description of one of the saddest and most shameful facts in German history.'[51] Philipp's claim, like Ludendorff's, that subversion of the army had begun long before the revolution was a reference to the mass strikes that had broken out in the factories in January 1918.[52] During a parliamentary debate on 26 February 1918, more than eight months before the war's end, the Secretary of State for the Interior, Max Wallraf, later also a prominent member of the German-national People's Party, claimed 'that international influences were at work' in the strikes, advocating 'violent manifestations against the ruling system'. The strikes, he warned, clearly aimed to 'give support to hostile powers … Anyone who dishonourably and disloyally attacks our brave warriors from behind as they carry out their sacred task makes himself an outlaw and must be punished with the extreme rigour of the law.'[53]

However, the idea that all these events were connected and formed part of a larger socialist-pacifist conspiracy to undermine morale in the army was not borne out by the facts. The strikes had been motivated by deteriorating conditions above all in the munitions factories, and were resolved by a series of agreements between the trade unions and the military leadership, leading to a more effective organization of production and supply and in particular to an improvement of wages and working conditions. In political terms, the strikes supported the mainstream Social Democratic demands for a peace with internal reforms and no annexations. They were not undertaken in order to push for a revolution. Food riots, overwhelmingly staged by women in 1915–16, were more difficult to deal with since they were more spontaneous than organized, but here, too, the restructuring of supply logistics helped mute the discontent. It was noticeable that the Majority Social Democratic Party played a central role in bringing the strikes and demonstrations to an end. Its support among the workers far exceeded that of its rivals on the left, whose influence on the workers was limited at best. And it did not seek to overthrow the Kaiser, simply to reform the political system over which he presided. Scheidemann only proclaimed the democratic Republic in November 1918 in order to head off the ultra-left attempt to establish a socialist one.[54]

Unfortunately, the Majority Social Democratic head of the first post-revolutionary government, Friedrich Ebert, actually contributed to the spread of the stab-in-the-back myth when he welcomed troops returning from the front on 10 December 1918 with the words: 'No enemy has overcome you.'[55] His intention was to praise the troops for the years of danger and privation they had endured, and to reinforce their self-esteem by emphasizing the fact that they had not, as he judged, been routed in a major battle or allowed the enemy to invade Germany itself. But the damage was done. And the impression of an undefeated army was reinforced by the sight of the orderly and disciplined columns of troops marching past Ebert, accompanied by military bands and cheered by crowds as heartily as they would have been had they been victorious. In fact, they were entirely untypical of the troops in general: while the bulk of Germany's armed forces were disbanding, laying down their arms, discarding their uniforms and finding their way back home in whatever fashion they could, the men who were parading in front of Ebert consisted of nine divisions, all of them of course greatly under strength, sent by the army leadership under Wilhelm Groener because they were 'trustworthy' and could be relied upon to defend the new government against further disturbances and revolutionary outbreaks.[56]

Ebert was not the only one to speak in such terms. The post-revolutionary Majority Social Democratic government's leadership in the state of Baden had already greeted the returning troops on 16 November 1918 with the words: 'You are returning unvanquished and undefeated.'[57] The local newspaper in Magdeburg reported on

12 December that 'an unbeaten army is coming home'.[58] By using such formulae, Ebert and other politicians, along with many journalists, intended to convey to their audience their belief that the German armed forces had been overcome only by the enemy's deployment of superior resources and had retained their discipline and elan to the end. Hindenburg himself, in his final order of the day, issued to the troops on 11 November, just before the signing of the Armistice, declared that his forces were 'leaving the fight upright and proud' after four years of successful defence of the Fatherland against 'a world of enemies', thus also invoking another myth, that the war had begun only because Germany had been 'encircled' by a group of hostile powers in 1914.[59]

For many ordinary Germans, greeting the marching columns with cheering and flag-waving, this was also the opportunity to thank the returning soldiers for their sacrifices; instances of public hostility towards them were rare, even in working-class areas, which after all had supplied many of the men who had fought at the front.[60] Too many ignored the inconvenient fact that this made little difference in the end in the face of the overwhelming superiority of the Allies in terms of equipment, supplies, manpower and military hardware. Coupled with the failure of the 1918 spring offensive and the advances made by the Allies from July 1918 onwards, this had a devastating effect on the morale of the troops, reflected in growing numbers of desertions, depleted strength and declining morale in the late summer and autumn. Supplies, logistics and resources are of course just as much a part of warfare as the actual fighting on the battlefront, as some seemed to forget, thinking it was somehow unfair for them to have played a role in Germany's defeat. Moreover, those who claimed that Germany was undefeated in 1918 were speaking as if Germany had fought alone, ignoring the influence of the collapse of Bulgaria and the Habsburg Monarchy, two of Germany's major allies, on the course of events in October and early November 1918.[61]

The march-past of orderly units returning from the front in Berlin and elsewhere obliterated the shameful spectacle of hundreds of thousands of soldiers 'demobilizing themselves' following the Armistice and returning home in disorder, looting and stealing along the way. It had been the troops, not the civilians on the home front, who had behaved unheroically at the end of the war and indeed for some months before. The declining morale of the German armed forces in the summer and autumn of 1918 was caused not by socialist agitators and conspirators working to undermine their commitment but by the catastrophic failure of the spring offensive, the shattering of the exaggerated hopes of final victory that accompanied it, and the increasing hopelessness of the struggle as Allied tanks and American troops poured into the fray in growing numbers. Four years of mechanized mass warfare had undermined the authority of the officer corps with the men, while depleted units, missing supplies and continued hopeless offensives had been lowering morale since July 1918. On 29 September Ludendorff had been forced to admit, without mentioning revolutionary or socialist influences at all, that 'the Supreme Army Command and the German army have reached the end . . . The troops can no longer be relied on.'[62] He knew, in other words, that the defeat was a military one.

The stab-in-the-back myth did not die down as the First World War became more distant in time. It played a major part in the propaganda of the German-national People's Party, the most successful right-wing conservative movement and critic of Weimar democracy until the rise of the Nazis at the end of the 1920s.[63] Nationalist journalists and politicians continued to try to discredit the Social Democrats and, by implication, the Weimar Republic, by alleging that they had supported labour unrest at home during the war.[64] In 1924 Reich President Ebert, who had led efforts to end the labour dispute, brought a legal action for defamation against a nationalist newspaper editor who had accused him of committing treason by supporting the striking munitions workers in 1918. The judge in the case, a conservative who, like the vast majority of the judiciary in the Weimar Republic, had begun his career under the Kaiser and shared his view that the Social Democrats were revolutionaries with no commitment to the Fatherland, manipulated the trial shamelessly, so that it ended with the acquittal of the defendant. Ebert himself was not required to testify, since he was, after all, the Head of State. He did, however, provide a statement to the court, denying the allegation. His supporters pointed out that he had lost two sons at the front, which made it unlikely, to say the least, that he would have wanted to stop the supply of munitions to the troops. During the trial he began to suffer from appendicitis, but delayed treatment because he did not want to appear to be attempting to gain public sympathy by claiming ill health: the delay proved fatal, and he died on 28 February 1925, a victim, even if only indirectly, of the stab-in-the-back myth.[65]

A second trial, held in Munich over five weeks from October to December 1925, focused on allegations brought by the nationalist campaigner Paul Cossmann (a Jew who had converted to Christianity and was later murdered by the Nazis) against a Social Democratic newspaper editor who had rebutted, in very personal terms, Cossmann's claim that the Social Democrats had stabbed the army in the back by fomenting unrest on the home front during the war, in particular the naval mutinies that had initiated the revolution in November 1918. Those called upon to testify in what the press called 'The Stab-in-the-Back Trial' included leading figures from the wartime military and naval leadership such as Groener, Hermann von Kuhl, and a number of other witnesses whose confidential testimony to the Reichstag committee was now brought into the public eye. The trial ended with the Social Democratic editor being fined a small amount; costs were awarded to the plaintiff. Its overall effect, however, was ambivalent. On the one hand, it brought a mass of detailed evidence to light on the conduct of the Social Democratic labour movement during the war, which by and large proved its patriotism and went against the thrust of Cossmann's accusations. On the other hand, since the nationalist press highlighted only the testimony given in support of these accusations, the trial did nothing to stop the further spread of the stab-in-the-back legend.[66]

When the Reichstag committee finally produced its report, issued in ten volumes in 1928, and printing huge amounts of the utterly contradictory testimony that its members had considered over the years since it was set up, it was too late to discredit the myth, which had now entered the discourse of the nationalist right as an unchallengeable truth. The enormous length of the report, and the fact that there were a number of dissenting statements by committee members, above all the Social Democrats and Communists, seriously weakened its impact. Still, such was the depth of the political divisions that racked the Republic that everyone took from it the conclusions they wanted to hear.[67] A rare conservative voice raised against the stab-in-the-back myth was that of the eminent military historian Hans Delbrück, a senior and much-respected figure in the Prussian Establishment (born in 1848, he taught for many years at the University of Berlin). A long-term critic of the 'chauvinism', as he called it, of the Pan-Germans, he thought their aggressive hyper-nationalism had poisoned the political atmosphere in Germany both during and after the war. It had come to be shared by the military leadership and thus prolonged the conflict by persuading them against seeking a compromise peace. And the insistence on a victorious peace had prompted the Western Allies to insist on the same, leading to the diktat of Versailles. If anyone was to blame for losing the war, he thought, it was Ludendorff, against whom Delbrück carried on a relentless public campaign. He accused the general of insulting the troops who had fought so bravely by implying they had abandoned the struggle under the influence of socialist agitators. As Germany's most highly regarded military historian, Delbrück was called before the Reichstag's committee investigating the causes of Germany's defeat, and as preparation for his testimony, he collected a large amount of evidence, including letters solicited from soldiers themselves. Most of them confirmed his view that Ludendorff's persistent rejection of a compromise peace had created a growing war-weariness among the troops. Instead of launching the hopelessly misconceived spring offensive in 1918, the army should have come round while it could to the idea of a negotiated peace without annexations. It was not surprising that the troops in the end had refused to fight on for a victory that might take years to achieve.[68]

Delbrück repeated these charges when he was called to testify as an expert witness in the Cossmann trial, pointing out that Erzberger was already en route to Compiègne on 7 November 1918 with Hindenburg's instruction to accept the terms offered, two days before the outbreak of the revolution, which therefore could not have exerted any influence on the signing of the Armistice. Germany had been defeated not because of subversion but because of the strategic failure of the 1918 spring offensive. This had led to a collapse in morale at the front, accentuated by the increasingly dire supply situation. Ludendorff and his allies were merely protecting their own reputations when they ascribed the poor morale of the troops to socialist agitation. Delbrück was listened to and reported in the press with respect, because he had no personal or political interest in attacking the stab-in-the-back myth. But the voice of his reasoned conservatism was already being drowned out by the shrill cries of the National Socialists by the time of his death in 1929.

IV

The stab-in-the-back legend was not necessarily or invariably antisemitic. In its classic conspiracist form, it was directed first and foremost against the socialists and revolutionaries who led the revolution that overthrew the Kaiser and established, with the help of liberal parliamentarians, the Weimar Republic. At the same time, however, the most radical versions incorporated a powerful element of antisemitic conspiracism. Even before the outbreak of the war, individuals and groups on the far right of German nationalist politics had levelled accusations of unpatriotic behaviour against Germany's tiny Jewish minority. In the course of the late nineteenth century, the long tradition of Christian antisemitism had been overlaid and in some respects superseded by a new, racist variant. Influenced by racial theories derived from Artur de Gobineau, by radical variants of Social Darwinism, by imperialist disdain for colonial subjects and by the new science of eugenics, a small number of politicians and journalists in Germany began to argue that Jews, including those who had converted to Christianity, were innately subversive and unpatriotic. These ideas were taken up by ultra-nationalist movements like the Pan-German League, which wanted to turn back the tide of representative democracy, restrict the power of the Reichstag and install an authoritarian government that would pursue an aggressive and militaristic foreign policy and establish Germany as the leading world power.[69]

The Jews, declared the Pan-Germans, were subverting German values, weakening the masculine aggression of German men through the encouragement of feminism, and causing chaos by undermining the stability of the German family. Their propaganda insinuated that the feminist movement was led by Jewish women, though in fact it was not – Jewish women had their own organization, largely separate from mainstream liberal feminism.[70] In this warped racist vision, Germany's Jewish men were rootless, unpatriotic, weak and effeminate. During the war, as young German men were being killed in their hundreds of thousands, fresh recruits were needed in ever greater numbers, and the patriotic associations and their supporters began to campaign against 'shirkers' who they thought had avoided military service, just as, in Great Britain, suffragettes turned nationalists handed out white feathers on the street to men who they thought should have enlisted in the armed forces.

Towards the end of 1916 this growing campaign against 'shirkers' was coming to focus above all on Germany's Jews.[71] Acting under this political pressure, the War Ministry initiated a comprehensive census of Jewish soldiers in the German armed forces on the front line. Jewish doctors and officers, it was alleged by influential figures on the nationalist right, had made sure that Jewish soldiers predominantly served behind the lines, away from danger. Flawed though its methodology might have been, and incomplete though the data were, the outcome confounded expectations by showing that 80 per cent of Jewish soldiers were serving at the front. Altogether, in fact, some 100,000 Jews (defined as adherents of the Jewish faith) did their military service during the war; 12,000 were killed and 35,000 decorated for bravery. Instead of trumpeting these results as evidence of the patriotism of German Jews, the Ministry suppressed the survey's findings, thus allowing the suspicion that Jews were 'shirkers' to continue unchallenged. In the meantime, the mere fact of the census, together with the accompanying antisemitic propaganda, sent shock waves through the Jewish community, prompting many Jews to emphasize more than ever their patriotic zeal.[72]

Not surprisingly, the suppression of the investigation's findings created the opportunity for the stab-in-the-back myth to become infused with antisemitism on the extreme right. Already in a decisive session of the Army High Command at Spa, in Belgium, on 9 November 1918, a right-wing general suggested sending troops armed with flame-throwers and gas grenades against refractory troops. Calling on a common antisemitic stereotype, he blamed their situation on what he saw as the fact 'that Jewish war profiteers and shirkers have fallen upon the army from behind and blocked off its supplies'.[73] However, under General Groener's leadership, the meeting rejected this view and decided not to use violent or indeed any other methods in a vain attempt to shore up the crumbling regime of Kaiser Wilhelm II, who left Spa by train for exile in the Netherlands the same evening.

Already on 17 November 1918, however, less than a week after the signing of the Armistice, Groener declared:

> For four years the German people remained unbroken against a world of enemies – and now it has let itself be overthrown like a corpse by a handful of sailors, into whom the Russian poison of Herr Joffe [the Soviet ambassador] and comrades had been injected. And who are the wire-pullers? Jews here, as there.[74]

Groener was most likely reflecting a wider current of opinion in the General Staff as he articulated this view. Another senior staff officer, General Albrecht von Thaer, had already claimed a few days earlier, in a clear reference to *The Protocols of the Elders of Zion*, that a secret lodge of Jewish Freemasons in Paris had decided to destroy 'not only all dynasties but also the Holy See and the Church'.[75] Similar views were expressed by the leader of the Pan-German League leader, Heinrich Class, who declared in February 1919 that 'Jewish influence' had been the 'driving force' in the defeat of Germany. The Jews were a 'foreign element' in Germany, and the League, as it had already done before the war, demanded the withdrawal of civil rights from the Jewish population. One of its leading members published statistics purporting to show that for every one Jewish soldier who had been killed during the war, no fewer than three hundred non-Jewish soldiers had died. These statistics were pure invention, of course, as the unpublished 1916 'Jewish census' had already demonstrated.[76]

But the accusation would not go away. As long as the outcome of the census remained unavailable, far-right politicians and newspapers continued to polemicize against wartime Jewish 'slackers' whose bad example had supposedly undermined the will of German soldiers to carry on fighting. The military officer who is said to have demanded and set in motion the 'Jewish census', Major-General Ernst von Wrisberg, whose role during the war had been to manage supplies to the front, was the first to elaborate on the antisemitic version of the stab-in-the-back legend, in a lengthy discussion of what he called 'attacks on the officer class'. In March 1919 he alleged that 'a part of the Jewish population stood behind the German revolution. No wonder, when this tribe is doing everything to annihilate a class that has long been a thorn in its eye.'[77] Wrisberg's allegations caused a good deal of controversy, and he was retired from the army later that year, but this did not stop him from repeating his claims in his autobiography, published in 1921, where he alleged that 'the trouble-making and subversive activity of the Jews in the domestic economy and in the army was to an enormous extent to blame for the misfortune that has fallen upon our Fatherland'.[78]

In the same year, Colonel Max Bauer repeated the same charge in his memoirs. The decline of morale in the reserve army in the last months of the war, he charged, had been caused by 'socialist-bolshevik teaching'. It was from these reserve units, he declared, that the revolution had spread; and most of these 'slackers' were Jews. Needless to say, he provided no concrete evidence for any of these allegations, though he assumed that the still-unpublished results of the 'Jewish census' would substantiate them.[79] Another male supremacist, the youth movement ideologue Hans Blüher, writing under the influence of the Austrian writer Otto Weininger, whose *Sex and Character* had put forward antisemitic views as well as anti-feminist ones, took a line characteristic of conspiracy theorists when he declared in 1922:

> It's no use today for the Jewish press to try and refute the 'myth of the stab-in-the-back'. You can prove and refute anything. But it's become a fact that every German has it in his blood: Prussianism and heroism belong together, just as Jewdom and defeatism do . . . The associative connection between the essence of masculinity and the essence of the German being, and between the feminine and the servile with the Jewish, is a direct intuitive feeling of the German people that becomes more certain from day to day. In this instance no 'proofs' for and against are of any use, even if a hundred thousand Jews had fallen for the Fatherland.[80]

Just as in the case of *The Protocols of the Elders of Zion*, therefore, so in the case of the stab-in-the-back legend, and beyond this, in the case of other conspiracy theories, too, ultimately facts did not matter. Even if these theories were demonstrably untrue, they none the less expressed an *essential* truth that in the end was not susceptible to empirical verification at all.

Propagandists such as these were indulging in unsubstantiated fantasy. One writer alleged in 1919 that the Jews had been 'everywhere': they had been 'dominant' 'in the government of Wilhelm II, in the Liberals, and in the socialist groups', an idea that had absolutely no basis in reality, least of all in the light of Kaiser Wilhelm II's own vehement antisemitism.[81] Far more common was the identification of revolutionaries with Jews. Arthur Hoffmann-Kutsche, indeed, in his book *Der Dolchstoss durch das Judentum* (*The Stab in the Back by the Jews*, 1922), took the myth far back into history when he described the nineteenth-century emancipation of the Jews in Germany as the starting-point of the 'stab in the back'.[82] The ultra-nationalist society the German Protection and Defiance League (*Deutscher Schutz- und Trutzbund*) claimed that 'the Revolution was made with Jewish money, led and carried out by Jewish spirits'. Others, including Ludendorff, alleged that Jews were particularly strongly represented among revolutionaries and left-wing socialists.[83] Some antisemites highlighted what they saw as 'the monstrous crowd of Jews in leading government positions' in the new regime established in Germany by the 1918 revolution.[84]

But attempts to demonstrate this were less than convincing. The left-wing, later Communist, Reichstag deputy Karl Liebknecht, for instance, an opponent of the war from the outset, appeared frequently in antisemitic lists of alleged Jews in the socialist movement but was in fact not Jewish at all. True, there were some Jews in leading positions on the left, including Rosa Luxemburg, co-founder of German Communism with Liebknecht; the Bavarian socialist leader Kurt Eisner; the leader of the Munich Soviet Eugen Leviné; and the pacifist socialist Hugo Haase, co-leader with Friedrich Ebert of the revolutionary council in 1918: not coincidentally, all of them were assassinated in the early months of the Weimar Republic. But the number of people of Jewish origin in the leadership of the left-wing parties was very small and, crucially, in becoming socialists or Communists they abandoned their Jewish identity, insofar as they had ever had one. Moreover, there was no evidence at all to back up allegations that they had somehow conspired to stab Germany in the back. In the absence of any real facts to support these fantastical claims, antisemites had to fall back on the allegation that power had been seized in the 1918 Revolution not by the Social Democrats but by 'secret Jewish wire-pullers' who were manipulating them. So, in other words, even if it could not be shown that these men had any Jewish family or other connections, they were still Jewish in the end, because their 'spirit' was Jewish even if their ancestry was not.[85]

V

Perhaps surprisingly, the idea of the 'stab in the back' was hardly used by the Nazis. It appears for example only once in the hundreds of pages of *Mein Kampf*, as part of a general attack on the Kaiser's rule for failing to recognize the threat posed by 'Marxism', or in other words Social Democracy, a movement which Hitler regarded as led by Jews.[86] A trawl through the collected editions of Hitler's proclamations, speeches and articles turns up only very meagre results.[87] For the Nazis, the Kaiser's regime had richly deserved its fate; the reason for its defeat had not been the stab in the back: it had been overthrown mainly because it lacked the will to survive. 'This defeat,' Hitler declared, 'was more than deserved' because the Kaiser and his government had not been prepared 'to apply thoroughly radical means' to win the war.[88] The Nazis still argued that the army had been in a position to win the war on the Western Front in November 1918, a claim not even Ludendorff had advanced ('I have never said the army was undefeated in the autumn of 1918,' he wrote in 1921). But because, unlike the conservatives who propagated the myth, they were not nostalgic in any way for the Bismarckian Empire, they were not very interested in harking back to the reasons for its defeat. Instead, they focused on what they saw as Germany's ills in the present, above all in the Depression that hit the country in 1929.[89] If the

Jews had played a part in the defeat of Germany in 1918, it was not, Hitler thought, through violent action or conspiracy but through contributing to the weakening of the German will to fight.[90]

On the only occasion on which he spoke at length about the reasons for the defeat in 1918 (9 November 1928, the tenth anniversary of the Kaiser's enforced abdication), Hitler put the blame squarely on the 'vermin' who had 'slowly ruined and poisoned us . . . the Hebrews'. Yet this process, in which the German people had been gradually made spiritually defenceless, faded into the background for him in comparison to the 'November criminals' who had signed the Armistice and the Treaty of Versailles. More important in his mind than identifying the causes of the defeat was the creation of a unified German 'people's community', reproducing the supposed 'spirit of 1914', in which the Kaiser had proclaimed that he did not recognize any parties any more, only Germans.[91] Hitler was wary of publicly blaming the loss of the war on the weakness of the home front in a more general sense not least because, especially after the fiasco of the failed beer-hall putsch in 1923, he was focusing his attention on winning votes; many of his potential supporters, women especially but also older men, had spent the war years on the home front, and it would not help his cause to accuse them of stabbing the army in the back or lacking the willpower to keep supporting it till the end.[92]

There was no doubt, of course, about the visceral antisemitism of the Nazi Party, and Hitler himself, from the very beginning. For Hitler, 'the international Jew' was 'the real organizer of the Revolution' of 1918. The overthrow of the Kaiser's regime had been prepared in order to establish 'the rule of the Jews', which, Hitler believed, had now come to pass in the form of the Weimar Republic. The 'so-called November Revolution' had been nothing but a 'Jewish putsch'. The Nazi newspaper, the *Völkischer Beobachter*, commenting on the 1925 trial, alleged that 'Jewry was the main factor in the stab in the back'.[93] But of course it was more or less unavoidable that the paper should use this term when reporting and commenting on a trial in which the concept took a central place. More generally, the Nazi press made no more than very occasional mentions of the stab in the back.[94] The Nazi propaganda machine preferred to concentrate its fire on the 'November criminals', the men who had (in their view) cravenly accepted the Armistice terms and betrayed the German race in the peace settlement. The weakness of will of the Kaiser and his regime had lost the war, but the treachery of the 'November criminals' had lost the peace.[95]

Beyond this, in their early propaganda and in the official Party Programme promulgated in 1920, the Nazis focused on what they portrayed as the economic criminality of Germany's Jews. A central allegation focused on the claim that Jewish businessmen had been 'war profiteers'. The war had in fact brought considerable dislocation to the German economy. Under the impact of an Allied economic blockade that lasted many months after the Armistice, food supplies in particular had run short, and over half a million Germans had died from malnutrition and associated diseases. As the military authorities had imposed ever harsher rationing, a vast black market had boomed behind the scenes, bringing substantial profits to the criminals who ran it. Of course, these were mostly non-Jewish (the Jewish population of Germany was under half of one per cent), but antisemites viewed such behaviour as evidence of a 'Jewish spirit' and so ascribed the entire black market to the manipulation of Jewish war profiteers. 'Jewish wartime inflation' was thus 'just as responsible for the shattering of the German will to fight . . . as was revolutionary agitation'.[96]

Yet this did not play very much of a role in Nazi propaganda during the years from 1929 to 1933, when the Nazis rose from being a fringe phenomenon to being the largest party. They had discovered in the national elections of 1928 that antisemitism did not resonate with the majority of voters. In 1933, of course, this all changed. However, though antisemitic rhetoric was ramped up once more after the Nazi seizure of power in 1933, Hitler now moved on from his earlier rhetorical assaults on the 'November criminals' to a more positive emphasis on the need to avoid in the coming war the mistakes made in the earlier one. The Nazi state would remove the Jews from Germany to guard against subversion from within; it would steel the people's will by educating them to embrace war with enthusiasm and commitment; it would install ruthless disciplinary measures in the armed forces to punish 'slackers' and 'defeatists'. Rather than continuing to attack the old Imperial elites for their supposed lack of willpower in 1918, a line that would have alienated them at a time when he needed their support, Hitler preferred to pull them along with him in the drive towards war and conquest.[97]

When he spoke or wrote about the First World War, however, which he did not do very often, it was less to bemoan Germany's defeat than to celebrate Germany's victories – Tannenberg rather than Verdun, for example – or to stress extreme examples of heroic sacrifice, notably Langemarck, where thousands of young Germans had gone into battle singing patriotic songs and been mown down by enemy machine-guns.[98] His own wartime service had after all been the greatest and most fulfilling time of his life. He preferred not to dwell on the defeat, which reminded him, and his audiences, of Germany's humiliation; rather, he focused on learning the lessons for the next war: overcoming the class divide that had undermined the German people's solidarity between 1914 and 1918; destroying democracy, which meant weakness of will, and replacing it with dictatorship, where Germany would be guided by a single strong, unshakeable will to power – his own; ruthlessly punishing 'shirkers', defeatists and deserters (more than 15,000 German soldiers would be executed for such offences during the Second World War); avoiding a two-front war (a goal which ultimately eluded Hitler); preventing a recurrence of the supply problems that he believed affected Germany during the First World War by conquering vast tracts of Eastern Europe and, especially, by using the grain and food in Ukraine, 'Europe's bread-basket', to maintain living standards in Germany itself; instituting generous family allowances so that troops at the front would not become anxious about the condition of their loved ones at home; strengthening the workforce by using foreign forced labour and so freeing up young men to fight at the front; and, not least, neutralizing what he thought were potentially subversive elements, above all the Jews, by forcing them to leave Germany and, in the end, by murdering them.[99]

For Hitler and the Nazi leadership, the genocide of Europe's Jews was to some extent an act of revenge for their supposed incitement of the 'encirclement' of Germany by hostile powers in 1914. Hitler blamed the First World War in large part on the machinations of Jewish 'international finance capital'. 'This race of criminals has the two million dead of the [First] World War on its conscience,' and 'once more hundreds of thousands', he said on 25 October 1941, 'so don't tell me we can't send them into the morass,' meaning kill them by driving them into the Pripet marshes, conquered by German armies after the invasion of the Soviet Union. Even more explicit was the statement of Heinrich Himmler on 4 October 1943, addressing the assembled SS hierarchy in Posen openly about the mass murders they had been carrying out: 'We would probably have got to the stage of the year 1916/17 if the Jews were still lodged in the body of the German people.'[100]

The idea of the stab in the back took on a very different form in 1944, following the failed attempt on Hitler's life by the military-conservative resistance on 20 July. Hitler tried initially to pin the blame on a small group of conspirators who thought that 'they could plunge the dagger into the back, as in 1918'. Although the phrase 'stab in the back' was used frequently by the Nazi leadership in the following days and weeks, however, it no longer referred to socialists or even Jews, but, as Himmler and the Gestapo uncovered the involvement of growing numbers of army officers and generals in the plot, it came to be employed in an exact reversal of its original formulation: it was not the home front that had stabbed the army in the back in 1918, not the 'deserters, Jews, asocials, criminals' who were to blame for Germany's defeat, but the generals themselves. Indeed, from this point up to the end of the war, the idea of the 'stab in the back' lost all its former specificities and was used by the Nazi regime to stigmatize anyone, whatever their position in society, their politics or their race, who was perceived to be undermining the increasingly futile war effort in any way.[101]

VI

The stab-in-the-back myth took a variety of forms both during and after November 1918. There was a very broad version, in which it was argued that the defeat in 1918 had been caused by the collapse of the home front in general, for economic and social reasons, damaging war production and weakening morale; nobody had intended this, it had just happened, above all as a consequence of the Allied blockade. Put in this way, the myth had not yet taken on the shape of a true conspiracy theory, which must necessarily include an element of deliberate intent. Yet it was this belief that had the most tangible impact on Hitler and the Nazis, as they developed from early on the purpose of conquering Eastern Europe in order to gain 'living space' (*Lebensraum*), meaning the annexation of vast agrarian areas in Ukraine and elsewhere, their colonization by German farmers, and their use to supply the German people with food so that they would not suffer as they had done under the Allied blockade in the First World War.

Then there was a narrower version, in which militarists and nationalists pointed the finger at the German left, accusing it of deliberately undermining the war effort by subversion, strikes, rioting and eventually revolution at home, in order to destroy the regime of the Kaiser and replace it with a socialist state. This really only emerged in its fully developed form after the revolution of 9 November 1918, although its exponents now claimed that socialist conspirators had infiltrated the armed forces before this, or undermined the will of the civilian population to continue supporting the war effort. Hitler and the Nazis, as we have seen, made relatively little use of this idea in their political propaganda. Their suppression of Social Democrats and Communists, who were arrested and imprisoned in their thousands and executed in their hundreds in 1933 and after, when the Nazis came to power, reflected above all the fact that these two political movements provided the bulk of active opposition to Nazism and therefore had to be destroyed.

Finally, there was an antisemitic version, in which socialist subversion was ascribed to the deliberately disintegrative work of Jews at home and abroad, reflecting the conviction that Jews everywhere were inclined by heredity to engage in subversion of the state and the German race.[102] It was this latter belief, rather than any specific antisemitic conspiracy theory that linked German Jews to their country's defeat in the war, that led the Nazi regime to work for the expulsion of Jews from the German 'national community', depriving them of their rights, pushing them to emigrate in numbers as large as possible, and eventually, during the war itself, arresting them, forcing them into ghettos, and murdering them in a genocidal campaign of extermination that soon extended far beyond the borders of Germany itself.

These three variants of the myth to some degree contradicted one another. The version of the myth that ascribed Germany's defeat to the collapse of the domestic economy, leading to the decline of morale on the home front and then in the armed forces themselves, implied that there was no chance that the armed forces could have carried on fighting longer than they actually did. In the other two variants of the myth, both of which treated the defeat as the outcome of a conspiracy deliberately aimed at causing Germany to lose the war, there was an implied counterfactual, according to which the army could have carried on fighting if the revolution had not broken out, thereby securing a compromise peace on terms better than those actually obtained; in the more extreme version, both army and people could have risen up in defence of the Fatherland, had the government rejected the peace terms and the Allies invaded.

The claim that the German government could have wrested better peace conditions from the Allies had the army not been prevented from fighting on by the outbreak of the revolution has recently been revived by the historian Gerd Krumeich, who has called it 'realistic' and asked rhetorically whether the stab-in-the-back thesis does not perhaps contain a kernel of truth.[103] But, as we have seen, the timing of Germany's military collapse and the outbreak of the revolution tell against this hypothesis. The morale of the German troops began to plummet, for military reasons, after the failure of the 1918 spring offensive, by July at the latest; by early September it was clear that the war was lost, and by early October the German army on the Western Front was already starting to disintegrate. The idea that the troops could have fought on in the defence of the Fatherland at a time when they were deserting in ever-growing numbers was, and is, a fantasy. And if they had done so, war-weary, weakened, poorly supplied and below strength, they would have been overwhelmed by the increasingly superior Allied forces, with fresh American troops continually coming to the front, and more tanks arriving every day with which the German defences could be ever more easily overrun. Ironically, given his later espousal of the stab-in-the-back theory, it was Ludendorff who, at least in the course of September and early October

1918, was being realistic here, not later historians. And it was Luden-dorff who abandoned the army and, indeed, the country, when the revolution broke out, donning blue spectacles and a false beard, and fleeing to Sweden, where he remained for the next few months until asked to leave by the Swedish authorities.

What was the effect of these various versions of the myth? For many millions of Communists and Social Democrats, of course, none of them meant very much at all. Nor, more broadly, for the moderate political parties that supported the Weimar Republic from the begin-ning, the Social Democrats, the left-liberal German Democrats and the Catholic Centre. All varieties of the legend had currency over-whelmingly on the nationalist right, which looked back nostalgically to the days of the Kaiser and the Prussian military monarchy best represented by Frederick the Great in the eighteenth century. On the extreme right, among the Pan-Germans and various small but often violent radical counter-revolutionary groups, most notably among the National Socialists, the antisemitic version predominated. The myth was therefore confined to a small, if vocal and influential, fringe of the political system of the Weimar Republic until the very end of the 1920s. It was not adopted by the great majority of the elector-ate.[104] Moreover, the Nazis' reluctance to use it in their propaganda further contributed to diminishing its influence. What undermined the legitimacy of the Weimar Republic was not so much the stab-in-the-back myth in any of its various forms as a much more general feeling that the advent of democracy had been accompanied by the national humiliation of the peace settlement and the war-guilt clause of the Treaty of Versailles, for which, therefore, whatever the reasons for Germany's defeat, it was ultimately responsible.

The stab-in-the-back myth was a far more specific conspiracy the-ory than the attribution to the Jews, all over the world, of instinctive, racially determined subversive and conspiratorial instincts by docu-ments like the *Protocols*. For one thing, it was confined mainly (though not exclusively) to Germany, and focused on specifically Ger-man historical events. For another, in its better-defined iterations, it pointed to particular groups in society, whether it was socialists, Communists and pacifists, or (an overlapping category in the minds of the extreme right) Jews at home, aided and encouraged by other

Jews abroad, above all in Britain, France and the United States. At the same time, it was not the kind of conspiracy theory that identified named or identifiable individuals who had allegedly caused Germany's defeat, except a few representative figures like Karl Liebknecht or Philipp Scheidemann, neither of whom was Jewish. For a still more narrowly focused type of conspiracy theory, directed against named individuals alleged to have been responsible for a specific event, we have to turn our attention from 9–11 November 1918 to another key turning point in German history, which took place on the night of 27–8 February 1933.

Communism
in
Germany!

The Truth about the Communist Conspiracy
on the Eve of the National Revolution

By

ADOLF EHRT

3

Who burned down the Reichstag?

Conspiracy theories often tend to cluster around violent and unexpected political events. A sudden death of a head of state, an assassination of a government minister, a bomb attack on a building or a crowd – these and similar, seemingly random occurrences demand explanation. For many, the idea that they could be the product of chance, or accident, or the deranged mind of a single disturbed individual, seems too simple to be plausible. Whatever the evidence seems to suggest, the authorship of such major outrages must surely have been collective, the planning long-term and meticulous. The killing of US President John F. Kennedy in Dallas in 1963 and the destruction of the twin towers of the World Trade Center in New York in 2001 are perhaps the two major vortices into which conspiracy theorists have been sucked in our own time, spewing out ever more elaborate hypotheses and pseudo-explanations as they re-emerge. Argument continues to rage, as the proponents of rival theories construct evidential edifices of such staggering detail and complexity that they are frequently almost impossible for the layperson to navigate.

Alternative histories of this kind are a product of the paranoid imagination, as identified in Richard Hofstadter's famous article. They have a long history. In 1933 another major and wholly unpredicted violent event occurred, in Berlin, the capital of Germany, as it was beginning to experience the transition from the Weimar Republic to the Third Reich. Hitler had been installed as Reich Chancellor in a coalition government consisting mainly of conservatives, but not yet in possession of dictatorial power, and in the middle of a general election campaign. The Nazis had already gone some way towards suppressing their most determined opponent, the German Communist Party, which at the previous election, in November 1932, had won a hundred seats in the Reichstag, the national legislature. German Communism was a powerful mass movement, but already by mid-February 1933 it had been forced to close its party headquarters in Berlin. It was obliged instead to use the committee rooms of the Reichstag for its meetings, held to organize the party's election campaign. Shortly before twenty to nine in the evening of 27 February 1933, just under a week before the election was due to take place, the leader of the Communist Reichstag delegation, Ernst Torgler, left the building after one such meeting, accompanied by another deputy and the secretary of the party delegation, Anna Rehme. Torgler, a witty and popular member of the Reichstag, handed the keys to the porter Rudolf Scholz as they left, exchanging a few pleasantries with him. The day porter had already been on his rounds, looking into the debating chamber at about half-past eight, finding everything in order. Coming on duty, the night porter Albert Wendt spoke briefly to the official messenger Willi Otto, who went upstairs, carrying his lantern through the darkened building, to empty the deputies' postbox. Otto left the gloomy corridors and staircases at around five to nine. Neither Wendt nor Otto had heard anything suspicious in the debating chamber or the echoing corridors.[1]

At three minutes past nine, a young theology student, Hans Flöter, was passing by the looming side elevation of the huge stone building on his way home from another day at the Prussian State Library when he heard the sound of breaking glass coming from the front of the building. At first he thought nothing of it, but as the noise continued he realized that a window was being systematically shattered. Going round to see what was happening, he saw a dark figure carrying a blazing torch climbing in through a window next to the front portal. Alarmed, Flöter made his way to the policeman who he knew from his regular journeys past the building was stationed nearby, and alerted him to the incident. Then he went home, having done his civic duty. The policeman, officer Karl Buwert, went towards the building and peered into the interior. He was joined by two passers-by, including a young typesetter, Werner Thaler. It was now ten past nine. They observed a mixture of shifting shadows and flickering flames moving from one window to the next behind the façade and ran along outside, following them. When the movement within the building stopped for a moment, the policeman fired his pistol, but failed to hit anything. He sent one of his companions to the nearest police station to summon the fire brigade. Flames could now be seen inside the building, attracting the attention of other passers-by, who also telephoned the fire brigade. More policemen arrived, having heard Buwert's shot. The Reichstag's night porter, Albert Wendt, was summoned and telephoned the secretary of the Reichstag's President, Hermann Göring.

By now, the fire engines were approaching the building, and their noise alerted the building's supervisor, who ran across with the keys. He went into the building with three policemen who were waiting outside, and the men made their way to the debating chamber, arriving shortly after twenty past nine. They saw flames running up the curtains behind the Speaker's chair, and passed several much smaller fires as they went with drawn pistols through the building. In the room where the stenographers usually sat a fire was burning fiercely. On reaching the restaurant, the men were met by a wall of flame. Returning through the debating chamber, they came across a half-naked young man, who was sweating profusely, and arrested him at gunpoint. 'Why have you done this?' the building's supervisor shouted at him. 'In protest!' the man replied. Enraged, the supervisor hit him twice. The young man was searched and his identity papers confiscated. They revealed that he was Marinus van der Lubbe, born in Leiden, Holland, on 13 January 1909. He was taken off to the nearest police station. It was twenty-seven minutes past nine. Nobody else was found at the scene of the crime. A mysterious figure seen leaving the building later turned out to be a man who had taken shelter from the cold in the doorway while he was waiting for his bus. An official police report submitted by Dr Walter Zirpins on 3 March concluded that van der Lubbe had been the sole perpetrator. Under interrogation, the young Dutchman had reconstructed the sequence of events precisely. No fire he had not admitted to having laid himself had been discovered anywhere in the building.

The fire brigade had arrived nine minutes earlier, and went into the building, putting out most of the smaller fires. When they tried to enter the debating chamber, however, the firemen encountered a sea of flames: the wooden panelling and furniture were blazing, and the heat was so strong that they were forced to turn back. The fire was sucking in air and creating a fierce updraught. Meanwhile, more fire engines began to arrive. Shortly after twenty to ten there were no fewer than sixty of them, taking water from the nearby River Spree to douse the flames, and by eleven o'clock the fires had all been extinguished. The debating chamber was burned out; all the wooden fixtures and fittings were no more than charred remains. The next morning, almost all that was left of the German national legislature was a shell.

One of the first outsiders to arrive at the scene was the British reporter Sefton Delmer, who had managed somehow to ingratiate himself with the Nazi leaders. He left behind a graphic account of the events that unfolded that fateful evening.

> The news that the Reichstag was burning came to me from one of the many petrol station attendants to whom I had given my card with a request to ring me if anything noteworthy happened nearby. There were no taxis to be seen, and I had already put my car in the garage a quarter of a mile away. So I ran, ran and ran the whole mile and a half from my office to the Reichstag. I got there at a quarter to ten – just forty minutes after the first alarm had been given. Already there were quite a few people standing around, watching the flames funnelling up through the great glass dome in a pillar of fire and smoke. Every minute fresh trains of fire engines were arriving, their bells clanging as they raced through the streets. An excited policeman told me, 'They've got one of them who did it, a man with nothing but his trousers on. He seems to have used his coat and shirt to start the fire. But there must be others still inside. They're looking for them there.'

Delmer spoke to as many people as he could, noting it all down, and was later able to reconstruct the reactions of the Nazi leadership in some detail. The news of the fire had first been spread by Ernst Hanfstängl, known to all as 'Putzi', a half-American, half-German playboy and barfly who had helped Hitler out following the beer-hall putsch in 1923 and had remained one of his friends ever since. A notorious practical joker, he often had difficulty in getting people to take him seriously. And so it was on this occasion too. As Delmer recalled,

> Hanfstängl, who was trying to sleep off an attack of flu in a room of Göring's presidential palace opposite to the Reichstag, had been awakened by the fire engines. He looked out of his window, saw the fire, rushed to the telephone and called Goebbels. 'The Reichstag is on fire,' he almost shrieked. 'Tell the Führer.' 'Oh, stop that nonsense, Putzi. It is not even funny,' answered Goebbels. 'But I am telling the truth.' 'I am not listening to any more of your stale jokes. Go back to bed. Good night!' And Goebbels hung up.
>
> The trouble was that just about four days earlier that merry little prankster Goebbels, to amuse Hitler, had played a telephone hoax on Hanfstängl. And when Hanfstängl called him with the Reichstag fire alarm he thought he was being hoaxed back. But Hanfstängl rang again. 'Look here! What I am telling you is the absolute truth. It is your duty to tell the Führer. If you don't I guarantee there'll be trouble!' Even now Goebbels would not believe him. However, this time he did pass the message to Hitler, who was in the next room.

As Delmer was talking to eyewitnesses at the scene of the fire, he saw two black Mercedes cars driving through the police cordon that had now been set up around the Reichstag.

> 'That's Hitler, I'll bet!' I said to a man beside me. I ducked under the rope the police had just put up to keep spectators back and rushed across to check up. I got to the Reichstag entrance Portal Two, it was just as Hitler jumped out and dashed up the steps two at a time, the tails of his trench coat flying, his floppy black artist's hat pulled down over his head. Goebbels and the bodyguard were behind him . . . Inside the entrance stood Göring, massive in a camel hair coat, his legs astride like some Frederician guardsman in a UFA film. His soft brown hat was turned up in front in what was called 'Potsdam' fashion. He was very red in the face and glared disapprovingly at me. How he would have loved to have thrown me out. But Hitler had just said 'Evening, Herr Delmer,' and that was my ticket of admission.

Göring made his report to Hitler, while Goebbels and I stood at their side listening avidly. 'Without a doubt this is the work of the Communists, Herr Chancellor,' Göring said. 'A number of Communist deputies were present here in the Reichstag twenty minutes before the fire broke out. We have succeeded in arresting one of the incendiaries.' 'Who is he?' Goebbels asked excitedly. Göring turned to face him. 'We don't know yet,' he said with that thin shark's mouth of his, 'but we shall squeeze it out of him, have no fear, Doctor.' He said it as though he resented an implied criticism of his efficiency. Then Hitler asked a question. 'Are the other public buildings safe?' 'I have taken every possible precaution,' said Göring. 'I've mobilised all the police. Every public building has been given a special guard. We are ready for anything.' I am sure that he meant this seriously and was not just putting on an act. Both Hitler and Göring then still feared the possibility of a Communist coup. With six million votes at the last elections and a large number of adherents in the trade unions the Communists were still a formidable power. And they had in the past tried to capture power by coups – just as the Nazis had.

Then, Göring's report done, we set off on a tour of the building. Across pools of water, charred debris, and through clouds of evil smelling smoke we made our way across rooms and corridors. Someone opened a yellow varnished oak door, and for a moment we peeped into the blazing furnace of the debating chamber. It was like opening the door of an oven. Although the fire brigade were spraying away lustily with their hoses, the fire was roaring up into the cupola with a fury which made us shut that door again in a hurry. Göring picked a piece of rag off the floor near one of the charred curtains. 'Here, you can see for yourself, Herr Chancellor, how they started the fire,' he said. 'They hung cloths soaked in petrol over the furniture and set it alight.' Notice the 'they.' 'They' did this, 'they' did that. For Göring there was no question that more than one incendiary must have been at work. It had to be more than one to fit in with his conviction that the fire was the result of a Communist conspiracy. There had to be a gang of incendiaries. But as I looked at the rags and the other evidence, I could see nothing that one man could not have done on his own.

We came into a lobby filled with smoke. A policeman stepped out and barred the way with outstretched arms. 'You must not pass here, Herr Chancellor. That candelabra may crash to the floor any moment.' And he pointed up at a crystal chandelier. In the next corridor Hitler fell back a bit and joined me. He was moved to prophesy: 'God grant,' he said, 'that this be the work of the Communists. You are now witnessing the beginning of a great new epoch in German history, Herr Delmer. This fire is the beginning.'[2]

The Nazi leaders clearly believed that the arson attack was part of a Communist plot. As Goebbels put it in his diary, they intended in his view 'through fire and terror to sow confusion in order in the general panic to grasp power for themselves'.[3] Göring ordered the mass arrest of Communists the same night, and Nazi stormtroopers, already enrolled as auxiliary policemen, fanned out across the capital, picking up known Communist Party activists and taking them off to makeshift prisons, basements, warehouses and torture centres. The Nazis' violent seizure of power was under way.

The next morning, the Cabinet, still with its majority of non-Nazi conservatives, met to draw up an emergency decree that abrogated civil liberties across Germany. Signed by Reich President Hindenburg the same day, it abolished freedom of speech, freedom of assembly and association and freedom of the press, suspended the autonomy of the federated states, like Baden or Bavaria, and legalized phone-tapping, the interception of correspondence and other intrusions into the rights of the individual citizen. It was of major assistance to the Nazis in clamping down on their opponents' campaigns in the general election, which gave the government parties a slim majority of 52 to 48 per cent. Far more importantly, however, the decree was repeatedly renewed all the way up to the end of the Third Reich in 1945. It was the first of the two fundamental documents on which the dictatorship of the Third Reich rested. The Enabling Act, passed by the Reichstag under massive Nazi intimidation and in the absence of the Communist deputies on 23 March 1933, assigned exclusive legislative power to Hitler and his ministers, thus bypassing the President and the Reichstag. It completed the process. By the summer of 1933 all opposition had been crushed. Nearly 200,000 Communists, Social

Democrats and other opponents of the Nazis had passed through the brutal regime of the concentration camps. All independent political parties had been forced to dissolve themselves, the Cabinet was almost exclusively Nazi in composition, and Hitler's dictatorial regime had been firmly established.[4]

The Third Reich, therefore, was built on the foundations of a conspiracy theory, the theory that the Communists had set fire to the Reichstag as the first act in a plot to overthrow the Republic. The most implacable opponents of the Nazis, they had garnered some 17 per cent of the vote in the last completely free elections of the Weimar Republic, in November 1932, increasing the number of seats they held in the national legislature while the Nazis had lost some of theirs. The Communist Party of Germany had never made any secret of its intention of destroying Weimar democracy and creating a 'Soviet Germany' on the lines of Stalin's Soviet Union. Violent seizures of power had been Communist practice in Russia in 1917 and, less successfully, in other countries in the following years, including Germany itself. It seemed obvious to Hitler that the destruction of the Reichstag could be the result only of a planned Communist conspiracy. The Nazi leadership proceeded therefore to charge a number of Communists with conspiring to burn down the German parliament building. Accompanied by a blaze of propaganda, this charge convinced many middle-class Germans that the decree was justifiable in the face of a threatened Communist coup.

By the time van der Lubbe was brought to trial before the German Supreme Court in Leipzig, he had been joined in the dock by Georgii Dimitrov, head of the Central Europe Section of the Communist International, and two other Bulgarian Communists who were in Berlin at the time, along with Ernst Torgler, floor leader of the German Communist Party in the Reichstag (on the grounds that he had been spotted leaving the building not long before the fire had started, though, as we have seen, there was a perfectly innocent explanation for this). Though the judge, Wilhelm Bünger, a well-known conservative and Saxon politician, attempted at every opportunity to shut him up, Dimitrov ran rings round the prosecution and mocked the Nazis' conspiracy theory with wit and panache. A decisive moment came with his cross-examination of

Hermann Göring, who as a witness called by the prosecution had given what he took to be evidence for the Communists' role in starting the fire. Dimitrov demolished its credibility and implied Göring was lying.

> Goering's anger mounted . . . : 'I did not come here to be accused by you.' Dimitrov: 'You are a witness.' Goering: 'In my eyes you are nothing but a scoundrel, a crook who belongs on the gallows.' Dimitrov: 'Very well, I am most satisfied.' At this point, Judge Buenger cut Dimitrov off, again accusing him of making propaganda, while not rebuking Goering at all. Dimitrov tried to put more questions, but the judge ordered him to sit down. Dimitrov had one last shot: 'You are greatly afraid of my questions, are you not, Herr Minister?' Goering's anger rose. He replied, 'You will be afraid when I catch you. You wait until I get you out of the power of this Court, you crook!' The judge, ever dutiful, said, 'Dimitrov is expelled for three days. Out with him!'[5]

The trial judges bowed to political necessity and found that the Communists had planned the fire. But, biased though they were, they were not mere Nazi stooges and still clung to at least some vestiges of legal propriety. So they dismissed the charges against Torgler and the three Bulgarians as insufficiently grounded in clear evidence.[6]

Van der Lubbe alone was found guilty. He was sentenced to death and executed in accordance with a Nazi decree that made arson subject to capital punishment even though it had not been at the time of the burning of the Reichstag – the first of many Nazi violations of fundamental legal principles.[7] The Nazis did their best to make political capital out of the general verdict of the court, but privately Hitler was furious. He quickly set up a new system of special courts, crowned by the so-called People's Court, to bypass the clearly unreliable traditional legal system and deliver the verdicts he wanted in further cases. But Torgler and the Bulgarians could not be tried again (double jeopardy was a principle even the Nazis were unwilling to violate at this point), and they were eventually released; after secret negotiations the Bulgarians made their way to the Soviet Union, where Dimitrov prepared to become the first Communist leader of Bulgaria after the war. Torgler, anxious to save his son from the violence that had been threatened against him by the Nazis, began working secretly for the Gestapo and eventually found a minor post for himself in the Propaganda Ministry, a move that caused him considerable problems after the war, when he eventually abandoned Communism and joined the Social Democratic Party in West Germany.[8]

II

Well before this time, Dimitrov and the Communist propaganda apparatus had developed their own conspiracy theory about the fire. The campaign was orchestrated by Willi Münzenberg, the Communist International's propaganda impresario, editor of a bestselling illustrated newspaper and organizer of countless Communist front organizations. Münzenberg's line was straightforward. The Nazis had benefited: so the Nazis must have started it (*cui bono* arguments of this sort are almost always a feature of conspiracy theories). Münzenberg and his team rapidly put together *The Brown Book of the Hitler Terror and the Burning of the Reichstag*, published later in 1933.[9] Aside from the numerous, undoubtedly genuine and often moving and shocking first-hand accounts of Nazi brutality by those who had suffered from it, the *Brown Book* presented ninety pages of documentation putting the case that a Nazi team of arsonists led by a prominent Brownshirt, Edmund Heines, had entered the Reichstag through a secret tunnel from Göring's official residence, set light to it in many places at once, then decamped back through the tunnel to safety, leaving the hapless van der Lubbe as a stooge to take the blame as suggested by 'his employers', the Nazis.[10] The book laid particular weight on the details supplied by a memorandum supposedly written by the Reichstag floor leader of Hitler's conservative Nationalist Party allies, Ernst Oberfohren, that put the blame on the Nazis.

The *Brown Book*, backed up by a sensational counter-trial *in absentia* of the supposed Nazi authors of the blaze, held before a carefully selected international bench of judges in London, put the Nazis on the defensive. Münzenberg had achieved a real propaganda coup and the allegations of the *Brown Book* were widely believed.

Here, it seemed, was a conspiracy theory that held water. None the less, after the war, in the course of a massive programme of denazification and prosecution, nobody managed to find any other guilty parties to stand trial for the crime for which van der Lubbe alone had been convicted. The amnesiac political culture of West Germany at the time worked against any attempt to identify Nazis who might have been involved. In East Germany, the *Brown Book* version continued to be regarded as the truth, and no point was seen in probing the issue any further. In 1956 its conclusions were tentatively supported by an investigation carried out on behalf of the West German government's political education service.[11]

Then, in 1959, a series of articles appeared in the news magazine *Der Spiegel* arguing that both conspiracy theories, the Communist and the Nazi, were wrong: van der Lubbe had acted without assistance. Three years later, the research presented in the articles was published in a greatly expanded form in a lengthy book by the previously unknown writer Fritz Tobias, entitled *The Reichstag Fire: Legend and Reality*. In well over seven hundred pages it presented a range of meticulously detailed evidential analyses backed by an enormous quantity of careful research in support of the thesis that van der Lubbe had lit the fire alone.[12] Among other things, Tobias produced contemporary evidence that demonstrated Oberfohren had not written the memorandum credited to him. He pointed out that van der Lubbe had always denied the involvement of anyone else in the arson and had greeted Dimitrov's claim in court to the contrary with open amusement.[13] The expert witnesses called before the court to explain how the fire had spread so quickly had testified that this had only been possible because fires had been laid with incendiary liquids at a number of points simultaneously – but of course they were testifying in support of the *Nazi* claim that the *Communists* had laid the fire; they knew that failure to conclude that van der Lubbe had not acted alone would have brought them into serious danger at a time when the Nazis were torturing and murdering thousands of their opponents. Nevertheless, under cross-examination by Dimitrov, the expert witnesses had conceded that given the fact that when he was arrested, van der Lubbe was panting and drenched in sweat, it was at least possible that he could have raced through the building setting fires in a number of different places within the space of a quarter of an hour. Other examples of major fires in large buildings cited by Tobias backed up the supposition that it would not have been difficult for one person to cause a major conflagration in the Reichstag within a short space of time.[14]

Ironically, indeed, a good deal of the evidence telling against a Nazi conspiracy was produced for the Leipzig court when it examined the Nazi thesis of a Communist conspiracy. This applied, for example, to the tunnel through which the arsonists were supposed to have gained access to the Reichstag and then fled once they had set the building ablaze. There was indeed a tunnel, and the court investigated it thoroughly. The maze of cellars and service rooms beneath the Reichstag building was so confusing that a policeman sent down to try and find the way to Göring's official residence got lost and had to be rescued by a search party. So many doors would have had to have been unlocked to allow the arsonists access to the Reichstag cellars and then locked again to conceal their activities on the way back that it would have been impossible to have carried out the deed expeditiously. Moreover, an inspection immediately after the fire revealed that the doors were all firmly shut.

When a group of journalists was led through the tunnel they discovered that the loosely fixed metal plates that covered the tunnel floor made such a noise when they trod on them that a group of stormtroopers would undoubtedly have alerted the night porter in Göring's official residence to their presence even had they been wearing felt slippers (and indeed an attempt was made to pass through the tunnel with such footwear, with the same noisy result). The night porter himself testified under oath that he had neither seen nor heard anything suspicious before the fire broke out. On the other hand, the evidence of the window through which van der Lubbe had gained access to the building, along with the testimony of witnesses who had heard the sound of the glass breaking as he climbed in, was irrefutable.[15] Tobias pointed out that no traces of flammable liquids or containers had been found at the site of the fire. Accompanied by a hundred pages of documentation from the trial and other sources and by maps and plans of the building, his book was a formidable challenge to both the Communist and the Nazi versions of events.

The vehement, sometimes angry and dismissive language in which Tobias advanced his theses clearly marked his book out as the work of an outsider to the historical profession. However, it received crucial backing when the respected Institute for Contemporary History in Munich, Germany's leading centre for research into National Socialism, commissioned the young historian Hans Mommsen (who later became the widely respected doyen of Third Reich historiography in Germany) to investigate the matter and come up with a verdict. In 1964 Mommsen produced a carefully researched and powerfully argued article backing Tobias's arguments. Seeing the Reichstag Fire as an unplanned event prompted Mommsen to argue that the Nazis were opportunists who seized upon potentially favourable chance occurrences to introduce key policies and further their own purposes. This became the so-called 'functionalist' interpretation of power in the Third Reich, as opposed to the 'intentionalist' view that saw everything as the outcome of Hitler's plans. This interpretation was subsequently applied to a wide range of questions in the history of Nazi Germany, including the origins of the Holocaust.[16]

The proponents of the conspiracy theory that saw the Nazis as responsible were not going to let the matter rest here. Münzenberg was long since dead; his body was discovered in 1940 in the French Alps, where he had been murdered on his way to the Swiss border following his escape from imprisonment, either by the Gestapo or by the Soviet secret police.[17] But by the 1960s this was long in the past, and a new generation of Communists and their fellow-travellers had come on to the scene to revive his conspiracy theory about the Reichstag Fire. The most active among them was the Croatian journalist Edouard Calic, born in 1910. While studying in Berlin during the war, Calic had been suspected, ironically, of taking part in 'plot-like conspiracies' of foreigners and spying for the British. He was imprisoned in the Nazi concentration camp at Sachsenhausen, near Berlin, but survived, and after the war stayed in Germany working as a journalist. He took a keen interest in the Reichstag Fire debate, arguing that the fire had been started by the SS under the command of Reinhard Heydrich.[18]

Calic declared himself outraged by the findings of Tobias, whom he defamed as a 'Nazi of the first hour'. He published evidence that he claimed proved that the Nazis had started the fire after all. However, critics soon began spotting anomalies that led them to believe much of this evidence was not genuine. For example, in 1968 Calic published transcripts of two alleged interviews with Hitler conducted in 1931 by a senior newspaper editor, Richard Breiting, and subsequently supposedly buried by him in a canister in his garden because he feared for his life should they be discovered.[19] The interviews purported to show that Hitler was already planning to burn the Reichstag two years before the event. 'In my opinion,' Hitler is recorded as saying to Breiting, 'the sooner this talking shop is burnt down, the sooner will the German people be freed from foreign influence.'[20] However, the interviews contained so many anomalies (treating Churchill and Roosevelt as figures of the first importance, for example, long before they were) that Hugh Trevor-Roper, Regius Professor of Modern History at Oxford and author of the standard work *The Last Days of Hitler*, immediately denounced the book as a forgery. Entitled *Unmasked* – a characteristic term used in many conspiracy theories – the 'interviews' published in the book were obviously made up in large part, if not completely, by Calic himself. Further analysis of the German edition showed that the language in which it was written contained many Croatian linguistic idioms translated directly into German. Calic's subsequent attempt to defend himself in the courts met with no success.[21]

Nevertheless, *Unmasked* was widely hailed by some historians on its appearance as a major revelation. Building on this success, Calic formed a committee to research the origins and consequences of the Second World War – the so-called Luxemburg Committee – and gained support from significant historians of the Third Reich such as Karl Dietrich Bracher and Walther Hofer (arch-'intentionalists') as well as the patronage of Willy Brandt and other prominent individuals. In 1972 and 1978 the Committee, led by the historians Friedrich Zipfel and Christoph Graf, produced two volumes of documents and commentary, adding up to nearly seven hundred pages and including old and new expert witness reports, the testimony of a number of firemen from the scene, excerpts from the testimony of van der Lubbe, and more than fifty pages of analysis of evidence concerning the underground passage, and restated the *Brown Book*'s central theses in massive detail. Tobias and Mommsen came under sustained attack from the two authors, who accused them of deliberately falsifying the expert reports.[22] A particular feature of these two documentary volumes was their claim that a whole series of allegedly inconvenient witnesses of the Nazis' sponsorship of the arson attack had died in the months following the event, above all in the 'Night of the Long Knives', Hitler's purge of the stormtrooper organization at the end of June 1934. Oberfohren had been found dead at his desk just a few weeks after the fire, and Breiting had died, supposedly poisoned by the Gestapo, in 1937. Such mysterious deaths of supposedly key witnesses or participants were to be an essential element in many of the conspiracy theories spun around President Kennedy's assassination many years later.

The two imposing volumes, which included a stout defence of the authenticity of the Breiting interviews and printed excerpts from another incriminating interview, supposedly with the press baron and minister in Hitler's coalition Cabinet, Alfred Hugenberg, were also accused of containing forgeries and falsifications, first in a series of articles in the liberal weekly *Die Zeit* in 1979 and then in a collective volume published in 1986 with contributions by Mommsen, Tobias and others. One of the contributors, Henning Köhler, presented extensive evidence in support of the view that the Hugenberg interview was a forgery. He called Calic's documentation 'falsification on a conveyor belt'.[23] Most of the printed documents were not made available to historians to check against the originals, or appeared only as excerpts; almost all of their authors were dead so could not be questioned about them; and they contained numerous contradictions with the known factual evidence.

Under pressure to submit the originals for forensic examination, the Luxemburg Committee produced a single page of a single document. It purported to be testimony from one of the alleged Nazi arsonists, Eugen von Kessel, written in 1933, shortly after the fire. But it turned out to be written on paper with a watermark dated 1935, several months after its alleged author's death.[24] Another of the forged documents drew its inspiration from a report of a talk with Göring recorded in the conservative local administrator Hermann

Rauschning's book *Conversations with Hitler*, published in 1940. Rauschning recorded that Göring had admitted his responsibility for the fire; but when Göring's attention was drawn to this passage during his trial by the International Military Tribunal in Nuremberg after the war, he said he had only ever met Rauschning twice, in passing, and would never have made such an admission to such a stranger.[25] In fact, there was nothing at all genuine about Rauschning's book: his 'conversations with Hitler' had no more taken place than his supposed conversations with Göring. He had been put up to writing the book by Winston Churchill's literary agent Emery Reeves, who was also responsible for another highly dubious set of memoirs, the industrialist Fritz Thyssen's *I Paid Hitler*; Rauschning's book has not been taken seriously by historians for many years.[26]

Calic himself was revealed by further investigations as having lied about his own past: his claim to have been imprisoned in Sachsenhausen in 1941 was shown to be false by evidence of his continued activity as a journalist in Berlin two years later. He was in fact only sent to the camp in February 1943. His assertion that he had obtained documentary evidence of the Nazi authorship of the Reichstag Fire from one of the 1944 military conspirators against Hitler when he had met him in Sachsenhausen was revealed to be pure invention since there was no record of the conspirator in question ever having been there. A libel suit brought by Calic against a newspaper in 1982 blew up in his face, with the court ruling that it was legitimate to call Calic a 'shady character' (*zwielichtige Figur*). Finally, on 9 March 2014, the newspaper *Die Welt* revealed that Calic had betrayed to the East German secret police, the Stasi, a key route through which East Germans were trying to escape across the newly built Berlin Wall to the West in 1961. How many people landed in an East German prison as a result is not known. Calic's contacts with the East German regime revealed him to be deeply embedded in the mental and moral world of Communism. A true disciple of Münzenberg, he evidently believed, as his master did, that forgery was justified by the political effect it produced.

In the end, therefore, Calic's falsification of the historical record only succeeded in convincing the bulk of the historical profession that Tobias was right. When combined with the latter's research, backed up by Mommsen's article, this seemed to lay the matter to rest, and through the 1970s and 1980s almost all serious historians accepted that Marinus van der Lubbe had set light to the Reichstag without any help. East Germany's professional historians did not intervene in the dispute, passing over both Tobias's work and its critics and preferring instead merely to join with Bulgarian and Soviet historians in publishing previously unavailable (and undoubtedly genuine) documents from their own archives.[27] In popular booklets and accounts of the fire, East German historians emphasized above all the fact that it had been the Nazis who had benefited from the fire as proof that they had caused it, mobilizing the *cui bono* argument once more in the service of a conspiracy theory.[28]

In the 1990s, however, dissenting voices were raised once more. In 1992 the political scientist Alexander Bahar, a student of the titular head of the Luxemburg Committee, Walther Hofer, produced a reissue of the Committee's documentation as, he said, an act of 'resistance against fascist tendencies' in the newly unified Germany (tendencies few others had managed to spot, it seems). Nine years later, together with Wilfried Kugel, he published a book more than eight hundred pages long, presenting the same arguments again on the basis of police investigation records, trial documents and interrogation protocols discovered in East German archives after the fall of the Berlin Wall. This new attempt to vindicate the *Brown Book* and its successors was roundly dismissed in a series of hostile reviews in the press. Even the more neutral reviews concluded that the new documentation, while it might contain some useful material, proved nothing.[29] Reviewers noted once more the presence of that staple of conspiracy theories, the mysterious deaths of key participants in the plot shortly after the event. Bahar and Kugel even suggested that the 'Night of the Long Knives' was triggered not least by the need to silence people who might have told the truth (though if this was the case, why wait nearly a year and a half?).[30]

It was relevant to note that Bahar had a long association with left-wing causes, including a 'quest for global equality', the name of a website to which he contributed under the pseudonym of Alexander Boulerian.[31] His collaborator Wilfried Kugel, described as a physicist and psychologist, was also registered with the Parapsychological

Association of America,[32] so it was hardly surprising that among the evidence the book presented was a report of a séance held in Berlin the night before the fire, in which the Berlin stormtrooper and later police chief Wolf-Heinrich von Helldorf asked a medium, 'Will our great plan to secure power succeed?' The hint that this vague question referred to the Reichstag Fire had no basis in reality, of course. Even more bizarrely, they added the suggestion that the clairvoyant might have hypnotized van der Lubbe into allowing himself to be used by the Nazis.[33] Bahar followed with a contribution to a volume of essays, published in 2006, which printed a brief vindication of Tobias's rejection of Nazi responsibility by a retired historian from the Institute for Contemporary History, Hermann Graml, alongside further attacks on Tobias and Mommsen by others and yet another lengthy documentary appendix.[34] But this did nothing to improve the credibility of his collaboration with Kugel, which, not for the last time in the history of conspiracy theories about Hitler and the Nazis, introduced an element of occultism and the paranormal into the workings of the paranoid imagination.

III

Though Bahar's and Kugel's arguments were greeted positively by some commentators, they soon ran into criticism from others. Their supposedly new documentation was at least genuine, it was conceded, but other historians, it was pointed out, had already used it and come up with no proof of Nazi guilt. This, and many other critical points, were made in a lengthy article in *Der Spiegel* and a short book by the journalist Sven Felix Kellerhoff, *Der Reichstagsbrand. Die Karriere eines Kriminalfalls (The Reichstag Fire: The Career of a Criminal Case)*, published in 2008 with a foreword by Mommsen. History editor at the conservative daily paper *Die Welt*, Kellerhoff systematically took Bahar's and Kugel's work apart, and with it the whole conspiracy theory that went back all the way through the Luxemburg Committee to the *Brown Book*. He pointed out once more that no traces of flammable liquids had ever been found in the building after the blaze. There was no evidence that the underground passage to Göring's official residence had been used. Kellerhoff noted that, of the named stormtroopers who had supposedly carried out the arson, one Hans-Georg Gewehr, had demonstrably no connection with the deed, while another, Adolf Rall, was in a remand prison at the time of the fire.[35] If, Kellerhoff asked pointedly, the Nazis had come through the passage, set the building alight, then escaped detection by going back the way they had come, then why did passers-by hear the sound of broken glass from someone smashing his way into the building through a window just before the fire began?

Kellerhoff dismissed the authors' attempt to discredit Tobias and the original article series in *Der Spiegel* by pointing out that although the magazine did indeed employ former Nazis and even ex-SS men (in positions that had no connection with the Reichstag Fire debate), the same was true of almost every organ of news and opinion in 1950s West Germany. Mommsen had also come under attack for allegedly having prevented the publication of an earlier report on the fire commissioned by the Munich Institute of Contemporary History from the Swabian schoolteacher Hans Schneider. Proponents of the conspiracy theory alleged this was because Schneider had proven Tobias's findings wrong and Mommsen did not want his report to come to light. He did indeed say that the publication of Schneider's report was undesirable for political reasons. But Mommsen actually drew attention to the report in his own article by thanking Schneider for his assistance and expressing the wish that it should indeed be published. There was no substance, therefore, to the allegation that he had tried to suppress it. And indeed, when Schneider's report eventually was published, in 2004, its disagreements with Tobias and Mommsen were far from convincing. In Kellerhoff's verdict, Schneider's report was 'a poor collection of material full of unsupported judgements'. This was hardly a ringing vindication of the claim of Tobias's critics that it was so damaging it had to be suppressed.[36]

Kellerhoff's book might have been thought to have finally set the matter to rest.[37] But a fresh attempt was made in 2014 to vindicate the original theses of the *Brown Book*. It came not from a source on the German left, but from an American lawyer and historian,

Benjamin Carter Hett, who had made his name with a well-researched and passionately written biography of Hans Litten, a left-wing lawyer. Litten's humiliation of Hitler in a cross-examination during a criminal trial of a group of stormtroopers towards the end of the Weimar Republic had led to his arrest on the night of the Reichstag Fire and treatment of such brutality in the camps that he eventually committed suicide. The book deservedly won the Fraenkel Prize for Contemporary History (I was on the jury that awarded it) and was later turned into a television docudrama. Hett's interest in the Reichstag Fire was evidently kindled by his work on Litten. His book, *Burning the Reichstag*, rested on files held in two dozen archives in several countries, including some, like the Stasi files, not consulted by previous researchers in the field. He also used private collections (notably the private papers of Tobias, who had died in 2011), correspondence and interviews. The book was an impressive piece of work that presented fresh evidence and put its theses forward with far greater sophistication than earlier defenders of the *Brown Book*'s arguments had done. It was well written and highly readable. But it was the work more of a prosecuting attorney than of a balanced and objective historian.[38]

In the first place, Hett's book failed to engage directly with much of the previous literature on the topic: Kellerhoff's book was mentioned only twice, for example, and his arguments were not confronted. Historians who accepted Tobias's conclusions were dismissed as ignorant or careless on the basis of a handful of extremely minor errors, a tactic which diverted attention from the major issues at stake. Instead of addressing these directly, Hett's preferred method was the classic courtroom tactic of discrediting the witnesses. Thus a key witness, the Gestapo chief Rudolf Diels, who did not believe there was a Nazi conspiracy to burn down the Reichstag, was discredited in Hett's eyes because the political police to which he belonged was pro-Nazi and corrupt, and anyway he was a womanizer and so immoral and unreliable, while a rival Gestapo official, Hans Bernd Gisevius, whose testimony in favour of the conspiracy thesis Hett approved of, was described as 'an early opponent of Hitler's rule',[39] although in fact he was busy in 1933 locking up Communists and other, genuine opponents of the Nazis. The judicial and police apparatus in Germany in 1933 was in any case not the Nazified institution it later became, as the thousands of prosecutions brought against violent stormtroopers, later quashed on Hitler's orders, clearly indicated. Hermann Göring indeed thought the police unreliable at this time, describing them as 'Marxist', or in other words Social Democratic, and enrolled the stormtroopers as auxiliary policemen to get round this difficulty. As Tobias had already pointed out, Diels knew perfectly well that the Nazis had been taken by surprise by the fire, and in other respects, such as, for example, his attempts to curb 'wild' concentration camps and torture centres set up by stormtroopers in 1933, his memoirs showed he was far from being a tool of the Nazis. As head of the Gestapo he was in a better position than almost anyone else to get at the truth in 1933. On the other hand, all of Gisevius's evidence was hearsay, and he was unable to bring any direct personal testimony to bear on the issue of who started the fire.[40]

Hett also launched a systematic assault on Tobias's integrity and motives. He portrayed Tobias as a Nazi who called Hitler a genius and, while acting as a German official in the Netherlands during the war, carried out activities that 'could have involved exposing Jews to deportation', an allegation typical of the innuendo that is the prosecuting lawyer's stock-in-trade as well as the conspiracy theorist's.[41] In fact, Tobias's passing reference to Hitler as a kind of genius is in no way suggestive of admiration for him; one can be an evil genius, after all. After the war, Hett claimed, Tobias was friendly with old Nazis, and a new edition of his book was published in 2011 by the far-right Grabert Verlag, which surely proved his Nazi affiliations. Actually, at the time of the agreement to publish, Tobias was terminally ill, and the book came out only after his death; and this was far from being the only case in which a far-right organization had published work by respectable historians without their informed consent.[42] By contrast, Hett did not mention the fact that the work of Tobias's critics appeared mostly in obscure publishing houses located on the far left of the political spectrum.

Fritz Tobias was actually a lifelong Social Democrat, not a Nazi, not even a crypto- or neo- or quasi-Nazi. In the very first sentences of his book, he told his readers that 'I lost my job, my profession and my home as a direct consequence of the Reichstag Fire. The same happened to my father.'[43] His father was a trade union official, and the family were all moderate Marxist Social Democrats. In the weeks and months after the Reichstag Fire Decree had suspended civil liberties, such people were thrown out of their jobs, no light matter at a time when Germany was still in the depths of the Depression and experiencing unemployment on a massive scale. Not infrequently they were imprisoned in one of the many improvised concentration camps that sprang up at this time. No wonder Tobias became obsessed with the Reichstag Fire, which had cost himself and his family so dearly. As the truth about the fire stubbornly eluded people even after the war, he began collecting information and documentation about it in an unsystematic way, inspired not least by the Social Democratic newspaper editor Friedrich Stampfer, who declared in 1957 that 'in 1933 we entered a new period of history in which the historian has to yield precedence to the criminal detective'. Tobias confessed himself surprised by the results of his investigation. But, he concluded, they were irresistible.[44]

Tobias was on also friendly terms with other people, including left-wingers like van der Lubbe's former comrades in the Netherlands. Benjamin Carter Hett, following earlier allegations by Calic, claimed that Tobias had allowed himself to be used as the mouthpiece of former Gestapo officials who feared prosecution in the 1950s for their supposed part in the fire. This was the origin, he alleged, of the entire argument that van der Lubbe alone caused the conflagration. To be sure, Hett was right to say that these men had some cause at least to distance themselves from any putative involvement in the fire; but in fact, as he himself pointed out, most of them had committed far worse crimes during the Third Reich, so one wonders why they would have devoted so much energy to an offence that paled into insignificance by comparison with deporting Jews to Auschwitz or exterminating civilians as supposed 'partisans' behind the Eastern Front.[45]

Hett suggested that Tobias had no independent motive for undertaking his project, a clearly absurd supposition in the light of its enormous length and complexity, not to mention the rationale he gave at the start of the book, which was clear for everyone to read. But his attempt to blacken Tobias's character went far beyond allegations of crypto-Nazism. Hett pointed out that Tobias was not just a civil servant but an officer in the state of Lower Saxony's Interior Ministry, working for the intelligence service, and in this capacity he used confidential information at his disposal to blackmail Hans Mommsen and the Institute for Contemporary History into suppressing Schneider's report and vindicating his own views by threatening to expose the Nazi past of the Institute's director Helmut Krausnick. Unfortunately, Hett failed to mention that actually Krausnick's 'Nazi past' was no secret, and did not in the end amount to very much – it was rare in postwar Germany for someone, especially someone in the professions, not to have a 'Nazi past'. He had only been a member of the Nazi Party from 1932 to 1934, and had spent almost the entire period of the Third Reich as a university student and archivist, serving in the armed forces only in the last few months of the war. His many contributions to the prosecution of Nazi war criminals over the years, and his pathbreaking publication into the crimes of the SS *Einsatzgruppen* ('Task Forces') behind the Eastern Front, rendered his formal membership of the Nazi Party during the Hitler Years more or less irrelevant.[46]

In any case, it beggars belief that an historian as combative and opinionated as Hans Mommsen should have abdicated his professional judgement in the face of orders from Krausnick and threats from Tobias. His article was surely not just 'a direct consequence of Tobias's campaign against Krausnick and his Institute', as Hett claimed.[47] Krausnick and the Institute, originally intending to produce research showing that Tobias was wrong, had not 'changed their position on the Reichstag fire' because of 'Tobias's threats':[48] they had changed it because the evidence presented by Tobias was simply too compelling to be ignored.

IV

More important by far than the motives of those who, like Tobias and Mommsen, argued that van der Lubbe had committed the arson attack on the Reichstag unaided, are the actual issues about the evidence for and against this thesis. These have to be tackled on their own merits. Hett's case essentially was the now-traditional one launched initially by the *Brown Book* and elaborated by its successors, namely that on the orders of Göring and Goebbels a group of Nazi stormtroopers entered the Reichstag through the tunnel from his official residence, set light to the building in various places with the help of flammable liquids, decamped back down the tunnel, leaving van der Lubbe to take the rap, and were subsequently mostly murdered to ensure their silence. This thesis had already been discredited by Tobias, with overwhelming evidence that Hett chose to ignore. Hett deployed a whole armoury of suggestion and innuendo that had no direct bearing on the case at all. He claimed that present-day experts in pyrotechnics whom he consulted dismissed the argument that the fire could have been started by a single person; but their opinion was worthless, since they had not even examined the detailed contemporary reports provided of the scene of the fire itself.[49] He provided convincing evidence that stormtroopers were trained in the use of fire-raising equipment such as kerosene and rags. But they used these on occasion to set light to advertising columns displaying posters hostile to the Nazi movement, and the fact that they were trained in fire-raising techniques in no way proved that this training was intended to prepare for the burning-down of the Reichstag, which was an entirely different matter nowhere mentioned in the sources presented by Hett. His book went into further detail about the stormtroopers' alleged murder of supposedly inconvenient witnesses, but it was completely unable to demonstrate that the fact that they were (allegedly) witnesses to the fire was the reason why they were murdered (the stormtroopers murdered many people for a whole variety of reasons, including refractory members of their own movement). Hett did admit that Oberfohren most likely committed suicide, but tried to rescue the views the conservative politician allegedly expressed in his (forged) memorandum, even though these were no more than hearsay, since Oberfohren had no direct knowledge at all of who had been behind the fire.

As for the stormtroopers' supposed recruitment of van der Lubbe as a stooge, all Hett could say was that he evidently met a Communist activist called Walter Jahnecke some days before the fire, that

Jahnecke *might have been* a police agent, and that his friend Willi Hintze, who also met van der Lubbe before the fire, on the evening of 22 February, in a Berlin flat, was definitely a police agent. This apparently made Jahnecke and Hintze 'plausible candidates for having brought van der Lubbe into the orbit of the SA [the Nazi Brownshirt or stormtrooper organization]'.[50] Other than this tissue of supposition, however (the two men were not even themselves members of the Brownshirt movement), there is no evidence at all to suggest the arsonist had any contact with stormtroopers before the fire. Surely it would have taken a lot more to secure the young Dutchman as a stooge in an operation as elaborate and dangerous as burning the Reichstag down than an evening spent in a Berlin flat with two men who both claimed at the time to be Communists and were generally believed to be so. And while the supposed Brownshirt leader of the arsonists, Hans-Georg Gewehr, was heard in later years to drop dark hints that he had taken part in the action, he was a notorious drunkard whose command over truth and memory was extremely shaky. When Gisevius named him after the war as a main suspect in the burning of the Reichstag, he believed him to be dead, but he was in fact very much alive, and emerged successfully from the historical woodwork to sue Gisevius for libel on learning of this allegation: and won the case.

Hett pointed out that the decree which suspended civil liberties had been prepared long before the fire which put it into action, as were lists of anti-Nazis to be arrested.[51] But this does not show that the Nazis planned to burn down the Reichstag, merely that they intended to suspend civil liberties, and that senior civil servants had drawn up contingency plans for their suspension well before the Nazis came to power. Lists of Communist Party members were also compiled by the police long before the fire, but again, this does not show that the fire was pre-planned, simply that the police expected at some point to arrest these people, hardly surprising given the Communist Party's record of violence and its publicly proclaimed intention of destroying the Republic and replacing it with a Soviet system. If the fire had been planned in advance, along with the arrests of Communists that followed, it is likely that the Nazis would have prepared it with a propaganda barrage claiming the

Communists were about to start a revolution. But no such claims appeared in the press, as Tobias pointed out: another indication that the fire took the Nazis by surprise.[52] Undoubtedly the Nazis were waiting for an opportunity to tighten their grip on Germany and move towards establishing a dictatorship. The Reichstag Fire turned out to be just that opportunity; but if it had not occurred, no doubt Hitler would have found some other pretext for the suspension of civil liberties.

Hett tried to discredit the thesis of van der Lubbe's sole responsibility by exposing very minor discrepancies in the timings offered by various eyewitnesses, leading to the conclusion that there wasn't enough time for him to have carried out the deed on his own; but while this might have been convincing had all the people concerned taken the time by electronic watches or clocks synchronized in accordance with a modern atomic clock, it is not convincing at all given the fact that the timepieces in question, all operated by clockwork, are likely to have varied significantly in the time they recorded at any given moment. Hett failed to deal with 'Putzi' Hanfstängl's evidence, yet why would Hanfstängl lie? His story was also corroborated, as we have seen, by the memoirs of the *Daily Express* reporter Sefton Delmer.[53] But Hett did not mention this testimony either, which was undoubtedly extremely inconvenient for his argument. Kellerhoff concluded that the policemen who had investigated the fire, Helmut Heisig and Walter Zirpins, were surely right in declaring that 'the question whether van der Lubbe carried out the deed alone may be answered in the affirmative without further consideration'.[54] If Nazis had really ignited the blaze that killed the Weimar Republic, then why did they not plant evidence of the supposed Communist conspiracy in the Reichstag building? This was their standard practice, used for example in their attempt to attribute to the Polish government an attack on a German radio station at Gleiwitz, on the German border, in 1939, which they in fact carried out themselves as a pretext for the launching of hostilities. They left bodies lying around on that occasion (concentration camp inmates dressed in Polish uniforms) and it would seem obvious that they would have done something similar if the Reichstag Fire had been a pre-planned operation.

Why did Sefton Delmer find the Nazi leaders in a state of panic when he arrived on the scene, instead of the calm satisfaction they would have displayed had the fire been planned? There is no indication at all that they were acting a part, and indeed they were far from capable of doing so. If Goebbels had been involved in preparations for the fire, why didn't he mention these in his private diaries, when he did mention, however indistinctly, preparations for far greater crimes later on, including the mass murder of Europe's Jews? Hett claimed that Goebbels must have deliberately omitted all mention of preparations for the fire, since he knew his diaries would be published, but at this stage, in 1933, he was publishing only carefully edited extracts: the intention to publish them all, signalled by his switch from writing to dictating the diaries, came only later. Even in 1938, when in public he portrayed the pogrom of 9–10 November as a spontaneous outburst of popular anger against the Jews, Goebbels recorded in his diary the fact that he himself had orchestrated the violence in accordance with Hitler's command.[55]

Crucially, Hett was unable to deal convincingly with the problem of van der Lubbe himself. Why would the Nazis have chosen the young Dutchman as their stooge when he was not even a paid-up member of the German Communist Party or any other Communist organization? There is no more evidence to back up Hett's claim that he was drugged by the Nazis during his trial to stop him revealing the fact that he had acted on their behalf as part of a larger group of arsonists than there is for Bahar's and Kugel's suggestion that he was hypnotized. Van der Lubbe had very poor eyesight as the result of an industrial accident earlier in his life, but he was not so blind that he could not recognize large pieces of furniture, doors and other obstacles in his passage through the Reichstag building. Contemporary reports described van der Lubbe as panting and sweating profusely when he was arrested, as he would have been had he rushed through the building rather than hanging around as a Nazi stooge waiting to be arrested, or acted in concert with others in a pre-planned division of labour spread across the entire building. No evidence was found at any time implicating others. Nor, once more, were any traces of flammable material discovered in the ruins apart from those owned to by the young Dutchman. And crucially, in endless hours of wearying interrogation, van der Lubbe never deviated from his story that he had acted alone, and never once accused the Nazis themselves of being behind the crime. His confession remains a compelling piece of evidence for his sole responsibility for of the fire, perhaps the most compelling of all.[56]

Rejecting the thesis of Nazi guilt does not commit one to seeing the fire as a wholly random event. In the early months of 1933 the Nazis would in the end have found any number of excuses to curtail civil liberties and eventually abolish them. Everything about the unrestrained violence and extreme, mendacious propaganda they had already unleashed on the German people during the election campaign that culminated in their (highly qualified) victory on 5 March 1933 suggests that the momentum towards the establishment of a dictatorship was fast becoming irresistible. Even van der Lubbe's act was not entirely a chance occurrence: a former anarcho-syndicalist, he had already tried unsuccessfully to set fire to a whole series of public buildings in protest against the political and social system he held responsible for the mass unemployment that was causing so much suffering and deprivation. Without the Depression, there would have been no reason to set the symbols of bourgeois rule alight.

What are the implications for democracy of the opposing arguments in this long-standing quarrel? According to Hett, Tobias's conclusion, that the Reichstag Fire was a 'blind chance, an error' that 'unleashed a revolution', amounted to 'effectively erasing from the historical record the Nazis' lust for power and the criminal ruthlessness with which they sought it'. Tobias's work therefore reeked of 'apologetic intentions', not least by pinning the blame for the blaze on a non-German.[57] But there was so much other evidence for the Nazis' lust for power and criminal ruthlessness that this is really beside the point. Hett presented no direct evidence for this misrepresentation of Tobias's purposes; there is plenty in Tobias's work to refute Hett's claim that he believed there was 'no long-term strategy . . . behind Hitler's entire bid for power'[58] – for example, the contextual section in Tobias's book entitled 'Germany 1932'. For Mommsen and Kellerhoff, on the other hand, the persistent attempts to vindicate the *Brown Book* and portray the Reichstag Fire as a carefully planned operation staged by the Nazis threatened to exculpate the role of the German people in the creation of the Third Reich by portraying them as victims of a deliberate conspiracy to seize power instead of accepting their complicity in the process.

There is no evidence that Tobias intended to provide excuses for the Nazis or underestimate their violence or their lust for power: on the contrary, he pointed out, in a passage not cited by Hett, that the Nazis committed far greater crimes later in their rule than the supposed destruction of the Reichstag, so that 'their guilt is too great for this supposed "exculpation" to carry any weight'.[59] Far from being a closet Nazi or only 'nominally a Social Democrat',[60] Tobias was a genuine and long-term member of the party. His real concern, typical for the moderate Social Democrat that he was, focused on the polarization of right-wing and left-wing views during the Cold War, which was reaching its height with the Cuban Missile Crisis that broke out in the same year that he published his book. He saw it as replicating the polarization of politics in Germany in 1932–3. In such a situation, he thought, a single event like the Reichstag Fire could lead to unimaginably disastrous consequences; and he ended his book with a quote from Bertrand Russell, whose uncompromising campaign against the stockpiling and threatened use of nuclear weapons he clearly supported.

V

Despite all the vast mass of evidence that has accumulated to show the implausibility of claims of a Nazi conspiracy to burn down the Reichstag, the conspiracy theorists continue to refuse to accept that such a major event could have been triggered by a single individual. Great excitement in the conspiracists' ranks has been caused by the surfacing of a notarized document, dated 8 November 1955, written by the former Brownshirt Hans Martin Lennings (1904–62), claiming involvement in the supposed plot. Lennings, a member of the Nazi Party since 1926 and a stormtrooper since shortly before Hitler's appointment as Reich Chancellor on 30 January 1933, knew Ernst Röhm, the leader of the stormtroopers, personally, and accompanied him on a number of ventures. Lennings's unit was employed 'for special purposes'. According to his denazification records after the war, he was visited by Hitler in hospital in the summer of 1930 after he had been injured in a brawl with members of the Communist Party. He was clearly, therefore, a trusted and valuable member of the Nazi stormtrooper organization. In early 1933, Lennings was engaged in covert surveillance of a rival (though unimportant) paramilitary organization, the *Christlicher Kampfschar* (Christian Fighting Squad).

Lennings claimed in his 1955 affidavit that between eight and nine o'clock on the evening of 27 February 1933 he had been ordered by Karl Ernst, leader of the east Berlin division of the Brownshirts, to pick up a young man from the stormtroopers' base in the Tiergarten area of central Berlin and take him to the Reichstag building, which was not far away. Together with two other stormtroopers, all of them in civilian clothing, Lennings had taken the young man, who had remained silent and calm throughout the short journey, to a side entrance of the parliament building and handed him over to another stormtrooper dressed in civilian clothes, who told them to get lost. As they did so, Lennings later claimed, they had noticed a 'peculiar burning smell' and observed faint but discernible wisps of smoke coming from the Reichstag. Lennings recognized the young man as van der Lubbe when his photo appeared in the newspapers. Realizing that the man was being falsely accused, since the fire had already started before he had been delivered to the building, Lennings, or so he claimed, had protested to his superiors, along with a few other Brownshirts, and as a result he had been arrested and forced to sign a false statement that they had been in error. A few days later, Röhm intervened and had the men released.

After the men he later claimed had been involved in the conspiracy, including Karl Ernst, had been murdered, Lennings fled to Czechoslovakia, but was extradited. Towards the end of 1934 and again in 1936 he was briefly imprisoned for criticizing the Nazi regime, and in particular for visiting the grave of one of the stormtroopers shot on Hitler's orders in the 'Night of the Long Knives'. After that, he kept quiet, and did not get into trouble again. In 1955 Lennings feared that he would be implicated in new legal proceedings over the

Reichstag Fire, and at the prompting of his priest, he decided to make a full confession of his part in the plot. It was not until July 2019, however, that his affidavit was discovered, in the archive of the District Court in Hanover, after a copy had been found in the papers of Fritz Tobias in Berlin. Its authenticity – though not the veracity of its contents – was confirmed by the Hanover prosecutor's office, and it was published in the local newspaper on 26 July 2019.[61]

Its publication made headlines in the national and international press. Benjamin Carter Hett declared that although previous documents allegedly by Nazis involved in the arson attack had proved to be forgeries, this one looked as if it was genuine. If that was the case, then the discovery discredited Tobias's claims completely. The media proclaimed the document to be clear proof that the Nazis had started the fire. The idea that the Dutchman had acted alone had been a 'Nazi narrative' concocted to protect the real perpetrators. It was particularly important that Lennings had seen fit to incriminate himself and appeared to have had nothing to gain from his confessions. And the fact that a copy had lain undisturbed and unused in Fritz Tobias's personal papers for decades suggested that the main proponent of the 'individual culprit' thesis had suppressed evidence that told against his argument.[62]

But the press, neither for the first time nor the last, was leaping prematurely to conclusions unsupported by other evidence. As Sven Felix Kellerhoff pointed out on the basis of over two hundred Berlin police files on the fire kept in the East Berlin Institute for Marxism-Leninism and released after the fall of the Berlin Wall, witnesses had reported seeing van der Lubbe in north Berlin before he walked into the city centre in mid-afternoon on 27 February 1933. Other witnesses had reported to the police that they had seen the young Dutchman wandering aimlessly around the centre of Berlin in the late afternoon of the same day, presumably waiting for the sun to set so that he could break into the Reichstag after dusk. There were no reports apart from Lennings's affidavit that van der Lubbe had been spotted in the stormtroopers' quarters in the Tiergarten, let alone held there for hours. Lennings had 'confessed' in the belief, widely shared in the mid-1950s, that he was helping Germans to shake off the stigma of guilt for their support for Hitler by pinning the blame for his dictatorship on a small clique of criminals. But his statement contradicted a mass of other evidence and was without value. Lennings had simply made his story up, and Tobias had discounted it simply because he had recognized this inescapable fact. Moreover, Tobias had gone to the trouble of talking to Lennings's brother, who described him as a habitual liar and fantasist, another reason for discounting his narrative.[63]

What the journalists and historians who were trumpeting the discovery of Lennings's affidavit as proof of a Nazi conspiracy were forgetting was that no historical document can be interpreted in isolation. The standard procedure for evaluating a document, laid down long ago by the great nineteenth-century German historian Leopold von Ranke, prescribed among other things a critical examination of its 'external consistency', that is, did it correspond to what other documents of the time revealed? If, like Lennings's affidavit, it ran contrary to every other relevant, genuine document relating to the Reichstag Fire, starting with the huge mass of police files, and going on to the proceedings of the Reich Supreme Court, then it must be discounted as false. Of course, the *Hannoversche Allgemeine Zeitung*, the newspaper that first printed the affidavit, consulted an historian on the affidavit's significance, but the 'expert' on the Reichstag Fire it interviewed was none other than Hersch Fischler, a long-time proponent of the conspiracy theory, and co-author of one of its central texts with Bahar and Kugel in 2001.[64] If they had consulted more widely, they would certainly have got a very different answer.

For Münzenberg, and later on Calic and the Luxemburg Committee, conspiracy theories came naturally in an atmosphere within a worldwide Communist movement that in 1933 had already seen Stalin launch show trials of plotters and saboteurs, just as he was soon to stage the monstrous purges that portrayed many leading Old Bolsheviks as part of a vast conspiracy to overthrow the Soviet Union. This tradition has long since come to an end, but it has been replaced with a new culture of conspiracy theory, rife in postmodern culture. Hett's book is permeated by it: the Nazis conspired to burn the Reichstag, Tobias conspired with ex-SS men to deny it, Krausnick and Mommsen conspired to deny the Nazis' guilt. The case of the Reichstag Fire is unusual in that it involves two diametrically opposed conspiracy theories that mirror one another so clearly that the same evidence has been used in support of both, including the much-vaunted tunnel from Göring's official residence to the Reichstag, for example, and the testimony of expert witnesses to buttress allegations that the fire was started by an organized group of arsonists rather than a lone individual. Attempts to prove that the Nazis started the fire display many key features of *event conspiracy theories*: the assumption that because an incident or occurrence was of enormous political importance it must have been planned in advance; the claim that witnesses to the event have mysteriously disappeared or been murdered so that they are no longer able to tell the truth about it; the belief that the people who benefit from an event must have caused it; the feeling that to make the claim that a tragic or criminal event was more or less a matter of chance somehow excuses or exculpates the perpetrators (or, again, those who benefit from it); the refusal to accept that a major historical event may have been triggered by a lone, obscure individual and not an organized group; the involvement of occult forces of some kind; and the forgery of documentary evidence in the conviction that it is allowable because the forger knows what really happened and is justified in creating the proof for his view in a situation where other, decisive proofs are for whatever reason not available.

Just as important is the fact that one of these two opposing conspiracy theories turned out very quickly to be untenable. Even several months into Hitler's Third Reich, the Nazi claim that the Reichstag was destroyed by Communists as a prelude to a violent revolution was in effect rejected by the German Supreme Court. As journalists sometimes say of a story that doesn't have enough evidence to justify it going into print, it 'didn't have legs'. And yet the Communist allegation that it was the Nazis who burned the building down has been revived again and again; indeed it continues to be warmed up and served to the reading public long after Communism itself has exited the stage of history. It is overwhelmingly the left, even the far left, that has stubbornly stuck to this version of events, but the argument, advanced by its proponents, that those who dismiss the idea of a Nazi plot must somehow be on the right, or are even 'old Nazis', is little more than a knee-jerk reaction. It is politically motivated rather than grounded in serious historical research. Such research of course sometimes gets things wrong, but that is not the same at all as deliberate falsification or suppression of the evidence. The argument for van der Lubbe's sole culpability for the Reichstag Fire is overwhelming. That, fundamentally, is why those who wish to argue that the fire was started by the Nazis focus not on the evidence itself but on the motives and character of people like Fritz Tobias, Hans Mommsen and Helmut Krausnick. This, too, is a common tactic of conspiracy theorists. But the reason why someone puts forward an argument has no bearing at all on the validity or otherwise of the argument itself. It may help explain why the argument is being advanced, but whatever the reason, the argument has to be confronted directly and on its own terms, irrespective of who has put it forward or why.

In the larger scheme of things, the Reichstag Fire was not, perhaps, the decisive, cataclysmic event it is often claimed to have been. Had the German parliament not burned down, Hitler and the Nazis would most likely have found another pretext for imposing a state of emergency and carrying out the mass arrest of Communists and Social Democrats. There are plenty of other examples of their seizing opportunities when they were presented with them. Hitler's dismissal of his Minister of War General Werner von Blomberg is a good example: he was ousted in 1938 when it was discovered that his new wife, a much younger woman, had worked as a prostitute and posed for pornographic photographs. It was particularly embarrassing for Hitler, who had been present at the wedding, and for Hermann Göring, who had been Blomberg's best man. A second top general, Werner von Fritsch, was also dismissed, after allegations that he had been conducting a homosexual affair began to surface (allegations that soon after proved to be false). The fact that these were largely chance occurrences did not, however, mean that Hitler, Göring and SS chief Heinrich Himmler did not intend to get rid of the two men in one way or another. Along with other senior conservative figures in the regime, they were proving too cautious for Hitler as he quickened the pace of foreign aggression and military preparation. Some reason would sooner or later have been found anyway: it's just that these sexual allegations provided the opportunity when it was most needed.

And so it was with the Reichstag Fire. As we shall now see, the flight of Rudolf Hess to Scotland in 1941, to all intents and purposes another chance and unexpected event, has also prompted conspiracy theorists to come up with a variety of explanations involving larger forces, groups of men acting in collusion, and behind-the-scenes plots.

4

Why did Rudolf Hess fly to Britain?

I

At a quarter to six on the evening of Saturday 10 May 1941, German time, a Messerschmitt Bf110E heavy fighter plane (commonly known as an Me110) took off from the manufacturer's airfield near Augsburg, in southern Germany, climbed upwards to sweep east of the River Lech and then set a course in a north-westerly direction, towards Bonn. After crossing the German border, it reached the Dutch Frisian islands at seven thirty-five and then altered course, flying in an easterly direction, clearly in order to avoid being detected by British radar. After some twenty-three minutes it changed course back to a north-westerly direction and began to make its way up the North Sea. Maintaining a low altitude, it passed over two German U-boats, which began to dive but then halted the manoeuvre when their spotters recognized the plane as friendly. The plane climbed to 5,000 metres and continued. At two minutes to nine, it made a ninety-degree turn to the left and flew directly towards Scotland, but the daylight was still too strong for it to avoid being seen by enemy spotters, so after a while it reversed course and flew back and forth until it was dark enough to continue safely. At twenty-three minutes past ten it reached the British coast near Bamburgh, in Northumberland and, descending rapidly, flew low enough over the countryside for the pilot to see people in the fields and wave to them as he passed overhead. After some minor course adjustments, the plane reached the west coast south of Glasgow at five to eleven, the pilot enjoying what he shortly afterwards described as a fairy-tale view of 'steep mountainous islands visible in the moonlight and fading twilight'. He turned inland, climbed again, and, unable to locate his intended landing-place, a small, disused private airfield at Dungavel House, the residence of the Duke of Hamilton, decided to parachute out of the aircraft. He turned the engines off, feathered the propellers, opened the cockpit roof, unfastened the side windows, and, turning the aircraft over, jumped out, pulled on the ripcord of his parachute, and fell to earth, hitting the ground hard and losing consciousness, while the Messerschmitt crashed and burst into flames a short way off. It was nine minutes past eleven.[1]

Writing to his son a few weeks later, the pilot, after recounting the details of his flight, then described what happened next:

> I woke up in a German-looking meadow, not realizing where I was and what was happening to me. When I first saw my parachute lying behind me, it became clear to me that I had arrived in Scotland, the first landing place of my 'Plan'. I was lying some ten metres from the front door of a house of a Scottish goatherd. People came running towards me, alarmed by the burning aircraft. They looked at me in a compassionate way.

The first person to arrive was David McLean, who lived in the house and came out when he heard the noise of the explosion. He was not in fact a goatherd but the head ploughman on a large farm. He helped the pilot up and, seeing his uniform, asked him if he was German. 'Yes,' the man replied in good English, 'I am Hauptmann Alfred Horn, I have an important message for the Duke of Hamilton.' Another man came up and then departed to fetch the police, while the German pilot, who had sustained minor injuries to his back and right ankle, was helped into the cottage. As the police were summoned, some men from the Home Guard arrived. They had spotted the Messerschmitt and seen the pilot jump out and open his parachute. They took him off to their base, where he was searched by two police detectives. From here he was transported to Maryhill Barracks in Glasgow. Officers began to suspect that he was, as one of them noted, 'a very important man in higher Nazi circles'. Meanwhile, the local RAF commander, alerted by the police, telephoned the Duke of Hamilton. 'A German captain has parachuted from an Me110 and wants to see you,' he said. 'Good heavens, what does he want to see me about?' Hamilton replied. 'I don't know, he won't say . . . I think you should go and see him.' Arriving at the barracks at ten in the morning on 11 May, Hamilton went in to the prisoner, who had requested that they meet without anyone else being present. The man identified himself immediately as Rudolf Hess, the deputy leader of the Nazi Party.[2]

Addressing the astonished duke, Hess said that he had come on a mission of humanity. Hitler, he told him, wanted to stop the fighting with Britain. Hamilton, he suggested, should 'get together with members of his party to talk things over with a view of making peace proposals'. Hamilton replied that even if Britain did make peace, war with Germany was bound to break out again within a couple of years. Leaving the room, he telephoned the Foreign Office and asked to speak to Sir Alexander Cadogan, the permanent secretary. As an official began to obstruct his efforts to get through, by a lucky chance Prime Minister Winston Churchill's private secretary, Jock Colville, came into the room and took over the conversation. Hamilton told him the gist of what had happened. Colville asked him what he proposed to do. The Duke suggested he should meet with the Prime Minister to discuss the business in person. Colville agreed. An experienced pilot, Hamilton flew to Northolt air base from Scotland, then made his way in another aircraft to Kidlington, near Oxford. From there he was taken by car to a country house where Churchill was spending the weekend.[3]

'Now,' said Churchill, as they met, 'come and tell me this funny story of yours.' As Hamilton filled him in on the details after dinner, the Prime Minister was 'taken aback' but insisted on watching a Marx Brothers comedy film that was about to be screened. Afterwards they discussed the matter some more, then, the following morning, they met members of the War Cabinet in London, where it was decided to send Ivone Kirkpatrick, a diplomat who had been an official in the British Embassy in Berlin and had met Hess several times, to confirm that it actually was him. In the meantime, Hess had been moved to a military hospital to deal with his injuries. Arriving there in the small hours of the morning, Kirkpatrick had Hess woken. He recognized him immediately and confirmed his identity without difficulty. Hess started to put his 'peace terms' to Kirkpatrick, declaring that any agreement would have to involve the return of the

German colonies taken by the League of Nations at the end of the First World War, but apart from that the British could keep their Empire if they let Germany have a free hand in Europe. At the same time, peace would have to be concluded with Mussolini's Italy.[4] Kirkpatrick knew, of course, that this was all utterly unrealistic; if this happened, a weakened Britain would be easy prey for a strengthened Nazi Germany, and Nazi demands would have escalated until, as Hamilton had predicted, war broke out again within a short space of time. Even the former Prime Minister David Lloyd George, who was relatively sympathetic to the Nazi regime, agreed: the 'peace terms' Hess brought with him were, he told the Soviet ambassador Ivan Maisky, 'absolutely unacceptable'.[5] The British government transferred Hess to London, where he was lodged in the Tower before being moved to less austere quarters while the authorities decided what to do with him. Uncertainty and confusion reigned over this last point, but one thing was clear to Churchill and his Cabinet: there was no point at all in taking Hess, his mission or his 'peace offer' seriously.[6]

II

Who was Rudolf Hess? Born on 26 April 1894, and so just forty-seven years of age at the time of his dramatic flight to Scotland, he came from a well-off family of merchants that originated in Wunsiedel, in northern Bavaria. Until 1908 he lived with his parents and two younger siblings in Alexandria, Egypt, where the family had a business, and then he was sent to Germany to attend school and receive private tuition. Following a year at a commercial academy in Switzerland, he enrolled as an apprentice at a firm based in Hamburg. On 20 August 1914, shortly after the outbreak of the First World War, he enlisted in an infantry regiment and fought in the First Battle of Ypres. After being decorated for bravery he saw more action at the Battle of Verdun, where he was wounded and hospitalized. After his recovery, he was posted to the Balkans, where Romania had recently entered the war on the Allied side, and was again wounded, this time more severely, with a shot through the torso that did not, fortunately for him, damage any vital organs. While convalescing, he applied for enrolment in the air force, which was more glamorous though also more dangerous than the infantry. After training, he joined a fighter squadron on 14 October 1918, but within a few weeks of his enrolment the war had come to an end and so he did not manage to see any action in the air.[7]

Like many demobilized servicemen, Hess, resentful at Germany's defeat, and at something of a loose end, now gravitated towards politics. He joined a small, ultra-nationalist group called the Thule Society, fighting left-wing revolutionaries in Munich, where he was once again wounded. After the situation had calmed down, he enrolled in the university to study history and economics, and it was here that he met Professor Karl Haushofer, an exponent of 'geopolitics' and advocate of Germany's territorial expansion. Hess became a close friend of Haushofer's son Albrecht, who also embarked on a career as a university teacher. In the febrile political atmosphere of post-revolutionary Munich, many far-right nationalist groups were touting for custom, and when he attended one of their meetings Hess fell under the spell of the leader of what was to be the most successful of them all, the National Socialist German Workers' Party, Adolf Hitler. Hess formed a student group of the Nazi stormtrooper movement, engaged in brawls at public meetings, and took part in Hitler's disastrous beer-hall putsch on 9 November 1923. After hiding from the police with the Haushofers, he eventually gave himself up and was sentenced to eighteen months in prison for his part in the attempted coup.[8]

It was in Landsberg, the fortress where Hitler sat out the relatively mild sentence meted out to him for the beer-hall putsch, that Hess became really close to the Nazi leader. Hitler devoted his time to writing his memoir and manifesto, *Mein Kampf*, dictating some passages to Hess, who carefully checked the rest. In the following years, Hess accompanied the Nazi leader on tours of Germany and generally acted as his factotum. When he was not ministering to the Leader's needs, he took up flying again, obtaining a pilot's licence in 1929 and acquiring his own light aircraft, donated by the Nazi daily paper, the *Völkischer Beobachter*. He flew frequently and became an experienced and proficient pilot, buzzing liberal and left-wing open-air election rallies to drown out the speaker's voice. When Hess got married, in December 1927, Hitler acted as witness, alongside Karl Haushofer. When the Nazi leader was appointed the head of a coalition government in January 1933 he rewarded Hess's loyalty by naming him deputy Party leader. Hess's new role meant, among other things, that he took the stand after Hitler's speech at the 1934 Party rally in Nuremberg, and in Leni Riefenstahl's film of the event, *Triumph of the Will*, he can be seen looking adoringly at the Leader, and, glowing with fanaticism, shouting ecstatically: 'The Party is Hitler! Hitler, however, is Germany, and Germany is also Hitler! Hail Hitler! Hail Victory! [*Heil Hitler! Sieg Heil!*]'[9]

Hess did not give up flying during his time as deputy leader, often entering races and competitions under a pseudonym. Alarmed at the danger of this activity, Hitler eventually banned him from flying. In his main role, Hess supervised state–Party relations through the Office of the Deputy Leader, run by the ambitious and indefatigable Martin Bormann. Power began to reveal an eccentric side to him, as he indulged in astrology, the occult, homeopathy and strange food fads.[10] More seriously, it began to become clear that he was being elbowed aside in the incessant struggles for power within the Nazi hierarchy. Hitler named Göring as his successor at the beginning of the war, demoting Hess to third in line.[11] Long before this, Bormann had taken over much of the work within Hess's office, including the supervision of civil service appointments.[12] After 1936 the deputy leader's functions within the dictatorship became mostly representational: introducing Hitler's speeches, welcoming delegations of German expatriates at meetings, and delivering the annual Christmas address.[13] While Bormann saw more of Hitler, Hess saw less, and he was frozen out of decision-making on key issues such as foreign policy, which became steadily more important as time went on, above all after the war had begun.[14]

By 1939, the self-appointed ideologue of the Party, Alfred Rosenberg, was describing Hess as 'indecisive', thought he was depressed, and observed that he no longer had much to do, since the Party apparatus had slipped out of his grasp.[15] Hess did, to be sure, retain the formal power to intervene in Party affairs if he felt inclined to do so, and his role in maintaining morale on the home front was far from negligible. A rabid antisemite, Hess pushed hard for harsh policies against Germany's small Jewish population. With his unconditional adulation for Hitler and his complete and oft-repeated faith in 'the National Socialist idea', he helped maintain the public's support for the Führer and his regime. He was widely regarded as one of the few honest and incorruptible figures in the Nazi leadership and so enjoyed a good deal of public approval.[16] All the same, as time went on he became increasingly marginalized in the Nazi leadership. His secretaries described him after 1938 sitting aimlessly at his desk shuffling papers or staring vacantly into space. If anyone addressed him, he appeared confused and disoriented.[17]

Hess was well aware of his loss of power. The decision to invade the Soviet Union, which was to come to fruition in the long-prepared 'Operation Barbarossa' on 22 June 1941, was taken without consulting him. While Hess later claimed to have known about it in advance, he most certainly was unaware of the details of the plan, including the date on which it was to be launched.[18] He became increasingly obsessed with the dangers, as he saw it, of Germany engaging in a war against the West and the Soviet Union simultaneously. Hitler had repeatedly made largely rhetorical 'peace offers' to the British government, and as far back as *Mein Kampf* he had considered that an alliance with the United Kingdom against the 'Bolshevik' regime in Russia was both desirable and possible. Hess therefore thought that if he could bring about a peace with Britain, this would fulfil Hitler's long-held dream of a British alliance and at the same time eliminate the threat of a war on two fronts.

Interrogating him on 10 June 1941, Viscount Simon, Lord Chancellor in Churchill's government, concluded that 'Hess's position and authority in Germany have declined and that if he could bring off the coup of early peace on Hitler's terms he would confirm his position . . . and render an immense service to his adored Master and to Germany.'[19] There was, Hess believed, a 'peace party' in British political circles that could be persuaded to use his 'peace offer' to overthrow the 'warmonger' Churchill and bring the war in the West to an end. The Duke of Hamilton, whom he did not know personally but admired as one of the first men to fly over Mount Everest, had been recommended by Albrecht Haushofer as a contact. Hess had readily agreed, since he thought he would get on with Hamilton, as they were both pre-war flying aces. In addition, the duke had been a leading figure before the war in the Anglo-German Society. There was nothing sinister about this: it was an innocuous, non-political organization very different from pro-Nazi groups such as the similarly named Anglo-German Fellowship. Haushofer was grossly mistaken in thinking that Hamilton was either a supporter of a separate peace or a man with significant political influence. Hess's mission was undertaken under false premises from the very beginning.[20]

Defying Hitler's ban, Hess had already begun the first, clandestine preparations for his flight not long after Hitler had started to plan the invasion of the Soviet Union. In September 1940 Hess gave permission to Albrecht Haushofer to send a letter to Hamilton suggesting a meeting with him. It was, however, intercepted by British Intelligence and did not reach its intended addressee until MI5 shared it with him in March 1941.[21] Undeterred by the lack of an answer, Hess had contacted the Messerschmitt company, whose boss Willy Messerschmitt he had known for many years, toured its factories inspecting various models, and arranged to make practice flights in the Me110. Accompanied in the two-seater for the first few flights, he mastered the machine's controls and decided that with some modifications to increase fuel capacity and the insertion of a radio compass to aid location it was suitable for the flight he was now planning. As early as 4 November 1940 he wrote to his wife, Ilse, telling her: 'I firmly believe that from the flight I will undertake in the coming days, I will return and the flight will be crowned with success.'[22] As it turned out, it was not until May 1941 that he finally undertook the mission, after two abortive attempts earlier in the year. On 9 May, when preparations were finally complete, he told his colleague Richard Walther Darré, the Minister of Agriculture, that he was going on a long journey and did not know when he would be back.[23]

III

Did Hess fly to Scotland on Hitler's orders? Certainly, Ernst Wilhelm Bohle, head of the Nazi Party's Foreign Organization and a friend of

Hess's, thought so.[24] Hess's son considered that the claim he flew on his own initiative 'contradicts the laws of logic'. That he was ordered to fly by Hitler was staringly obvious – anything else was inconceivable.[25] Quite a few subsequent students of his flight have also been certain that Hitler must have known about it in advance. The freelance military historian John Costello declared firmly in 1991 that Hess was carrying 'an authoritative peace offer' from Hitler.[26] According to J. Bernard Hutton (author of several books on spying and subversion), 'Hess's historic flight to Britain was made with Hitler's full knowledge and approval. The venture was discussed endlessly before Hitler sanctioned it.' The 'peace offer' he brought with him was serious, he says, and if Churchill had accepted it, the course of history might have been very different. Hutton entitled his chapter on the hours after Hess landed in Scotland 'History Hangs in the Balance'.[27] But he confessed in his Preface that 'this book may read like fiction', and neglected to supply any evidence to back up these assertions. His account of Hess's alleged conversations with Hitler is pure invention.[28] Hutton also rather undermined his credibility by claiming in a passage ascribing the venture to the influence of Karl Haushofer that 'it is probable that Haushofer possessed psychic powers' – another example of the appeal the occult sometimes possesses for the paranoid imagination.[29]

The naval historian Peter Padfield has pointed to Haushofer's subsequent claim that Hess embarked on his flight with Hitler's approval. But Haushofer's belief rested on no more than hearsay. Most likely, Haushofer simply did not suspect that Hess was proposing a lone mission without sanction from above – the idea would have seemed too bizarre. Even if he was aware that Hess was acting entirely on his own initiative, Haushofer, as a man closely involved in the escapade, had every incentive to exculpate himself after the event by claiming that he had been convinced that Hess was acting in accordance with Hitler's wishes. Once more, speculation takes over as Padfield claims that 'the idea must also have appealed to Hitler'. But there isn't actually any evidence to support the theory that he knew about it at all.[30] Hess himself never deviated from his initial admission that the flight had been entirely on his own initiative.[31] His wife also always insisted that the flight was his own idea and nobody else's.[32] It would surely have strengthened his position when he was being interrogated by the British if he had said Hitler had ordered the flight, but right at the outset he denied any such thing. Viscount Simon asked him during his interrogation on 9 June 1941: 'Would you tell me, do you come here with the Führer's knowledge, or without his knowledge?' Hess replied 'Without his knowledge', adding: 'Absolutely (Laughs).'[33]

In order to get round the problem this evidence poses for the theory that Hitler ordered the flight, some writers have hypothesized that Hess remained obdurately silent about a prior agreement with Hitler that if his mission failed, he would never admit it had been undertaken on the Führer's orders. But this is nothing more than a supposition; there is absolutely no evidence to support it. Moreover, the idea of a pact of silence is implausible in the extreme. Hitler after all had previously banned him from flying because he considered it too dangerous, and there is nothing to suggest he ever reconsidered this prohibition.[34] General Karl Bodenschatz later recalled that Hitler had asked him: 'How was it possible, General, that the Luftwaffe permitted Hess to fly even though I had explicitly banned it?'[35] If Hitler had personally ordered the flight, he would at the very least have chosen an airfield closer to where he was at the time; Augsburg was relatively remote from the centres of Hitler's activity, which of course was one reason for its choice. Hess remained convinced to the end of his life that Hitler was a great man and National Socialism a great idea. But it is simply not credible to claim that he was deliberately lying when he said the initiative for his expedition had been his alone, and then continued to lie to the end of his days, when he had every reason to enhance Hitler's posthumous reputation by naming him as the author of his 'peace mission'.[36]

All the available contemporary sources make it clear that Hess's flight took Hitler completely by surprise: Hutton's account of the Nazi dictator's impassive reception of the news, repeating word for word the story as related by the German popular historian Wulf Schwarzwäller, is as fictional as his seemingly verbatim rendering of a conversation between Hitler and Hess before Hess took off.[37] The first the German dictator knew about the escapade was when Hess's adjutant Karlheinz Pintsch arrived on the late morning of Sunday 11 May at Hitler's Bavarian mountain retreat, the Berghof, near

Berchtesgaden, bearing a letter Hess had handed to him shortly before taking off, with instructions to give it personally to Hitler. After overcoming some obstruction from the staff at the Berghof, Pintsch managed to get through to the Führer and hand him the envelope containing the letter. Albert Speer, Hitler's architect and one of his closest associates, was leafing through some sketches when Pintsch approached him. 'At this moment Hitler descended from his room upstairs. One of the adjutants was called into the salon. While I began leafing through my sketches once more, I suddenly heard an inarticulate, almost animal outcry. Then Hitler roared: "Bormann, at once! Where is Bormann?" '[38]

After a while, according to Speer, Hitler regained at least the appearance of composure. '"Who will believe me when I say that Hess did not fly there in my name?"' he asked. Telephoning the flying ace Ernst Udet, he was relieved to hear his opinion that the plane did not have enough fuel to reach its goal (Scotland, as Hess had told him in his letter) and would have crashed into the sea on the way. Hitler's interpreter Paul Schmidt, indeed, noted that 'Hitler was as appalled as though a bomb had struck the Berghof; "I hope he falls into the sea!" I heard him say in disgust.'[39] Hitler told Alfred Rosenberg that he felt physically sick when he read the letter. He was, he said, flabbergasted by its contents as he read them.[40] According to Speer, Hitler never got over his deputy's 'disloyalty', even insisting later that one condition for peace with Britain, if it came, would be that Hess should be hanged. 'The Leader,' Joseph Goebbels, who arrived at the Berghof on 13 May, reported in his diary the next day, 'is completely shattered. What a spectacle for the world!' He was, the Propaganda Minister added the following day, 'bitter beyond measure. He'd never expected it.'[41] Goebbels instructed the puppet German media to mention the flight as little as possible.[42] Hans Frank, Nazi boss of the occupied Polish 'General Government', told his staff a few days later, after hearing Hitler give the news to regional Party leaders on 13 May: 'I have never seen the Führer so deeply shocked.' Another witness at the meeting reported Hitler breaking down in tears.[43]

The fact that so many sources reported the rage, followed by depression, that Hitler displayed when he heard the news of the flight, has not stopped conspiracy theorists from claiming that this reaction was a mere piece of play-acting, designed to fool people into believing that the news came as a surprise.[44] In his dramatic narrative reconstruction of the flight, James Leasor suggested that 'there seems little doubt that Hitler knew about Hess's attempts to be a go-between', quoting a number of contemporaries who took this view. 'Without Hitler's knowledge and consent,' he argued, 'Hess could never have made twenty trial flights from Augsburg.' He suggests that the all-pervasive surveillance operations of the Gestapo would have picked up on Hess's preparations.[45] But the Gestapo, as modern research has shown, was in fact a small organization whose surveillance was far from all-pervasive, although historians' opinion at the time when Leasor was writing still considered that it was.[46] If Hitler had not been complicit in the mission, Leasor says, then he would surely have vented his wrath on the people who had helped his deputy in his escapade ('there seems little doubt that their punishment would have been severe'). In fact, Hitler did have everyone who had assisted Hess in preparing the flight arrested, starting with his adjutants and going on to include the Haushofers and Hess's astrologer. He would not have done this had Hess been acting with his approval. Pintsch was indeed imprisoned, but ultimately, like Hess's other accomplices, and indeed like others who had been in the know but failed to prevent the flight, he was saved by the fact that he had obviously assumed that his boss had been acting on Hitler's orders.[47]

And then there is the letter Hess left for his adjutant to give to Hitler after he had taken off, in which he outlined his motives and intentions, a letter that surely would not have been necessary had Hitler been aware of the flight in advance. Attempts, for example by John Harris – a chartered accountant who has written five collaborative conspiracy-theory books on Hess, variously with Richard Wilbourn, a farm manager, and Meirion Trow, a schoolteacher and author of detective novels, true-crime stories and historical works – to prove that Hess flew with Hitler's approval, fail to get round this fundamental obstacle.[48] The hint by Lothar Kettenacker, former Deputy Director of the German Historical Institute in London, that Hess may have told Hitler in advance about his impending flight, is pure speculation.[49] As Hitler's biographer Ian Kershaw points out, if Hitler had really wanted to make a peace offer to Britain, he would have chosen someone more versed in foreign relations than Hess, and would have used a method of transmitting it other than a risky solo flight to Scotland. He most certainly would not have chosen the marginal figure of the Duke of Hamilton as his interlocutor. He knew, too, that news of Hess's escapade would deeply damage the regime's credibility among the German people, as indeed it did (a popular joke circulating at the time had Hess brought before Churchill, who says: 'So you're the madman, are you?' To which Hess replies: 'Oh no, only his deputy!'). Hitler had no incentive to put out peace feelers to Churchill at this time in any case: he was fully engaged in planning the invasion of the Soviet Union, which he and his generals were confident would enjoy rapid and complete success. The last thing he would have wanted was to enter into complicated diplomatic negotiations with Britain when Operation Barbarossa, the largest land invasion in history, was only weeks away.[50]

But lack of evidence has not stopped conspiracy theorists from insisting that Hitler had given the order to Hess to fly to Scotland. Missing papers, censored documents and closed archives all feature prominently in historical conspiracy theories, which, Harris and Trow claim, 'will never go away as long as there are locked files, top secret classifications and official obfuscation'. In sensitive cases such as the Hess flight, there is always 'plenty of scope for all sorts of vital evidence to be "mislaid" '. Despite their concession that 'speculation on what exactly *is* missing is largely fruitless', it remains likely for example, in their view, that key correspondence has been removed from the Haushofer archives. Official records containing 'vital evidence on the wartime record of the head of the Red Cross in Geneva, Karl Burckhardt, who undoubtedly had a hand in bringing Hess to Britain', are unobtainable, they complain. Of course, Harris suggests, the missing correspondence, if it emerged, would most likely reveal the truth.[51] But unfortunately no such correspondence has turned up. Speculation of this kind can be found in many other conspiracy theorists' writings. Padfield even asserts that 'there is documentary evidence that papers which were once in the files have been removed', although of course there isn't.[52] Official 'secrecy', as Harris and Trow complain, 'bedevilled the research' they attempted to carry out.[53] 'The details,' Padfield, admits, 'may never be known'; so where the details aren't known, imagination has to serve as a substitute. All of this is pure speculation. In the case of the Reichstag Fire conspiracy theory, it is key witnesses who have supposedly gone missing; in the case of Hess's flight to Scotland, it is key documents; but the conspiracist frame of mind behind both suppositions is essentially the same. The hint in both cases is that they have been deliberately hidden or, more likely, destroyed, in order to conceal the truth from posterity.

As an alternative to claiming the truth is buried in missing documents, conspiracy theorists also frequently cite genuine sources then accord them a weight far beyond what they will actually bear. They join the dots between authentic pieces of historical evidence to create a picture that isn't in the least plausible. Padfield correctly points out, for example, that there were many points of contact between the people he supposes were involved in the conspiracy to bring Hess to England.[54] But does listing them amount to proof of a conspiracy? Guilt by association is no substitute for documentary evidence of actual collusion. One oft-cited example must suffice to illustrate what the points of contact listed by Padfield actually involved. The German diplomat Ulrich von Hassell's diaries record that Albrecht Haushofer had gone to Geneva to see Carl J. Burckhardt (to give his name the correct spelling). Burckhardt later said to Hassell's wife that the British still wanted peace with Germany, though not while Hitler was in charge. And Hassell himself had discussed the possibility of peace the previous January with Burckhardt, who had told him that he was convinced 'that sentiment was favourable in the English Cabinet' in the matter of peace with Germany.[55]

None of this had anything to do with Hess, of whom there is not a single mention in Hassell's diaries in this connection. They related in fact to the German resistance movement, of which Hassell was a member, along with Albrecht Haushofer. Both were involved in the failed attempt to kill Hitler on 20 July 1944; both were arrested and shot, though in Haushofer's case not until the very end of the war. Hassell's approach to Burckhardt was part of the ongoing efforts of the resistance to find a way of bringing the war to an end, efforts that also included a persistent though unsuccessful search for interlocutors in the British Establishment. Burckhardt's claim that members of the British War Cabinet supported a separate peace was itself of course nothing more than wishful thinking. Similarly, Harris's and Trow's theory that Hess's flight was arranged in pursuit of Burckhardt's supposed peace feelers is also purely speculative (their narrative is littered with phrases such as 'I believe that', 'it is likely that', 'I have it on good authority', and so on). The fact was, however, that Hassell recorded in his diary after the news reached him of the Nazi deputy leader's landing in Scotland:

> The flight of Hess has now shattered every possibility of advancing our cause through Haushofer. After some weeks he was to go once more to Burckhardt, who meanwhile was to have got in contact with the British again. Then we were to have used the accumulated evidence to good purpose. This is now out, as Haushofer has been arrested.[56]

In other words, there is absolutely no evidence that Burckhardt knew anything about Hess's intended flight. The evidence, Harris and Trow suggest, lies 'buried perhaps in a dusty vault at the Foreign Office in Whitehall or perhaps long ago disappeared in a Civil Service incinerator'.[57] At least they use the word 'perhaps'.

The most thorough and level-headed Hess biography, by Kurt Pätzold and Manfred Weissbecker, makes short shrift of theories that are based either on unsubstantiated speculation about individuals who knew Hess, such as Albrecht Haushofer, or the misinterpretation of documents like the Hassell diaries, or speculation, hearsay and evidence from people such as Hess's adjutants, who, when interrogated after being arrested by the Gestapo, had the strongest possible interest in denying that their boss had acted without Hitler's approval.[58] Beyond this, conspiracy theorists frequently cite each other as authorities for their claims. Thus, for example, Harris and Trow claim that 'the historian Peter Padfield established' the 'likelihood' that Hitler knew in advance of Hess's flight.[59] In return, Padfield praises Harris's 'superb' work and claims that it 'blows apart Hess's own account of the flight'.[60] Conspiracy theorists tend to do this because they regard serious historians as 'official' or 'traditional', enabling them, or so they think, to ignore the work they have done on topics such as the Hess flight. But if such theorists are to produce work that convinces, they have to confront historians' research on its own terms, and deal with the documentary evidence that actually exists.

All these conspiracy theories are based on the assumption that Hess, like van der Lubbe, could not have acted on his own. For the paranoid imagination, this is simply unacceptable: individuals such as these must have been part of a wider, secret plot of which they were a part, or even a tool. If the argument that Hitler knew in advance about Hess's flight does not hold water, then perhaps someone else in the Nazi hierarchy was involved. Certainly, Hess could not have made these preparations without the knowledge of at least some people, including his adjutant Karlheinz Pintsch, who knew about his intention from January 1941 but kept it secret.[61] But were there others? According to the ubiquitous Edouard Calic, Hess's flight was organized by Reinhard Heydrich without Hitler's knowledge, though quite what Heydrich's motive might have been is unclear.[62] The type of Me110 combat plane used by Hess, he claimed, could surely not have carried enough fuel to complete such a long journey: it must have stopped for refuelling, or been replaced on the French or Belgian coast by another, implying collaboration from the German Luftwaffe. But the identification marks on the remains of the crashed plane were the same as those photographed on the plane at Augsburg before the flight. Moreover, there is incontrovertible evidence to prove that the plane used by Hess was equipped with auxiliary fuel tanks and was quite capable of flying from Augsburg to Scotland without stopping to refuel. Nor is there any mystery about the fact that it was not intercepted during his flight across Germany: the Me110 was easily recognizable as a German aircraft and so would not have aroused any suspicion, as the reaction of the two submarines over which it passed in the North Sea showed.[63] And there is certainly not a shred of evidence to support the surreal claim that Hess was accompanied across Germany by a plane flown personally by Heydrich.[64]

IV

Conspiracy theories about Hess's flight have grown in number and variety over the years.[65] They began almost as soon as the plane had landed. The first in the field was Dr James Vincent Murphy, who published *Who Sent Rudolf Hess?*, a forty-eight-page pamphlet, just a few weeks after the flight. Murphy was an Irish journalist and translator (and a lapsed Catholic priest). He was based in Berlin from 1929 onwards.[66] After leaving for the UK during the Depression, he produced a short biographical study, *Adolf Hitler: The Drama of His Career*, written at the request of the publishers Chapman and Hall, in 1934. The book's aim was to explain to English-speaking readers how Hitler had come to power, at a time when he was still not very well known in the UK. Its verdict on Hitler was relatively favourable. As Murphy admitted:

> What I may call the negative aspects of the Hitler achievement have been ignored in this book. And that for two reasons: first because enough has already been published in the English language by opponents of the Hitler regime; secondly because negative criticism is an obstacle rather than a help to the understanding of an historical movement.[67]

Murphy went on to make at least a few concessions to Hitler's critics. 'Criminal and even official hooliganism' were 'early excesses' of German National Socialism which, if it followed the pattern of Italian Fascism, he thought, might well disappear as Hitler's government became firmly established. 'Only the future can tell.'[68]

But overall, Murphy praised the 'positive achievements' of the Nazis and claimed they had come to power with the support of the great mass of the German people. He presented the antisemitic policies of the Nazis as not only explicable but also justified. The Jews were 'shrewd Asiatics' (in fact, German Jews were highly acculturated; this was a breathtakingly racist categorization).[69] The Jews dominated 'German industry and commerce' (apart from steel and coal, which, he claimed erroneously, were largely state-owned), while 'the chief direction of the great public banks has hitherto been almost a Jewish monopoly', with 50 per cent of private banks also being in Jewish hands (these figures were wild exaggerations; the German-Jewish economic elite was tiny, as well as being deeply divided by religious and political cleavages). This, he concluded, meant that 'less than 1 per cent of the German population, representing a group of people alien in race and tradition, have a very strong and almost decisive voice in the financial and commercial affairs of the country'. The same was true, he thought, of the academic professions, literature, culture and the arts. He went on to parrot the Nazi claim that socialism and Communism, along with the Weimar Constitution, were Jewish creations, though he failed to note the contradiction with his simultaneous assertion that capitalism in Germany was also dominated by Jews.[70]

Not surprisingly, reviewers of the book in the UK regarded Murphy as 'an ardent Hitlerite' and criticized his acceptance of Nazi propaganda, especially about the Jews.[71] But reactions were not all negative, particularly not in Germany itself. Impressed by the book, and aware of Murphy's track record as a translator of German texts, the German Propaganda Ministry offered him the job of producing English versions of Hitler's speeches and brought him over to Berlin. He soon began criticizing other translations of Nazi propaganda, including an abridged version of *Mein Kampf* published in English a few years earlier, so the Propaganda Ministry commissioned him to produce a full translation of the book. Under pressure of time, Murphy secured the collaboration of a young woman, Grete Lorke, whom he had met at the house of a mutual acquaintance. Lorke had been a German exchange student in Madison, Wisconsin, and admired Murphy's work. But, by an astonishing chance, she was also secretly a member of the 'Red Orchestra', a Communist resistance circle, and, among other things, in effect a Soviet agent. She persuaded her superiors that a good, unexpurgated English translation of Hitler's book would help alert the world to the threat he posed.[72]

Lorke discovered that the Irishman had a serious drink problem which meant she had the opportunity to fill in the gaps he left in his translation without his paying too much attention. She managed to insert phrases and expressions that emphasized the vulgar and rabble-rousing character of the original, which she felt had been smoothed over in Murphy's accomplished literary rendering.[73] At this point, however, things began to go seriously wrong. The Irishman was forced to resign from his post in the Propaganda Ministry when he refused to translate parts of Hitler's speeches that contained personal attacks on British politicians such as Foreign Secretary Anthony

Eden. Unfortunately for Murphy, the Ministry also repudiated the translation of *Mein Kampf* and impounded Murphy's manuscript drafts. Fearing for his safety, he left for London. But he had virtually no money. The translation of *Mein Kampf* offered a way out, but the drafts were still in Berlin, and Murphy was rightly afraid to return. So his wife, Mary, went instead. Fortunately, Murphy's former secretary in Berlin still kept a handwritten draft and Mary Murphy returned to Britain with it in her suitcase. The translation was published on 20 March 1939 by Hurst and Blackett. But Murphy's bad luck continued, for public opinion in Britain had turned decisively against Hitler following the German invasion of Czechoslovakia just five days earlier, and Murphy's Foreword was unequivocally condemned by reviewers as scandalously 'pro-Hitler'.[74]

This, then, was the man who was the first to publish a conspiracist account of Hess's flight. Murphy's initial response to the flight, in an article published in the *Daily Sketch* newspaper on 14 May 1941, was to claim that Hess had fled Germany of his own volition as a 'protest against the disastrous consequences of Ribbentrop's influence over Hitler'; in his view, the Nazi Foreign Minister Joachim von Ribbentrop was pushing the German dictator in an anti-British direction, against Hitler's personal inclinations.[75] A few weeks later, however, Murphy reconsidered the issue in a pamphlet, published by Hutchinson, with the title *Who Sent Rudolf Hess?* On the garishly coloured cover, the publishers noted in bold type that 'the author was for four years (1934–38) an official of the German Propaganda Ministry in Berlin. He knows the inner workings of the Nazi machine and the persons who control it.' In a Preface dated 8 June 1941, Murphy noted: 'This little book was already in the press when the Nazis launched the peace initiative which had been heralded by the advent of Rudolf Hess,' adding: 'At the moment one cannot say whether it will hang fire or not.'[76] In fact, of course, 'the Nazis' had not launched any 'peace initiative', either officially, at Hitler's command, or unofficially, as part of a wider conspiracy involving Hess.

Murphy made a number of assumptions in his pamphlet that were to resurface in much of the subsequent conspiracist literature. They included 'the fact that Hess's melodramatic appearance in Scotland was timed to coincide with the mass raid on London' by German bombers as an act of 'psychological aggression'. This was intended, Murphy suggested, by 'the group behind Hess' in Germany to soften up British opinion for their 'peace initiative'. Murphy alleged that Hess had long masterminded the Nazi Party's programme of penetrating other countries through the encouragement of 'Quislings' and 'Fifth Columnists', or in other words Nazi sympathizers.[77] It was indeed, he claimed (on the authority of Hess's brother Alfred), Rudolf Hess who had written the sections of *Mein Kampf* dealing with propaganda, *Lebensraum* ('living space', or in other words the conquest of Eastern Europe) and the British Empire (not a view for which there is any direct evidence).[78] In 1934, Hess had issued an appeal for a peace movement to be formed by the ex-servicemen of the world and Murphy had translated it at his request. Retrospectively, Murphy saw this, however, as a 'propaganda stunt' whose purpose was to gain Hitler time for rearmament and recover the international standing he had lost through his direction of the murders that had just been carried out of a number of political rivals in the 'Night of the Long Knives'.[79]

Hess's involvement in all this, Murphy claimed, was through the Foreign Organization of the Nazi Party, which he created and which was led by Ernst Wilhelm Bohle, a man with whom Murphy had worked closely.[80] Murphy still ascribed Hess's flight to what he regarded as a feud between Hess and Foreign Minister Ribbentrop over who exactly was in charge of Nazi foreign policy under Hitler. But now he had revised his opinion to the extent that he considered it only 'partly' responsible for the escapade. Murphy regarded Ribbentrop as 'the Svengali who practices the art of post-hypnotic suggestion on the Berchtesgaden somnambulist' (yet again, as so often in conspiracy theories, as we have seen, there is a hint of the uncanny here). 'Most of Hitler's decisions on war,' he added, 'now originate with Ribbentrop.'[81] Ribbentrop was indeed deeply anti-British, but to ascribe to him such influence was a clear exaggeration. Still, Murphy's belief that the leaders of the German armed forces had been extremely uneasy about the speed of Hitler's drive to war was accurate enough. From conversations with the late army chief Werner von Fritsch, Murphy had come to believe that Germany's military leadership, backed by big business, foresaw that the next war would be an 'orgy of destruction without purpose'. The mass bombing of cities would 'lead to no decisive military results' and end with the aristocratic military caste being overthrown in favour of Nazi 'gangsters'.[82]

In Murphy's view, Hess was an honest German patriot, 'endowed with a good share of common sense'. His associate Bohle considered that Ribbentrop was mistaken when he asserted that his pro-German 'friends' in aristocratic circles in Britain 'were not representative of British public opinion'. Nevertheless, despite Ribbentrop's scepticism, the Nazi leaders still considered them influential. 'Do the Nazis think that the policy of appeasement . . . still has influential support among the British public?' Murphy asked: 'Undoubtedly they do. Do they believe that military victories alone will win this war for Germany? Some do, but others don't. Those who don't are responsible for Hess's mission to Britain.' The bombing raid on London on the night of Hess's flight showed that Hermann Göring, head of the Luftwaffe, was also among them. Both the raid and the flight 'were part of a policy that had been thought out months ahead. The dramatic method of the approach was quite in Hitler's Wagnerian style. It was the first step in a new peace offensive. And undoubtedly Hitler was a party to it.' The aim of the peace offensive was to head off growing opposition within Germany to the continuation of the war, which would surely result in the break-up of the Nazi Party that Hitler and Hess had created together.[83]

It was important to remember, however, Murphy continued, that the Nazi 'peace offensive which had been heralded by the advent of Rudolf Hess' was 'a combine for world penetration' based on the subversive activities of the Deputy Führer's Foreign Organization of the Nazi Party. It might 'take over for a spell' from the military, naval and airborne campaigns against Britain, but only with the idea 'that by psychological, political and economic infiltration they will prepare the ground for the final military effort which will make the Nazis lords of the world. That is the purpose,' he concluded, 'of all the peace plans that are being put forward at the moment.'[84] In this respect, Murphy was surely right: any separate peace concluded with the Nazis would only have postponed the reduction of Great Britain to the status of a German client state, rather than preserving its independence, its economy and its possession of a global empire. There are no signs of any sympathy with Hitler and the Third Reich on Murphy's part here; if anything, the opposite. Murphy's pamphlet was clearly intended as a warning against any attempt to conclude a separate peace with Germany.

Yet his conspiracy theory was all surmise and speculation. As we have seen, the evidence tells against the supposition that Hitler knew about Hess's flight, and the same is true of other figures in the Nazi hierarchy such as Göring, who was as surprised as anyone when news of the Deputy Führer's landing came through (Murphy was seemingly unaware of the official German declaration that Hess was a madman who had been acting on his own initiative and without the knowledge of anyone else in the Nazi hierarchy). The coincidence of the bombing raid on London with the date, though not the hour, of the flight, was just that: a coincidence – though it is a key characteristic of conspiracy theories that coincidences don't happen, they are planned. Perhaps because he knew members of Hess's staff like Bohle, Murphy vastly exaggerated the extent of the power and influence Hess was wielding by the time he boarded his plane, and indeed long before. The generals' opposition to Hitler's forward military policy had evaporated by 1941, following the German armed forces' stunning victories in the West the previous year. Murphy thought that, if nothing else, the growing involvement of the United States on the Allied side had convinced the Nazi leadership that the German war effort was doomed, prompting the supposed 'peace initiative' with Britain, but he was wrong here too. Murphy's theory that Hess's flight was part of a secret plot hatched by the Nazi leadership convinced few people even in 1941, and has not stood the test of time.

V

Murphy's theory disappeared from view almost as soon as he had propounded it. Others, however, were more influential, and more persistent. This was particularly the case with conspiracy theories emanating from the Kremlin, where Stalin had long harboured suspicions about the intentions of the British. They were capitalists, so were the Germans: it was obviously in their interests to conclude a separate peace. From early on in the war, the international Communist movement, acting under Stalin's orders, had dismissed the conflict as a quarrel between two capitalist nations in which international Communism had to remain neutral. The policy had changed, however, following the defeat of France in June 1940, after which Stalin had urged the formation of a 'people's government' in Britain to carry on the struggle against Fascism.[85] Any kind of movement towards a separate peace between Britain and Germany would be evidence in Stalin's suspicious mind of a joint plan of the capitalist nations to turn on the Soviet Union and had to be stopped.

Such were the considerations governing the reaction of international Communism to the Hess flight. Leading figures in the Communist Party of Great Britain, notably Harry Pollitt, rushed into print alleging that Hamilton had known Hess well and was a Nazi sympathizer. Aircraft production minister Max Beaverbrook endorsed this view when he told the Soviet ambassador shortly after the flight: 'Oh, Hess, of course, is Hitler's emissary.' But the proofs he adduced to back up this theory were far from convincing: he asserted (falsely) that Hamilton was a 'Quisling', part of a 'peace party' that wanted to accede to Hitler's undoubted (in fact, however, non-existent) desire to conclude peace with the United Kingdom.[86] Allegations in the Communist Party organ *World News* that Hamilton was a 'Quisling' prompted the duke to sue the paper for libel, and since it presented no evidence in support of the allegation, the defendants were obliged to withdraw it and print an apology.[87] But the Communists did not abandon their suspicions. The German invasion of the Soviet Union on 22 June 1941 then prompted the ever-suspicious Stalin to claim that the British were in cahoots with the Germans and that Hess had flown to Scotland with their connivance – else why had he not been immediately shot, or at least put on trial?

The Party newspaper *Pravda* (*Truth*) even claimed on 19 October 1942 that Hess's wife had been brought to London to join him, suggesting that Hess might indeed be representing the Nazi government in Britain. A few days later, to back this up, it printed a photograph of her playing the piano in London – but this was in fact Myra Hess, a popular British concert pianist of the day and no relation to any of the other parties involved.[88] Undeterred, Stalin repeated the suggestion to Churchill at a Kremlin dinner on 18 October 1944, when, despite the British Prime Minister's detailed exposition of the affair, he raised his glass in a toast to British Intelligence, which had 'inveigled Hess into coming to Britain'.[89] This theory was repeated in 1991, when the Soviet Intelligence Service put forward the claim that Hess had been lured to Britain by letters faked by MI5; but this claim was based on information from the late Soviet spy Kim Philby, a notorious liar; and Philby never made any mention of it in public, not even in his memoirs. A statement alleging MI5 involvement made to the Soviet authorities by Karlheinz Pintsch while he was in their custody after the war reflected nothing more than the characteristic tendency of Soviet interrogations to force the prisoner by whatever means to say what the secret police wanted.[90] A British Secret Service plot to lure Hess over to Scotland would in any case have been as much a waste of time as the flight itself. Finally, Peter Padfield's theory (already, as we have seen, advanced by Murphy) that the heavy air raid launched against London on 10 May 1941 had the purpose of diverting the RAF from Hess's flight further north falls down on the fact that the raids began only *after* Hess had crossed the British coast.[91]

Still, we need to explain why Hess's plane was not intercepted or shot down by the RAF when it reached British airspace. Surely this was highly suspicious: it must prove that there were people in high places in the UK Establishment who knew about the flight in advance and issued orders for the plane to be allowed to land. Unfortunately for this theory, no orders have ever been found instructing the RAF to let Hess pass unhindered through the skies over Britain. On the other hand, orders *were* issued to shoot his plane down, confirmed after the war by more than one of the pilots involved. The fact – mentioned by some conspiracy theorists[92] – that anti-aircraft batteries were ordered not to open fire on the aircraft as it entered and crossed British airspace, is not evidence of a plot but reflects the RAF's knowledge that fighter planes had been sent to intercept it: it was standard practice in this case to avoid firing in case one of the pursuers was accidentally hit from the ground.[93]

Despite his care on the long flight over the North Sea to avoid detection by British radar, Hess did not escape the notice of the Royal

Air Force, which had deployed a string of twenty-two radar stations along the coastline. British aircraft carried an instrument aboard that enabled ground radar to identify them as friendly, and of course Hess's Messerschmitt did not carry such a device, so when, at eight minutes past ten on the evening of 10 May 1941, it appeared as a blip on the radar screen at Ottercops Moss, to the north-west of Newcastle, it showed up, therefore, as an enemy aeroplane. By this time, Hess had finished flying back and forth while he was waiting for dusk to descend, and had commenced the final leg of his journey. The sighting was reported to the central operations room in Middlesex and was soon joined by three more. The blip was identified as a single aircraft. Northumberland was far less densely covered with fighter bases then the counties further south, but orders to attack the plane were passed to two Spitfires flying over the Farne Islands. However, they were unable to make visual contact. At twenty past ten, another Spitfire was scrambled from 72 Squadron base at Acklington. The pilot, Sergeant Maurice Pocock, took off and climbed to 15,000 feet, where the enemy aircraft had been reported by the radar operators, but was also unable to see it, and returned to base.

Hess had avoided detection because he had noticed a layer of mist below the altitude at which he was flying, and descended to a very low level so that the Spitfires could not see him from above – so low, indeed, that a Royal Observer Corps post on the ground actually heard him pass overhead. Another post, however, at Chatton, in Northumberland, did spot the plane's silhouette and correctly identified it as an 'Me 110 at 50 feet'. As Hess continued on his way, virtually skimming the treetops, a string of observer posts also reported seeing an Me110, flying fast and low, at about 300 mph. There was no reason why a single German aircraft of this type should be flying in this area, however, particularly because the Me110 was known not to carry enough fuel to make the return journey to Germany. There surely must be some kind of mistake. Nevertheless, a two-seater Defiant night-fighter was ordered to take to the air to investigate. Slow compared to the Messerschmitt, and equipped with turret-mounted weaponry instead of forward-facing guns, the Defiant followed Hess, who had climbed again and turned inland after reaching the west coast. He spotted the Defiant from afar, but he was already making his final run towards

Dungavel and preparing to jump. It was too late to stop him, and his plane crash-landed before it could be caught.[94]

So there was no conspiracy to let Hess pass British defences and reach Scotland. In any case, the claim, advanced by the Soviets, that there was a serious 'peace party' in Britain engaged in negotiations with Hess, was always hard to sustain. To begin with, there was no 'welcoming committee' awaiting Hess when he landed; not even Hamilton was there to greet him. Even if Hess bailed out instead of landing on the airstrip he was aiming for, there is no evidence of any-body looking out for him in Scotland or anywhere else. According to Alfred Smith, another conspiracy theorist, the 'Peace Party included representatives from royalty, the landed aristocracy, business and financial interests and politicians of Cabinet rank'.[95] It stretches cre-dulity beyond breaking point, however, to imagine that a significant group of politicians and civil servants in Britain, either seriously pro-Nazi or merely anti-war or Appeasement-minded, could have engaged in such a ramified plot without any of them admitting that it existed, either then or later. So implausible is this idea that even serious Hess conspiracy theorists have dismissed it. Peter Padfield, for example, points out that while there were people in the British Establishment holding one or other of these views,

> no proof had surfaced of a coherent group with plans to oust Church-
> ill and in contact with Hess. If such proof exists in the 'Hess' or 'Peace
> feelers' files closed until 2017, it is strange that the former Foreign
> Office men in charge of Hess's case do not remember it. Hess's arrival
> made such a sensation [that] the antecedent causes are not likely to
> have been forgotten by those who must have known of them had they
> been referred to in the official files.[96]

The sheer impossibility of so many people, from Hamilton down to RAF radar operatives, from politicians to civil servants, keeping the matter so completely secret that no evidence of it ever saw the light of day has convinced most students of the subject that the idea of Hess being invited over by a 'peace party' is a non-starter. Nor is there any evidence of a plot in 1941 to oust Churchill, whose position as Prime Minister by this time had become unassailable.

Since there isn't really any evidence for an organized group engaged in a conspiracy to overthrow Churchill and conclude a separate peace, a number of authors have decided that the idea of a 'peace party' was put about by the British Secret Service to lure Hess to Britain on false pretences.[97] But their accounts amount to little more than speculation. In some cases this involves an attempt to engage readers by naming as part of the plot individuals who became famous after the war – Ian Fleming, for example, the later creator of the fictional secret agent James Bond. Harris and Trow, who put forward Fleming's name, attribute the connection to 'Donald McCormick, who died last year . . . and had access to information either still classified or long ago consigned to the incinerator'.[98] 'The paper trail quite properly demanded by historians,' they admit, 'is not there.' The men involved, Harris and Trow claim implausibly, 'have carried their secrets to their graves'. The tissue of coincidences and connections they spin is no substitute for facts, and 'it may have been' and 'could have been' are no replacement for actual evidence.[99] In similar fashion, Alfred Smith laid considerable weight on the alleged withholding of key documents by the British authorities as an explanation for the lack of documentary backing for his conspiracy theories.[100] But since Hess's flight was a failure, what would have been the point in keeping British involvement secret decades after the war was over?

In 1994 the investigative journalist Louis C. Kilzer, who subsequently published a book, *Hitler's Traitor*, purporting to expose Martin Bormann as a Soviet spy, produced a variant on the 'fake peace party' theory in his book *Churchill's Deception: The Dark Secret that Destroyed Nazi Germany*.[101] Kilzer argued that Churchill had deliberately encouraged Hitler to believe that he was about to conclude a separate peace with Germany, thereby prompting him to feel confident enough to launch an invasion of the Soviet Union in the belief that Britain would soon be out of the war. This 'peace party conspiracy' was supposedly used by the British authorities to trick Hitler into sending Hess to Scotland on 10 May 1941, little over a month before the launching of Operation Barbarossa against the Soviet Union. Unfortunately, the evidence Kilzer presents for Churchill's supposed orchestration of the conspiracy is as threadbare and unconvincing as the evidence he also presents for Hitler's supposed authorization of Hess's flight.[102]

The 'fake peace party' line concocted by MI5 is followed by other conspiracy theorists writing about Hess's flight, for example Rainer F. Schmidt, who asserts that Churchill also knew about the flight in advance, and that it was planned by Foreign Secretary Anthony Eden and his officials (though what might have been their motivation is unclear). Harris and Trow also share the view that it was all staged by the British Secret Service.[103] However, Rainer Schmidt's theories were comprehensively demolished in 1999 by the British historian Ted Harrison, who showed that they rested on unnamed sources, newspaper articles written long after the event and similarly unreliable pseudo-evidence. MI5 documents released in the 1990s did not include any correspondence between Hess and the British security services, while the exchange between Hamilton and Haushofer had not reached any conclusion by the time Hess took to the skies. The idea that MI5 orchestrated the whole affair rests on an almost comical overestimation of the power and efficiency of the British Secret Service in 1941, when it is generally agreed to have been poorly organized and suffering from low morale.[104] And finally, what would have been the point of luring Hess to the United Kingdom? No proponent of the 'fake peace party' theory has ever been able to provide a convincing answer to this question. Hitler certainly wasn't going to try and ransom him; Stalin's suspicions of the British would have been redoubled to no purpose; and the likelihood of the flight persuading Hitler to change his mind on the aims or conduct of the war was vanishingly remote. And none of these theories can overcome the fundamental problem that Hess was generally agreed by 1941, not only in Germany, to be one of the least important and most marginal members of the Nazi hierarchy.

As David Stafford has pointed out after an examination of the evidence on the British government's reactions to the flight: 'The disarray between Churchill and the Foreign Office over how to handle Hess's arrival in Scotland stands as overwhelming evidence against any . . . theory about some carefully planned conspiracy. For why, if it was so cunningly prepared, was there no strategy in place to exploit it?' Yet Stafford goes on at the same time to claim that the notion of a 'peace party' in the UK was the product of a disinformation campaign devised in order to persuade Hitler that it wasn't necessary in the end to invade Britain. This is a theory, however, for which there is no evidence at all, and which lacks any kind of plausibility since Hitler had clearly abandoned his invasion plans several months earlier, if indeed they had ever been serious in the first place.[105]

VI

The obvious absence of hard evidence to support the 'fake peace party' theory has apparently led at least one of the theory's proponents to take desperate measures to bolster it up. Like others, the conspiracy theorist Martin Allen argued that the flight was orchestrated by the British Secret Service. If Hitler could be brought to believe there was a serious 'peace party' in the UK, then it was more than likely that he would launch an invasion of the Soviet Union, which in the long run was the only hope for Britain in its war with Germany. Using Hess and his friends the Haushofers as intermediaries, Hitler tried to make contact with this non-existent 'peace party', in the end deciding that the only way this could be done was by getting someone to fly to Britain and negotiate in person. Initially this individual was to be the head of the Nazi organization for Party members who lived abroad, Ernst Bohle, but – driven by ambition – Hess decided at the last moment to go in his place. After the war, Karl Haushofer was murdered in order to stop him revealing the 'Hitler/ Hess peace overtures' at the Nuremberg War Crimes Trials.[106]

But this whole theory is based on a tissue of invention and falsification. To begin with, Hess's long and meticulous preparations for his flight precluded the possibility that he only stepped in at the last minute. The Haushofers were not in any way close to Hitler and he would not have used them as intermediaries. Haushofer in fact committed suicide in a secluded rural retreat, with his wife, by taking arsenic, on the night of 10 March 1946.[107] The British authorities had no objection to his being interrogated. And, of course, there is no evidence that Hess flew to Scotland on Hitler's command. Worse than any of this, the documents in the British National Archive files on Hess used by Allen in support of his theory have been revealed as blatant forgeries (among other things, by the simple method of forensically testing the paper on which they were written, which turned out to have dated from after the war) or have been found not to have existed at all. Almost as implausible is the allegation, raised in another book by Allen, that SS chief Heinrich Himmler was murdered on his arrest by the British shortly after the end of the war in order to prevent him from revealing secrets that the British authorities wanted kept hidden.[108] Martin Allen's father, Peter Allen, made a similar kind of claim in his book *The Crown and the Swastika: Hitler, Hess and the Duke of Windsor* (1983) – the involvement of the ex-King Edward VIII is another characteristic example of the tendency of some conspiracy theorists to try to arouse interest in their work by involving famous people.

The exposure of forged documents in the files on Hess and related topics in the British National Archives led the archive's authorities to tighten security measures around readers, who from 2006 onwards have been required to write their notes in bound, stapled or stitched-together booklets to prevent them slipping single pages containing forged documents into the files. Allen, of course, has denied creating the forged documents himself, though he was investigated by the police, and it was reported that the Crown Prosecution Service refrained from pressing charges only because of Allen's ill health.[109] In any case, however, his work is full of unsubstantiated speculations and dubious interpretations that render it unfit for use as a guide to the topics with which it deals. This has not prevented it from being translated into German and published by the extreme right-wing, historical 'revisionist' Druffel-Verlag, which has leapt at the chance of spreading the notion that the British government was concealing inconvenient truths about Hitler's so-called 'peace initiatives' during the war, implying that it was Churchill and not Hitler who insisted on the continuation of the conflict.[110]

Both the real and the fake 'peace party' conspiracy theories reflect on the part of some of their proponents the existence of a far more wide-ranging conspiracist mentality. *Hess: The British Conspiracy* (1999), by John Harris and Martin Trow, displays a typical conspiracist attitude when it dismisses the accounts of 'traditionalist historians' on Hess's flight.[111] Like other conspiracists, Harris and his collaborators question accepted accounts of other events in modern history such as the death of Diana, Princess of Wales. 'The world since 1945,' they declare, 'has become hardened to conspiracies great and small . . . a tangled web of secrecy, contradiction and confusion obscures the core of fact.'[112] Of course, some conspiracy theories turn out not to be true. But many others, in their view, clearly are. And yet, they continue, 'the traditionalists still cling to their narrow view of events'.[113]

'The fact is,' Peter Allen darkly suggested, 'that behind all the significant events in recent history have been an army of anonymous spies who have exerted far greater influence on history than those who wrote it.'[114] Such conspirators have had no qualms about silencing those who might have exposed their machinations.

> Heydrich, too, was assassinated in 1942 on the orders of British intelligence, while Bedaux [a friend of the Windsors] died of an overdose of sleeping tablets. Even the Duke of Kent, who had certainly been in contact with his brother the Duke of Windsor in Lisbon, died in a mysterious plane crash that the Germans insisted had been arranged by British Intelligence – everyone was silenced.[115]

Heydrich was indeed assassinated in 1942, but by Czech resistance agents and because he was acting with particular brutality and cunning in his capacity as governor of occupied Bohemia and Moravia; while there was in fact nothing very mysterious about the death of either the French-American Nazi collaborator Charles Bedaux in prison in 1944 while awaiting trial for treason, or the Duke of Kent, who was killed in an air training crash in 1942.

As Ernst Haiger, an acknowledged academic expert on the Haushofers, remarks caustically in his devastating exposure of Allen's work: 'A man is said to have committed suicide, but in fact he was killed by British agents to silence him: this story reminds us of Martin Allen's book on the "murder" of Heinrich Himmler.'[116] Fear of being assassinated apparently also stopped others from revealing the truth: Peter Padfield, for example, claims that 'a key informant allegedly substantiating his theory of a British Intelligence plot refused at the last moment to deliver the crucial evidence', one of many who suspiciously kept silent about the affair.[117] Speculations such as these are the bread and butter of conspiracy theories: key witnesses 'mysteriously' disappear in an obvious attempt to cover up their conspiratorial origins. Yet again, conspiracists seize on a major and widely known event in modern history sparked by a single individual and argue instead that it must have been the result of collective action and planning behind the scenes. If only the evidence were available, it would conclusively prove them right. Unfortunately, however, all the evidence goes to show that Rudolf Hess acted alone, on his own exclusive initiative, and claims to the contrary are entirely without foundation.

Is there any larger political thrust behind conspiracy theories about British involvement in Hess's mission, whether it was articulated by a genuine 'peace party' or a fake one dreamed up by the security services? For some conspiracy theorists, the flight of Rudolf Hess represented a real opportunity to bring the war to an end, save Britain from making the sacrifices that ultimately proved necessary to defeat Hitler, including the loss of the British Empire after the war, and leave the Nazis and the Soviets to slug it out in a war of mutual destruction that would have left the Soviet Union crippled. Representative of this point of view is Peter Padfield, one of the most persistent of the Hess conspiracy theorists. The peace offer Hess brought with him, he insists, was genuine. It was the warmonger Churchill who squandered the historic chance Hess offered:

> The terms he carried – from Hitler – would have given Britain peace with some honour. Churchill, committed to the defeat of 'that man' Hitler, and Nazism, had to bury the message and write off the messenger; in doing so he almost single-handedly deflected the course of history – for realists would have accepted Hess's terms. This is the real significance of his story: as a pivotal moment when history did not turn as might have been expected.[118]

A few have gone even further. For Alfred Smith, for example, Hitler had never wanted a war with Britain in the first place (his book is entitled *Rudolf Hess and Germany's Reluctant War 1939–41*) and Hess's flight to Scotland on his behalf was a last desperate attempt by the Nazi leader to stop the warmonger Churchill in his tracks. 'Hitler,' he declares, 'had no ambitions in the West.' Indeed, if Hess's mission had not been thwarted, the Holocaust would never have happened. As it was, it went ahead, while the result of the war for Britain was the humiliating loss of the Empire and the domination of the world by Russia and America.[119] So it was Churchill who was ultimately responsible for the Holocaust then, not Hitler – an allegation that betrays a breathtaking ignorance of Nazi policies in occupied Poland from September 1939 onwards, and Nazi planning for the future of Eastern Europe in 1940–41. At their furthest extreme, such views represent a clear sympathy with Nazi Germany and a regret that the war had ever happened at all: it is notable, for example, that Ilse Hess's book claiming her husband was a 'prisoner of peace' silenced by the warmonger Churchill was translated into English and published by The Britons, an organization that also, some years before, had produced one of the earliest English translations of *The Protocols of the Elders of Zion*.[120]

Nostalgia and regret about the outcome of the war for the United Kingdom are based on illusions. The fact is that, even without the financial and geopolitical impact of the Second World War, the British Empire's days were numbered. It was being undermined by the inexorable rise to superpower status of the USA, and by the steady growth of independence movements in the colonies, which required countermeasures that would in the long run have been politically and economically impossible for London to sustain even without the financial burden of the war. And in any case, as we have already seen, a separate peace between Britain and Germany in 1940 or 1941 would, as Churchill realized, have meant the eventual subjugation of Britain and the Empire to Hitler and the Nazis, with catastrophic results, not least for Britain's Jewish population.

The argument that Hess's mission, if successful, would have avoided the Holocaust is also advanced by Lynn Pinknett, Clive Prince and Stephen Prior in their book *Double Standards: The Rudolf Hess Cover-Up*, published in 2001. They argue that Hess's flight was arranged between a British 'peace party', an organization that included Hamilton, who was waiting for him at his house (which Hess failed to reach, of course); the 'peace party' would have mounted a coup, replacing Churchill with Sir Samuel Hoare (a noted pre-war Appeaser), who would then have concluded a separate peace. This would have avoided a Soviet takeover of Eastern Europe after the war, since the USSR and Nazi Germany would have ended the conflict in a state of complete exhaustion. Hess, they claim, was a 'moderating influence' on Hitler, so a separate peace, with Hess returning to Germany in triumph, would have saved millions of lives, since he 'was opposed to violent action against the German Jews'. None of these claims rests on any credible evidence. Hess was a rabid antisemite, Hamilton was not waiting for him on 10 May 1941, and there was no 'peace party'; the rest is pure speculation.[121]

The credibility of Pinknett and Prince is further undermined when one turns to their own biographies. They are, to put it simply, professional conspiracy theorists, with previous publications on 'The Turin Shroud: In Whose Image?' (it was apparently forged by Leonardo da Vinci), 'The Templar Revolution' and 'The Stargate Conspiracy'. Their co-author Prior claimed to have been working as an *agent provocateur* for the British security services and to have been imprisoned on fake terrorist charges in 1969. He was, he said, also involved in a 'secret project' with Michael Bentine (a comedian, famous for his performances in radio's postwar comedy series *The Goon Show*), who was also engaged in 'intelligence work' (in fact, Bentine had served in MI9, a unit formed to assist resistance movements against the German occupying forces on the European Continent). Among the authors' acknowledgements was a note of thanks to Trevor Ravenscroft, 'author of the controversial *Spear of Destiny*, which centred on Hitler's fascination with the occult'. Despite the apparently rational arguments in a book stretching to more than five hundred pages, the authors in the end belong firmly in the world of professional conspiracism.

Even stranger is *Rudolf Hess: Truth at Last* (co-authored by Harris and Wilbourn and published in 2019 by the aptly named Unicorn Publishing Group). The book advertises itself as presenting 'the untold story of the Deputy Führer's flight to Scotland in 1941', despite the fact that Harris and his collaborators had already told the story four times in their previous books on the subject. Among other 'revelations', the book tells the story of how MI6 orchestrated the flight with the help of a Finnish art historian, Tancred Borenius, who was sent to Switzerland as an intermediary in a bid by the 'peace party' in the UK to bring about a deal with Germany. This involved a plot to overthrow the British government and – a topical note in the era of

Brexit – install a new regime that would support the creation of a 'federalist' Europe. Unfortunately, the authors fail to include a single source reference in the book, which is shot through with unsupported speculation, suggestion and innuendo. Instead, there is a lot of 'we think that' and 'we believe that'. And the book ends with the demand for a judicial inquiry into the affair, so it does not deliver 'the final truth' after all. Parts of it, beginning with the Introduction, which is cast in diary form, are clearly fiction. At this point, conspiracy theories about Hess's flight pass over into the realms of fantasy; it no longer really matters whether any of them can be proved or have any basis in a verifiable documentary record. What counts is their entertainment value.

VII

Hess's mission was founded on his own illusions, not on other people's intentions. It did not take long for him to realize this uncomfortable fact. It soon became clear that his flight to Scotland had achieved nothing. In a kind of megalomania induced by years of addressing crowds of adoring Nazis, he had enormously overestimated his own importance and almost comically misjudged the significance of his action. Ignorant of the true political situation in Britain, he had hugely underestimated the cohesion and determination of Churchill's government.[122] He plunged into a deep depression, already noted by Viscount Simon when he interrogated him on 9 June 1941. In the early hours of 14 June, Hess asked to be let out of his first-floor room, and rushed on to the landing, throwing himself over the banisters. But although he broke his leg on the flagstones below, he survived. He showed distinct signs of paranoia, and told people he was being poisoned. His behaviour unleashed a lengthy debate on his mental state: many put this together with what they assumed was his already deranged condition before his flight, and concluded that he was insane.[123] On 26 March 1942 he was moved to Maindiff Court Hospital in South Wales, where he remained under guard for the rest of the war. On 4 February 1945, realizing Germany had lost the war and Hitler was doomed, he tried to commit suicide again, stabbing himself in the chest with a bread knife, but to no effect. After prolonged behind-the-scenes discussion, it was decided to include him among the principal defendants in the Nuremberg War Crimes Tribunal, although he had not been directly responsible for war crimes and crimes against humanity; he was charged only with crimes against peace. He tried to convince the Allied prosecutors and officials that he had lost his memory, and pretended not to recognize either his former secretary, Hildegard Fath, or indeed the former Reich Marshal, Hermann Göring. Sentenced to life imprisonment, he was incarcerated in Spandau jail, in the north-western part of West Berlin. Here he remained for the rest of his life.[124]

In the long years of Hess's imprisonment in Spandau, his family and friends made repeated efforts to secure his release, not only on humanitarian and compassionate grounds (which became more compelling as he grew old), but also, and perhaps above all, on political ones. A particularly active advocate of Hess's release was the lawyer Alfred Seidl, who acted for his defence in the Nuremberg War Crimes Trials. There could be no doubt about Seidl's Nazi beliefs. In 1935 he had gained his doctorate with a dissertation under the supervision of Edmund Mezger, a pro-Nazi criminologist who believed that the purpose of punishment was 'the elimination from the national community of elements which damage the people and the race'.[125] Replete with quotations from the Nazi lawyer Roland Freisler, later to become notorious as President of the People's Court during the trial of the resistance members involved in the bomb plot of 1944, Seidl's dissertation parroted the Nazi doctrine that punishment should be directed not against the offence but against the will and disposition of the individual who committed it.[126] A member of the Nazi Party from 1934 until he joined the Wehrmacht in 1940, Seidl acted not only for Hess at the Nuremberg Trials but also for Hans Frank, the brutal and corrupt ruler of German-occupied Poland, and others, including Ilse Koch, the wife of a concentration camp commandant, whose sadistic conduct earned her the nickname 'the beast of Buchenwald'.

A central part of Seidl's courtroom tactic was to justify the Third Reich and its policies. After the war he became a conservative politician and served as Interior Minister in the Bavarian government in 1977–8. Seidl worked closely with the extreme-right-wing politician

Gerhard Frey, founder of the 'German Union', an unsuccessful neo-Nazi movement, and publisher of the *National-Zeitung*, a neo-Nazi newspaper, for many years. In 1981 he was co-founder of the self-styled Contemporary History Research Centre in the Bavarian town of Ingolstadt, which devoted itself to minimizing the number of Jews murdered in the Holocaust and denying German responsibility for the outbreak of the Second World War.[127] Not surprisingly in the light of his political affiliations, Seidl described Hess as a 'peace envoy' whose genuine peace mission, undertaken on Hitler's behalf, was brusquely rejected by the Allies, whose aggression had (of course) caused the war in the first place.[128]

Rudolf Hess's son Wolf-Rüdiger Hess – 'Wolf' was the nickname generally given to Hitler – campaigned for decades for his father's release from Spandau. He was joined by many others, including the writer and sometime far-right politician David Irving, who at the time he wrote his book *Hess: The Missing Years 1941–1945* had yet to make the transition to fully-fledged Holocaust denial that ruined such reputation as he had ever possessed of being a serious historian.[129] Irving accepted the standard accounts of the reasons behind Hess's flight, including the political marginalization of the 'Deputy Führer', pointing out that 'Hess attended not one of Hitler's historically significant planning conferences' during the war. He had in effect become a 'bystander'. Irving agreed that Hess had acted alone, and that his self-appointed peace mission was a 'fool's errand'. The book's focus is not so much on the flight itself as on Hess's fate after his arrest, when Irving alleges he was plied with drugs and driven mad. Hess in Irving's view was a 'martyr to a cause' and 'a prisoner of mankind'.[130]

Hess came across to his fellow-prisoner in Spandau, Albert Speer, Hitler's Munitions Minister, who was serving a sentence of twenty years for the use of slave labour and other crimes, as odd, eccentric and unpredictable, but not insane; Speer indeed told him it would not do his reputation any good to pretend he was mad. The former Munitions Minister realized Hess had suicidal tendencies, which the prison authorities already knew from his previous behaviour in prison in the UK.[131] After the release of the final prisoners in 1966, Hess was the only inmate of the six-hundred-cell jail. Appeals for his release on compassionate grounds were rejected by the Soviet Union, which had joint responsibility for him, along with Britain, France and the United States. He made another suicide attempt, in 1977, and continued to fear he was being poisoned. Gradually, the conditions of his incarceration were improved. But his health deteriorated, and in extreme old age he became incontinent, plunging him once more into a deep depression. He had been reading the lengthy judgement passed on him by the Nuremberg War Crimes Trials, and, after many decades, at long last began to feel guilty.[132] On 17 August 1987, at the age of ninety-three, he succeeded in a final suicide attempt, hanging himself with an electric extension cord from the window of a summer house that had been made available to him as a place to read in the prison garden. A letter was found in his pocket, apologizing to his secretary for pretending at the Nuremberg trial not to remember who she was, and thanking his family for everything they had done for him.[133]

Spandau prison was immediately demolished in order to prevent it from becoming a place of pilgrimage for Nazis, old and new. One part of the site was covered in a car park, another built over by a supermarket for British soldiers and their families, which they inevitably named 'Hessco' (after the supermarket chain Tesco). Hess was buried in a secret grave, but his body was disinterred in 1988 and reburied in the family plot at Wunsiedel. This did indeed become a place of pilgrimage for the ultra right, not least because of the epitaph inscribed on the grave: *Ich hab's gewagt* ('I dared it'). In 2011 the local council decided not to renew the family's lease on the grave, and so, with the consent of the family, the body was disinterred again, cremated, and the ashes scattered at sea. The gravestone was destroyed.

VIII

Hess was scarcely cold in the ground when claims were raised that he had been murdered. According to his son Wolf-Rüdiger, Hess was too weak and feeble to have hanged himself. He had been murdered by the SAS on the orders of British Prime Minister Margaret Thatcher in order to prevent his release. The suicide note was a forgery. Hess had been unjustly imprisoned. The British had steadfastly refused to recognize that in reality he should have been awarded the Nobel Peace Prize for his efforts in 1941. In 1956 he had expressed his regret for 'the mass annihilation of people of Jewish descent' by the Nazis (though the document in question was in fact written in his name by the Spandau prison pastor and there is no evidence that Hess himself had approved it). As for Churchill, Wolf-Rüdiger endorsed David Irving's venomous portrayal of the British statesman as a drunkard and mass murderer.[134] Others claimed that Hess had been killed to stop him revealing the fact that he had come to Scotland at the invitation of the (non-existent) British 'peace party' whose existence the authorities wished to conceal; or at the invitation of MI5 or MI6; and that the frustration of his mission by Churchill had led to the loss of millions of lives in the war and the Holocaust – conspiracy theory piled on top of conspiracy theory.

The claim that Hess was murdered was comprehensively debunked in an investigation undertaken by Detective Chief Superintendent Howard Jones in 1989.[135] The autopsy on his body, performed immediately after his death, showed no signs of involvement by anyone apart from himself, and a second autopsy confirmed it (a later medical investigation claimed there was no evidence of hanging, but the model of hanging it applied was unrealistic, taken from formal execution procedures, with a hangman's knot and a drop).[136] An examination of the handwriting on the suicide note confirmed it was genuine, although one conspiracy theorist claims that it was indeed written by Hess with intent to deceive in order to discredit the prison authorities (how exactly this would have worked, however, is a mystery).[137] Later testimony by Abdullah Melaouhi, a medical orderly in Spandau, made too much of the lengthy time he had taken to reach Hess in the summer-house when the alarm was raised; the claim that this was the result of deliberate obstruction on the part of the authorities was without foundation. Hess, the orderly claimed, was too weak to perform the operation of self-strangulation, but the same orderly had supervised his exercises on a gymnasium bicycle every morning during the previous years and surely knew that he was relatively robust for his age. In any case, if Hess was murdered in order to stop him revealing that he had flown to Scotland with the connivance of leading figures in the British Establishment, then why did the British repeatedly press in the last years of his life for his release from Spandau on compassionate grounds? And why had he not told this story before? He had, after all, plenty of opportunities to confide, for example, in a prison pastor, or in his fellow-inmate Albert Speer; but he never did so. The inescapable conclusion is that in the end he didn't have any dark secrets to reveal at all.[138]

Even more bizarre is the theory that there had at some point been a body-switch and that the prisoner in Spandau was Hess's double, murdered by the British to stop him talking. The former Spandau surgeon Hugh Thomas alleged that the real Hess had been shot down by a German fighter plane out of reach of radar, and another man substituted for him, on the orders of SS chief Heinrich Himmler, aided and abetted by Hermann Göring. Both men saw the Deputy Führer as an obstacle to their own aggrandizement of power. The man who landed in Scotland was

> a counterfeit Hess – a *Doppelgänger* – who would start by making peace overtures as though they came from Hitler, but then, when some progress had been made, would put forward the very proposals that Himmler himself had been cultivating – namely that peace should be made with himself rather than Hitler as Führer.[139]

Hess's memory loss, his claim not to recognize his former secretary, the absence of scars on the body of the prisoner of Spandau that were known to have been present on the body of the real Hess, all these were cited by Thomas as proof of the substitution.

There were numerous problems with this hypothesis, however, starting with the fact that the theory that Hess had been killed in 1941 was pure, unadulterated speculation, and going on to the fact that nobody who had known him, including for example Albert Speer, had ever voiced even the slightest suspicion that the man they met after the war was not the man they had known before and during it. Wolf-Rüdiger Hess poured scorn on Thomas's 'abstruse hypothesis'.[140] Even the idea that Himmler and Göring were collaborating in the conspiracy was deeply implausible, given the well-known rivalry between the two men.[141] Thomas did not ask why the double had agreed after Nuremberg to spend the rest of his life in prison, remaining there uncomplainingly until his death, never revealing the fact that he was not the man everyone thought he was. Thomas brought forward no evidence of any factor (blackmail, for instance) that might have provided even a veneer of plausibility for the doppelgänger theory. When the prison chaplain asked Hess about Hugh Thomas's book, he 'laughed heartily'. Medical testimony indicated that bullet scars fibrosed over after a time and therefore were not immediately obvious even to a medical officer conducting a physical examination.[142] But the scars were in fact there on Hess's body, though very small and easily overlooked – as confirmed by his wife, Ilse, following a prison visit.[143]

Thomas's assertion that the man in Spandau was considerably shorter than the real Hess was easily refutable: Hess's medical records from the First World War give his height as 5 feet 10 inches, not 6 feet 1, as Thomas claims, and the height given in his post-mortem examination, 5 feet 9, reflects the well-known fact that with increasing age people tend to shrink.[144] The details Thomas supplied of the prison, the prisoner and the circumstances of the prisoner's death were full of errors, as the governor of Spandau at the time noted.[145] In any case, leaving points like these to one side, the theory of the double was definitively disproved in 2019 when a sample of Hess's blood that had been taken in Spandau and preserved was subjected to a DNA analysis with blood taken for comparison from his living relatives. The investigation found a 99.9 per cent match. There could be no doubt at all that the prisoner of Spandau was indeed Rudolf Hess.[146]

The most widely circulated conspiracy theories involving Hitler's deputy Rudolf Hess – the real or fake plot by Hitler and/or the British Secret Service to bring the war to an end, and the murder of Hess decades later to stop him revealing it – aim not least to convince both the historical profession and the general reader of their validity by presenting a large amount of (plausible and often apparently) genuine evidence to back them up. To some extent, indeed, they have met with a degree of success.[147] On the wilder shores of conspiracism, however, there flourish conspiracy theories that don't stand a chance of being taken seriously by historians. Representative of this literature are the works of Joseph P. Farrell, which include numerous books on what he calls 'the cosmic war', such as SS Brotherhood of the Bell: NASA's

Nazism, JFK and MAJIC-2: The Nazis' Incredible Secret Technology, one of a number of publications in which he argues that Unidentified Flying Objects or UFOs, such as the one involved in the legendary 'Roswell incident' of 1947, when an alleged flying saucer is said to have landed at Roswell, New Mexico, are in reality sent out from hidden Nazi bases. His books can be fitted into the category of 'alternative science' or (as Farrell himself calls it) 'alternative research'. His interests extend to conspiracy theorizing about the assassination of US President John F. Kennedy and contributions to the literature linking ancient monuments such as the Egyptian Pyramids to supposed visits to Earth by aliens from outer space.[148]

Most of what Farrell has to say about Hess derives from texts by other conspiracy theorists, including Abdullah Melaouhi, Wolf-Rüdiger Hess, Padfield, Picknett and Hugh Thomas, all of whose theories he accepts more or less without question, even when they contradict one another. Conspiracy theorists have a tendency in this way to feed off each other's work. The conclusions Farrell draws from this literature are, however, very much his own. In Farrell's version, the 'peace party' becomes the 'British deep state, represented by the Duke of Hamilton and the Duke of Kent', Hess's flight mistakenly misses the waiting reception party, the double is implanted with 'false memories', the real Hess is drugged up and sent to his doom with the Duke of Kent to die in a plane crash, and the fake Hess is eventually murdered to stop him talking (Farrell makes much of the fact that the man who carried out the official autopsy, Dr James Cameron, bore the same clan name as the doctor, Ewen Cameron, who examined the supposedly fake Hess at Nuremberg); moreover, Farrell says, emphasizing the claim by italicizing it, 'both Camerons did their medical studies *in the same medical school in Glasgow*'. Any anomalies can be explained by the fact that '*Hess, and/or his double, became the first, and most infamous, example of mind-control on record*' – not insane, then, or feigning insanity, but hypnotized, brainwashed or telepathically manipulated from afar. To add to the story, Farrell also suggests that the real Hess's peace offer included the resettlement of European Jews in Palestine as an alternative to the Holocaust, so that 'someone' '*wanted* the genocide to proceed' – Farrell actually hints that this was the Zionist movement itself, 'given the pattern of examples of Nazi-Zionist complicity documented in this chapter' (in fact, this 'complicity' rests on a tissue of conjecture, and neither Hess nor anyone else can have been aware of the Nazi extermination programme because it did not start until the late summer of 1941, though the ghettoization of Jews was already being carried out before this in occupied Poland).[149]

Farrell is already seriously off the rails by this stage in his book, but his arguments become fully fantastical when he declares that the division of Antarctica must have been included in the 'peace plan' Hess brought with him to Scotland. This has a bearing on the theory of a number of UFO enthusiasts that Hess was murdered to prevent him from revealing the contents of a file that Hitler had entrusted to him – the 'Omega File' – that contained details of secret Nazi bases under the Antarctic.[150] Already in 1946/7, he hints, an Antarctic expedition led by the American admiral Richard Byrd must have been looking for Nazi bases underneath the ice-cap; why else would it have gone there? At this point the inevitable murder mystery makes an appearance, in the shape of the 'strange' death of Byrd's adult son in 1988, killed apparently because he possessed a secret 'that others feared might have come out'.[151] The thought that Byrd's expedition might have had a scientific purpose is silently passed over, as is the fact that the admiral had already taken part in three Antarctic expeditions before the war. Admittedly, Farrell's reference to possible Nazi bases under the Antarctic (even small ones) remained inconclusive; but then hints, suggestions and innuendo are part of the stock-in-trade of conspiracy theorists. In the end, speculations such as these are of more interest to the student of conspiracism than they are to the historian. What is interesting from this point of view is the extent to which multiple conspiracy theories intersect in the world of 'alternative knowledge' and its communities, where belief in one conspiracy theory is likely to be shared, whether in full or not, by believers in others, as we shall now see.

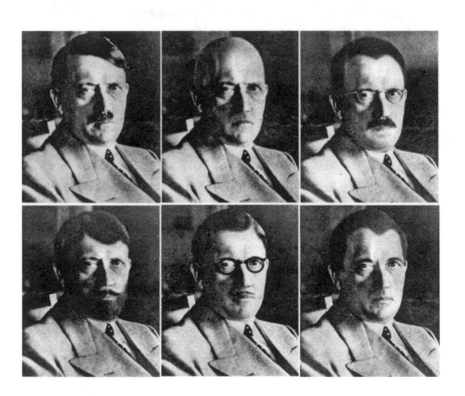

5

Did Hitler escape the bunker?

At 10.26 pm on 1 May 1945, Hitler's death was officially announced over German radio. Admiral Dönitz, his designated successor, told the *Wehrmacht* that the Führer had been killed 'fighting to his last breath against Bolshevism'. The Nazi leader's demise instantly hit the headlines all over the world. The previous evening General Hans Krebs, last chief of the German High Command, realizing all was lost, had crossed the front line in Berlin to negotiate a ceasefire, secure the recognition of the Dönitz government, and preserve a remnant of the Reich in what was left of the ruined German capital. He was authorized to say, he told the Soviet general Vasilii Chuikov, that Hitler had committed suicide the previous day. But Chuikov, sticking to the agreed policy of the Allies, insisted on unconditional surrender. Returning to the bunker in despair, Krebs, too, committed suicide, like hundreds of other Nazi officials, government ministers, generals and senior civil servants during these final weeks and months. Meanwhile, seeking to protect itself from charges of negligently allowing the Nazi leader to get away, the Red Army printed the report of Hitler's suicide in its newspaper *Red Star*.[1]

But bulletins issued by the Soviet leadership in the Kremlin a few weeks later told a very different story. And in a private meeting with the American envoy Harry Hopkins, Stalin declared on 26 May 1945: 'Hitler is not dead, but is hiding somewhere.' He might well have fled to Japan in a submarine, the Soviet leader added.[2] In fact, junior Red Army officers had earlier reported to Western journalists that Hitler's body had been one of four charred sets of human remains found in the Reich Chancellery garden in early May. On 5 June, Red Army staff officers told their American counterparts again they were 'almost certain' that Hitler was dead and that his body had been identified. Four days later, however, the Soviet commander Georgii Zhukov issued a denial on Stalin's instructions. Why did Stalin brush aside the reports of his own front-line troops? The reason was political: for the Soviet leader, the claim that Hitler was still alive bolstered his argument that it was necessary to be tough on the Germans in case there was a revival of Nazism. The Soviet leader wanted to scotch Dönitz's claim that Hitler had died a hero's death by portraying him as a coward who had fled the scene of his defeat and was skulking in some corner or other of the world, like a criminal trying to evade his responsibilities.[3]

As the confusion continued, the rumours began to multiply. Repeated sightings of the Nazi leader were reported, many of them logged by the FBI in the file they soon opened on the case:

> Some said he had been murdered by his own officers in the Tiergarten; others that he had escaped from Berlin by air; or from Germany by submarine. He was living on a mist-enshrouded island in the Baltic; in a Rhineland rock-fortress; in a Spanish monastery; on a South American ranch; he had been spotted living rough among the bandits of Albania. A Swiss journalist made a deposition to testify that, to her certain knowledge, Hitler was living with Eva Braun on an estate in Bavaria. The Soviet news agency Tass reported that Hitler had been spotted in Dublin, disguised in women's clothing.[4]

His presence was reported in Indonesia or, alternatively, Colombia. American Intelligence even prepared illustrations of what he might look like in disguise. For if Hitler was indeed still alive, there was a risk that he might emulate his predecessor the Emperor Napoleon and return to lead a fresh set of armies against the victorious powers. The thought was too terrible to contemplate.[5]

In September 1945, while Stalin was busy sowing uncertainty among the Western Allies, Dick White, the head of MI5, had lunch with two young fellow-intelligence officers, the historian Hugh Trevor-Roper and the philosopher Herbert Hart. 'Over the third bottle of hock,' as Trevor-Roper's biographer Adam Sisman puts it, White gave Trevor-Roper full powers to investigate the matter, telling

Trevor-Roper's superiors that unless the job 'is done by a first-rate chap, [it] won't be worth having'.[6] Trevor-Roper was rightly regarded as first-rate, but his investigation was not quite the lone enterprise it was subsequently portrayed as: the British Intelligence services had been concerned with the fate of the Nazi leader for many weeks, and had already gathered a good deal of information about his death, though they had waited for some time before using it, in the vain hope that the Soviet side would give them access to its own material and allow them to interview captives from the bunker under the Reich Chancellery who were now in Soviet custody.[7] Trevor-Roper was able to make use of the Intelligence material, along with fresh reports that were gathered by the security services, as his investigation proceeded. With the assistance of colleagues, he tracked down survivors of the final weeks in the bunker, examined its interior, found Hitler's final appointments diary, and located a copy of the Führer's last will and testament.[8] In November he presented his findings, writing them up subsequently into a book, *The Last Days of Hitler*, which, after official permission had been obtained, was published by Macmillan on 18 March 1947. It immediately became a global bestseller, enabling Trevor-Roper to buy himself 'a grey Bentley, which he parked ostentatiously in Tom Quad' at his Oxford college, Christ Church.[9]

To provide the basis for his conclusions, Trevor-Roper had obtained personal testimony from a wide range of eyewitnesses, carefully checking their statements against one another's, as he said, and concluding that the discrepancies he discovered made it clear that their stories had been neither co-ordinated nor rehearsed.[10] Yet his investigation, conducted under heavy pressure to reach his conclusions as quickly as possible, was hurried and incomplete. He was unable to contact a good number of the people who had been in the bunker in the last days of the Reich, especially those who were still in Soviet custody. Some of those he said he had interrogated later denied having spoken to him or claimed they had told him lies (though they may also have been lying when they said this).[11] Much of the testimony he cited was hearsay. His claim, advanced in his bestselling book, to have carried out the investigation alone was misleading. Above all, he had no access to any of the material the Soviets had compiled on Hitler's death, based on the testimony of eyewitnesses of the disposal of Hitler's body.

Nevertheless, the broad outline of his findings was confirmed in the 1950s as a result of a claim for the restitution of a rare Vermeer painting in Hitler's personal art collection that prompted a local court in Berchtesgaden, where the Nazi leader's private residence was registered, to begin proceedings to declare him officially dead. The court launched a major investigation, lasting some three years. A number of eyewitnesses who had been in Soviet custody had by this time been released and lived in the West, including, crucially, Hitler's valet Heinz Linge, who had helped dispose of the Nazi leader's body. Along with a large number of people whom Trevor-Roper had failed, or been unable, to contact, he was interviewed. As a result of this very thorough investigation, the court finally issued a death certificate for Hitler towards the end of 1956.[12] Unfortunately, however, although the certificate was widely publicized, the voluminous records of the investigation itself remained hidden from the public under German privacy laws and were not made available to researchers until many years later.

In the meantime, Soviet obfuscation continued with a short book on the subject published in 1968 by the wartime interpreter and journalist Lev Bezymenski, *The Death of Adolf Hitler: Unknown Documents from Soviet Archives*.[13] It was full of inaccuracies; among other things, it claimed falsely that Hitler had poisoned himself, a claim advanced in order to show Hitler died a coward's death, and buttressed by photographs of a corpse that was most certainly not that of the Nazi leader. It was not until the fall of Communism and the collapse of the Soviet Union in 1989–90 that the full range of Soviet documentation on Hitler's death came to light. Towards the end of 1945 Stalin, like his British counterparts, had ordered an investigation of the circumstances of Hitler's death, together with an assessment of his personality and private life between 1933 and the end of the war. It was carried out by People's Commissar Sergei Kruglov and a team from the secret police under the codename 'Operation Myth' and completed in December 1949. The most important part of the 413-page typed manuscript was the testimony of Heinz Linge along with that of Otto Günsche, Hitler's personal adjutant, who were both in Soviet captivity and were forced to write down their reminiscences. Both had been in the bunker up to the end. The manuscript did not fit in with the official Soviet account of the war, however, so it was kept under lock and key and discovered only after the fall of Communism, when it was used by the journalist Ulrich Völklein and the Hitler-researcher Anton Joachimsthaler, already notable for his minutely detailed and critical account of the evidence relating to the Nazi leader's early life.[14] The new evidence, updating Trevor-Roper's findings, was effectively summarized in 2002 in a smooth narrative by the conservative journalist Joachim C. Fest, a highly competent historian, whose book was subsequently used as the basis for the successful German movie *Downfall*.[15] The Soviet report was eventually published in German and English in 2005.[16] By this time, a number of those present in the bunker in the final days and weeks had written their memoirs, so the amount of testimony and evidence available today is far greater than that which Trevor-Roper was able to assemble.[17] Nevertheless, in their broad outlines, Trevor-Roper's findings were vindicated by the evidence that has come to light in the seventy years or more since the publication of *The Last Days of Hitler*. Particularly important was the fact that the Soviet investigations, conducted at roughly the same time but kept secret for over forty years, arrived independently at much the same conclusions as those reached by the British historian, as had, indeed, the Berchtesgaden court in the mid-1950s.

What were these conclusions? During the final weeks, Hitler had consistently rejected the arguments of those in his entourage who wanted him to escape from the bunker and go into hiding, either in his mountain retreat at Berchtesgaden, or in some other remote part of the Reich as yet unconquered by the Allied armies. Eyewitnesses reported that he recognized all was lost: his main concern was now his place in history. Two days after his fifty-sixth birthday, on 22 April 1945, he told his generals and his staff he would shoot himself, repeating this to Propaganda Minister Goebbels over the telephone. On 24 April he informed his personal friend Albert Speer that his partner, Eva Braun, wanted to suffer the same fate. Their bodies would be burned to avoid desecration, a decision that was strengthened in Hitler's mind when he learned of the indignities to which the bodies of his fellow-dictator Mussolini and his mistress, Claretta Petacci, had been subjected after they were shot by Italian partisans on 28 April 1945. Hitler sent his adjutant Julius Schaub to Berchtes-gaden to burn his private documents kept there after he had done the same in Berlin; he married Eva Braun in a short ceremony in the bunker on 29 April 1945, certifying to the presiding official, as his own laws demanded, that he was of Aryan descent, and dictated his last will and his political testament to his secretary. After testing out cyanide poison successfully on his dog Blondi, Hitler and his new wife retired to his study on 30 April 1945. After a brief interval, Linge, accompanied by Martin Bormann, entered the room and found Hitler's body on the sofa, oozing blood from a hole in his right temple, his pistol on the floor beside him; Eva Braun's body was next to his, giving off a strong smell of bitter almonds: she had taken poison. No such smell emanated from the corpse of her husband.

Following instructions issued earlier, Linge, Günsche and three SS men wrapped the bodies in blankets, took them up into the Reich Chancellery garden, and, watched by Bormann, Goebbels and two generals, they doused the bodies in petrol and set them alight. At six in the evening Günsche sent two SS men to bury the charred remains in a pit, where Red Army troops unearthed them a few days later. The Soviets took the surviving part of Hitler's jawbone and two dental bridges in a cigar-box to a technician who had worked for Hitler's personal dentist and identified the bridges from his records as belonging respectively to Hitler and Eva Braun. This was all that was left of the bodies. A complete skull alleged to be that of Hitler later turned up in Moscow but was demonstrated in 2009 to belong to a woman. 'The earthly remains of Adolf Hitler,' as Ian Kershaw concludes in his monumental biography of the Nazi leader, 'it appears, were contained in a cigar-box.'[18] Once she was certain Hitler was dead, Magda Goebbels had her six children poisoned, and went up into the garden with her husband, where both took poison and were shot twice by an SS man to make sure they were dead; their bodies, too, were set alight, but there was not enough petrol to consume them, and their remains were easily recognized by the Red Army troops who arrived the following day. The rest of the bunker's inhabitants, including Bormann, made their way out through an underground railway tunnel close to the bunker. Some were shot in the fighting that raged about them as they emerged at Friedrichstrasse station, some were captured, others managed to escape, Bormann, it was generally thought, among them; his body was not discovered until 1972, when construction workers unearthed it; it was quickly identified through dental records and its identity confirmed in 1998 by DNA analysis.[19]

II

The confusion sown by the Soviets, the inadequacies of Trevor-Roper's account, however minor, and the absence of key eyewitness testimony for several years after the end of the war provided room for concluding that Hitler's death remained unproven. Sensational American magazines like the *Police Gazette* made a career out of running stories on the Nazi leader's survival. The French magazine *Bonjour* was particularly active in advancing claims that Hitler was still alive: claims that crumbled as soon as they were subjected to the test of whether the people whose evidence they relied on had actually been present in the bunker in late April 1945. The variety and persistence of such stories was striking. *Bonjour* paid particular attention to the theory that Hitler and Eva Braun and, indeed, the dog Blondi had been substituted by doubles at some point late in the war (Hitler's secretaries vehemently denied this was possible; they would have recognized the substitutions, they pointed out).[20] The real Hitler's health was deteriorating fast during the final months, as the Parkinsonism from which he suffered made him shuffle rather than walk and caused an uncontrollable tremor in his left hand, but the symptoms, it was suggested, were less serious than supposed, the sick man was the substitute, and Hitler had fled the bunker through the rubble of Berlin, taken the last plane out, reached Denmark and embarked with Eva Braun on a submarine that had taken them to Argentina. Plausibility for this theory was provided by the fact that two submarines, the U-530 and the U-977, had indeed arrived in Argentina after the end of the war. Inspected on arrival, however, the U-530 turned out to be carrying nothing but a bulk cargo of cigarettes, which *Bonjour* confidently declared had been supplied to Hitler and his entourage (ignoring the well-known fact that Hitler neither smoked nor allowed smoking in his presence). The commander of U-977, Heinz Schaeffer, who had sailed to Argentina to avoid having to surrender to the British, later published a book devoted to denying the charge that he had been carrying Hitler into exile.[21] However, this did not deter the conspiracists. 'Nazism is not dead in Europe,' claimed Ladislas Szabó, author of *Je sais que Hitler est vivant*, in 1947: 'The world is in danger. Its peace is newly menaced by Adolf Hitler.'[22]

These and many other theories were investigated thoroughly by the American historian Donald M. McKale in his book *Hitler: The Survival Myth*, published in 1981. McKale pointed out that stories of Hitler in Argentina had been circulated widely in the late 1940s by, among others, the French daily *Le Monde*, the popular biographer Emil Ludwig, and the evangelical preacher Garner Ted Armstrong and his father, who predicted Hitler would return by 1972 to begin a new war against the West (though they later changed their minds). Yet, McKale noted, all these claims 'relied on supposition and insinuation, no documents and no testimony from actual witnesses'.[23] Nevertheless, Hitler's survival had entered popular mythology by 1950. The idea that Hitler had simply succumbed to the pressure of events and committed suicide was surely not acceptable to some people. The suggestion that Hitler had survived, in McKale's view, fed a 'new mythology' that helped justify the continued presence of Anglo-American and French troops on German soil. For the Soviet Union, this mythology helped justify its continuing control over Europe east of the Iron Curtain. Yet the more the mythology proliferated, the less credible it became: Hitler, it was reported, was living in a Tibetan monastery, or in Saudi Arabia, or had been spotted in a café in Austria, or was in a secret prison in the Urals.[24] A retired German miner, Albert Panka, complained in 1969 on his eightieth birthday that he had been detained three hundred times since 1945. 'I'm fed up with being taken for the other fellow,' he told the press, adding that he was 'not a retired Führer'.[25]

Of all these theories, however, it has been the claim that Hitler and Eva Braun escaped to Argentina that has enjoyed the widest and most persistent currency.[26] Under its dictator Juan Perón, Argentina was known to encourage ex-Nazis to escape – usually over the 'ratlines' in the Alps, often with the assistance of a Vatican bishop, the Austrian

Alois Hudal – and contribute their expertise to building the national economy.[27] The kidnapping in Argentina by Israeli agents of Adolf Eichmann, the main organizer of the 'Final Solution', and his trial in Jerusalem in 1961, the capture in Brazil in 1967 of the former commandant of the Treblinka death camp, Franz Stangl, and the uncovering of a network of senior ex-Nazis in South America, including the Auschwitz camp doctor Josef Mengele, all made it seem possible that the most senior Nazi of all might be hiding in South America too. In fact, neither Eichmann's interrogation before his trial, nor the very extensive tape-recordings kept by a Dutch journalist of his conversations with him during his exile in Argentina, threw up a single mention even of the possibility that Hitler might still be alive, let alone living in their midst; but this troubled the theorists no more than did the evidence assembled by Trevor-Roper or the testimony of Hitler's entourage in the bunker.[28]

McKale concluded that the myth of Hitler's survival was more than a harmless or eccentric fantasy:

> That he had masterminded a plot to throw the world off his tracks, revealing again his unique evil genius, is a dangerous theme that remains with us. It is now the preserve mainly of the entertainment industry, and thereby seemingly harmless enough on the surface. But by ignoring the 'fact' of Hitler's death, such depictions, wittingly or not, leave the impression for present and future generations that Hitler, although the worst mass murderer in history, had been a sort of superman who fooled the world one final time . . . His alleged survival against impossible odds, they imply, is proof of something nearly inhuman and godlike. This is the kind of myth-making that could potentially spark an unconscious desire among some for a 'new Hitler' – a charismatic and legendary figure who could lead a mass protest against oppressive evils like Communism or decadent Western culture.[29]

Four decades after McKale published his investigations, such fears may seem exaggerated. Hitler has not become a hero-figure except to a tiny minority of neo-Nazis on the furthest lunatic fringes of politics. Even here, the theory of his escape from the bunker has been far from universally accepted; some commentators on the neo-Nazi

Stormfront website have pointed out that it said little for Hitler's courage that he fled ignominiously from the bunker instead of sticking it out to the end. More generally, any hint of admiration for Hitler is political suicide. When Lutz Bachmann, the founder of the anti-Islam movement Pegida, whose Monday demonstrations in 2014 attracted thousands of participants in Dresden and elsewhere in East Germany, had himself photographed as Hitler, he was forced to resign the moment the picture was made public, though he was subsequently reinstated, claiming that the photo was a forgery.[30]

The idea that Hitler survived in one form or another has of course played a part in fantasy literature, film and the entertainment industry for many years. The 1978 movie *The Boys from Brazil* imagined the former Auschwitz doctor Josef Mengele re-creating genetically exact copies of Hitler from samples taken from the Führer's blood; a 1978 episode of *The New Avengers* starring Patrick McNee and Joanna Lumley had neo-Nazis trying to release Hitler from suspended animation; the 1963 movie *They Saved Hitler's Brain* portrayed a similar scenario; its title was famously parodied in the episode of *The Simpsons* entitled *They Saved Lisa's Brain*; the 1970 film *Flesh Feast* imagines that a group of Nazis have got hold of Hitler's body in order to clone it, though the scientist in charge, played by Veronica Lake, undertakes the experiment only to wreak on Hitler her revenge for the death of her parents in a concentration camp by throwing flesh-eating maggots at his face; Armin Müller-Stahl's *Conversation with the Beast* (1996) has Hitler emerging from an underground bunker aged 103, to be interviewed by an investigative journalist who ends up shooting him. Timur Vermes's recent novel *Look Who's Back*, in which Hitler awakes after decades to come back to a contemporary Germany whose realities he views through the ideological blinkers of Nazism, belongs in this company too. In most of the movies the effect, whether it is suspense or comedy, is gained by the juxtaposition of the figure of ultimate human evil with decent and heroic people trying to prevent him gaining ultimate victory, which they do by killing him by one means or another, thus achieving the justice and revenge Hitler cheated in 1945; *Look Who's Back* has a more disturbing message, as Hitler gradually achieves acceptance in contemporary German society.

III

Fantastic imaginings of Hitler's survival can serve as a convenient or even entertaining plot device in fiction and film. But for all the thoroughness of McKale's demolition of the survival myth, writers and journalists of various kinds have not stopped claiming that there is a factual basis to the story of his escape from the bunker. Despite all the evidence to the contrary, more book-length arguments for the survival of Hitler in Argentina have appeared in the twenty-first century than in the whole of the fifty-five previous years. Indeed, 'since 2009', the most recent serious treatment of the subject has noted, 'the historical debate regarding Hitler's death has been dominated by conspiracy theories'.[31] Even before this, conspiracy theorizing on the subject of Hitler's death was becoming more frequent and more insistent. The valve engineer and businessman Hans Baumann, who came to the USA from Germany as an exchange student in 1953, author of *The Vanished Life of Eva Braun* (2010), and Ron T. Hansig, author of *Hitler's Escape* (2005), collaborated on a new edition of Hansig's book in 2014. The authors challenge what they say is the 'official story, widely accepted, at least by the Western Allies, that Hitler committed suicide on April 30, 1945'.[32] As so often in conspiracy theories, accepted professional scholarship is dismissed as 'official', as if thousands of historians and investigative journalists had all been suborned by governments to tell lies, or been fooled by state-controlled propaganda. Hitler and Eva Braun, according to Baumann and Hansig, actually did escape the bunker, leaving doubles behind, and flew to Spain, travelling from there to Argentina, where they probably lived out their lives in 'peace and comfort'.[33] Like many others before them, Baumann and Hansig use Hitler's marked physical deterioration in the final months as evidence of his substitution by a double. 'The aim of this study,' the authors insist, 'certainly is not to glorify Hitler, or to make him out as a latter-day hero, but to show him as a coward, escaping justice. History provides ample proof of the incredible death and destruction he caused to the Jews, to Germany and to the rest of Europe and Russia.'[34] They repeatedly express their regret that he avoided punishment for his crimes.[35] Nevertheless, they comment that he 'certainly had a brilliant mind', 'was very gentle with children, women and animals', and was generous towards the British, allowing them to escape at Dunkirk and sending peace terms to them with Rudolf Hess in his ill-fated flight to Scotland. His invasion of Russia was launched in self-defence as 'Stalin was planning to attack Germany'.[36] Not so bad after all, then. He might have been able to live in Argentina in peace and comfort, but for such a brilliant mind it must have been hard, however many children, women and animals he had around him to be gentle with. 'Any lifestyle of enforced idleness in a foreign country,' they remark perceptively, 'must have been unbearable for a person who, in the past, could command millions.'[37]

In advancing these views, Baumann and Hansig rely on the various early postwar statements by Stalin and senior Soviets, and among other sources, on the three-volume *Gestapo Chief* by Gregory Douglas. This work purports to print extracts from a lengthy US Intelligence debriefing of Gestapo chief Heinrich Müller in the late 1940s in which Müller, whom Baumann and Hansig describe as a career policeman and intelligence officer who was not an antisemite, offers new information on Auschwitz (Müller denies it was a death camp) and Hitler (Müller says he escaped from the bunker, thus proving their thesis). But the two authors have not delved deeply enough into the background of this work. To begin with, 'Gregory Douglas' was actually one of a number of pseudonyms of Peter Stahl, a man who allegedly claimed to be Müller's nephew. Stahl, or Douglas, had far-right connections, particularly with the Druffel-Verlag, which published his supposed Müller documents in German in 1996. Stahl was in fact a conspiracist who had written about other supposed plots as well. Among his publications was *Regicide: The Official Assassination of John F. Kennedy* (2002), which claimed to present documentation from a recently deceased senior CIA officer 'proving' Kennedy was shot by CIA conspirators. With a background in the murky trade in Nazi memorabilia, a large quantity of which are fake, Stahl was widely accused, particularly in Holocaust denial circles, of having fabricated the Müller and Kennedy documents.[38] The historian Johannes Tuchel established in 2013 that Gestapo chief Heinrich Müller had been killed in Berlin in 1945 and buried in a mass grave, ironically, in a Jewish cemetery, after being identified by the grave-digger by his uniform and medals.[39]

Perhaps even more persistent in propagating the theory of Hitler's escape from the bunker has been the American writer Harry Cooper. Here the central figure in the conspiracy is not Hitler himself but Martin Bormann, who by 1945 was the most important official in Nazi Germany under Hitler himself. Hitler, Cooper says, 'did not commit suicide in the bunker. He and Eva Braun got out.' But, he suggests, they did not escape of their own volition: they were 'forcibly drugged' on Bormann's orders and taken to Argentina, where they lived in hiding on the Bariloche estate in the Andean foothills. Cooper's *Hitler in Argentina: The Documented Truth of Hitler's Escape from Berlin*, published in 2006, is a collection of photographs, documents and narratives, mostly from the immediate postwar years, centred on the racy memoirs of Don Ángel Alcázar de Velasco, who claimed to have met Hitler in Argentina and to have had several encounters with Bormann ('Martin was the first to speak, *"Man, you've grown old, Angel." "And the years have made a difference to you too, Martin,"* I countered with a chuckle').[40] The compilation includes a photograph purporting to be of an elderly Hitler, his face half covered by a handkerchief. It features prominently on the back cover; Hitler's eyes are described in an accompanying radio programme in enthusiastic terms ('There is an ancient echo of fire and passion . . . It's a very hypnotic eye'). In fact, the photograph, entitled originally 'Forty Winks', is of a British old-age pensioner, taken from Kurt Hutton, *Speaking Likeness* (1947). A photographer for the magazine *Picture Post*, Hutton notes he shot it with a Leica using a combination of natural light and a photoflood from the ceiling. 'Forty Winks was caught as I strolled round an old people's home in search of local colour,' he says.[41] The copyright is held by Getty Images, though Cooper claims it as his own.

Cooper is also the author of *Hitler's Spy Web in South America* (2017) and *Escape from the Bunker: Hitler's Escape from Berlin* (2010). Both books were released through a self-publishing organization now owned by Amazon and based in Scotts Valley, California. According to Cooper's advertising copy on amazon.com, his work presents of distributing were a forgery that had already been exposed some years previously. He pointed out that Henry Ford had withdrawn his support for the claim of their authenticity.[64] More importantly, in the same year, representatives of the Jewish community in Bern, Switzerland, launched a prosecution of the Swiss National Front, a fascist organization that had distributed the document at a demonstration the previous year. The prosecution was initiated under a local statute outlawing the distribution of immoral, obscene or brutalizing texts. Lead expert defence witness was Ulrich Fleischhauer ('a professional anti-Semite and probably a Hun, [he] has made statements impugning my personal character and veracity,' Graves complained). In Germany, the Nazi press claimed Graves was Jewish, or was being paid by the Jews, or was even a pseudonym of Lucien Wolf. Following a lengthy series of expert witness testimonies by prominent academics and scholars, including exiled Russians such as the Menshevik intellectual Boris Nicolaevsky, confirming that the *Protocols* were falsified and liable to arouse hatred of Jews, the court ruled that the *Protocols* were plagiarized, obscene and a forgery, and found for the prosecution. The judge declared that the document was 'risible nonsense' and regretted that the court had been obliged to spend an entire fortnight discussing such an absurdity.[65]

This was not the end of the story, since the defence issued a formal appeal against the verdict and the appeal was upheld by the Swiss Supreme Court in November 1937. This was anything but a vindication of the *Protocols*, however, as the judges ruled that they were indeed forged and falsified but concluded none the less that they did not violate the provisions of the statute on obscene literature because they were in the end to be classified under the heading of political propaganda. Costs were awarded against the defendants (i.e. the supporters of the *Protocols*' authenticity) and the court publicly expressed its regret that the law did not offer Jews adequate protection against false allegations of the kind presented in the *Protocols*. The Swiss fascists and antisemites of course trumpeted the final outcome as a triumph, and condemned their Jewish accusers as behaving in exactly the way the *Protocols* had predicted; but the overall effect in terms of publicity was anything but favourable to the antisemites' cause.[66]

Graves had felt unable to appear as a witness in the trial, because the faithful transcription of a file given to me by a highly placed Nazi agent during WW II. He came to Sharkhunters, our history organization covering WW II submarine history, with his story that he helped Martin Bormann escape Germany after the war and that he met with Adolf Hitler years later. He has been thoroughly checked out and he was who he said he was, and his claims have been substantiated by countless files from the US and other nations' Intel agencies.

This was, of course, Don Ángel Alcázar de Velasco, who was in fact a well-known fantasist. Velasco's claim to have spent the final three months of the war in the Führer bunker is clearly bogus, since nobody else who was there ever reported having seen him. Rather than admitting the truth, however, Cooper reacted allergically to the exposure of the Don, threatening his critics with prosecution for spreading fake news ('Jail them all!'), though under what law was unclear. Reflecting this situation, the sceptical *Tomatobubble* website carries a legalistically phrased disclaimer by Mike King, the author of the website's article 'The Hitler-in-Argentina Myth', certifying

> that we hold Cooper's record of historical research, and the integrity of his resumé, in the highest regard. Our use of the word 'hoax', and the logically related insinuation of profit motive, both in our blog and in a recent interview with Red Ice Radio, was really meant to apply to the deliberately outlandish claims of most of the other 'Argentinists', not Cooper. We should have been clearer about that distinction. Although we strongly maintain our disagreement with the conclusions which Cooper has reached in regard to Hitler escaping to Argentina, we apologize to Mr. Cooper for any erroneous perception that Cooper is not a man of integrity or that he is not sincere in his belief.[42]

It seems likely that this disclaimer was issued in response to a legal threat from Cooper or his representatives.

It is clear, indeed, that Cooper's *Hitler in Argentina* is not a deliberate hoax or designed to fool anybody. It is published by Sharkhunters International, which Cooper, who personally founded the organization in 1983, insists is non-political and devoted mainly to the serious study of U-boats of the Second World War. But Sharkhunters

International does offer tours to Nazi sites in Germany and, indeed, tours to alleged Nazi sites in Argentina. It sells Nazi memorabilia, and has advertised in pro-Nazi and antisemitic publications such as *National Christian News* ('Talmudism is Treason!') and *The Spotlight*, run by the white supremacist, antisemite and Holocaust denier Willis Carto. The investigative journalist Roger Clark has alleged that 'Harry Cooper regularly mixes with neo-Nazis, antisemites and Holocaust deniers and takes part in many broadcasts publicising their views.' Members of the Sharkhunters over the years have included Leni Riefenstahl, director of the Nazi propaganda film *Triumph of the Will*; Leon Degrelle, the Belgian fascist leader; Manfred Roeder, a German neo-Nazi and Holocaust denier classified as a terrorist by the German Office for the Protection of the Constitution; and Charles Ellis of the neo-Nazi white-supremacist movement the National Alliance. Cooper himself spoke at the 1996 convention of the *Barnes Review*, a Holocaust denial publication run by Willis Carto and named after Holocaust denier Harry Elmer Barnes. The serious U-boat enthusiasts of the website uboat.net have banned posts by and about Sharkhunters because these 'generally contain obnoxious remarks'.[43] Cooper is a frequent contributor to Rense Radio, run by Jeff Rense: he broadcast on it twenty-three times between January 2013 and December 2014 alone, according to one report. The Jewish Anti-Defamation League has described Rense's website as 'virulently antisemitic'.[44] Interestingly, the website also frequently presents material on UFOs, 9/11 conspiracy theories and paranormal phenomena, as well as 'anti-Zionist' content, showing how many different kinds of 'alternative knowledge' coexist and interact with one another.

Right-wing political motives often lie behind seemingly innocent attempts to prove Hitler's survival. The Austrian writer Werner Brockdorff, for example, who claimed he had spent 'twenty years studying the sources and travelling in many lands on different continents' gathering the facts about Hitler's supposed escape to Argentina with Martin Bormann and Eva Braun, called himself a Nazi hunter; but his idyllic picture of Mr and Mrs Hitler, undefeated and undetected, living in domestic bliss to a ripe old age in South American exile, was not that of the conventional Nazi hunter, obsessed with tracking down evil and bringing it to justice. Brockdorff was in fact a pan-German nationalist, hostile to both sides in the Cold War, who argued that Hitler had been protected by the CIA and that the Russians had deliberately misled the world about his true fate.[45] As we shall see, far-right or neo-Nazi political affiliations can be identified in a number of other exponents of the genre too.

IV

While these authors devoted themselves to assembling documentary material and individual testimony to buttress their argument that Hitler and Eva Braun had escaped to Argentina, Simon Dunstan and Gerrard Williams, in their book *Grey Wolf: The Escape of Adolf Hitler: The Case Presented* (2011) and the accompanying television programme and DVD of the same title issued the following year, took a different approach. Dunstan was the author of over fifty books of largely technical military history, including monographs on the Centurion, Chieftain and Challenger tanks, and had made several military history programmes for the History Channel; Williams was a journalist who had worked for the BBC and Sky News, mainly on desk jobs. Their book was presented not as a critical assemblage of evidence but as a connected historical narrative extending over nearly three hundred pages, accompanied by some fifty pages of endnotes and bibliographies. The book claimed to be based on years of meticulous research, including recently discovered and freshly declassified official documents. Rather than arguing, as most proponents of the survival story did, that Hitler *might* have escaped the bunker, that doubles *were probably* put there in his and Eva Braun's place, that they *most likely* escaped to Argentina in one U-boat or another, and so on, Dunstan and Williams presented the story as proven fact, leaving the arguments about the evidence to brief discussions in the endnotes, although from time to time they printed a narrative passage in italics to indicate its derivation not from hard evidence but from 'deductive reasoning'.[46] And unlike most of the other proponents of the survival hypothesis, the two seasoned writers knew how to tell a story.

In a lengthy Preface to the book, the two authors tell how they started off wanting to make a 'thought-provoking' television documentary examining conspiracy theories about Hitler's supposed escape from the bunker. But they gradually became convinced that the survival story was not theory but fact. Their argument follows the familiar lines of the existing literature: the bodies in the bunker were doubles; Eisenhower and Stalin both said they did not think Hitler was dead; nobody actually witnessed the suicide; the postwar FBI files contain reports of sightings and follow-up reports of 'Hitler in Argentina'; there is a Nazi ranch at Bariloche, 1,350 kilometres south-west of Buenos Aires, where Hitler and Eva Braun lived. In their search for evidence, the two authors went to Argentina, and though 'everyone we spoke to about the possibility of Hitler living there after the war believes it was eminently possible and in many cases definitely true', they did not manage to meet and identify anyone who could be confirmed to have actually encountered him in the flesh.[47] They dismissed Trevor-Roper's report as a work of political expediency created by a man who, as his later endorsement of the bogus *Hitler Diaries* showed, was unable to tell truth from fiction or to know when he was being lied to.[48] The inmates of the bunker in the final weeks, including the secretaries, were all fooled by the presence of the doubles into believing Hitler had stayed on and eventually killed himself, though why a double should have committed suicide remains a mystery.

Grey Wolf brings a few novelties to the table. It claims that Professor Alf Linney, a 'facial recognition expert' at University College, London, has 'proven scientifically' that the famous picture of Hitler reviewing a troop of Hitler Youth on 20 March 1945 is actually the picture of Hitler's double.[49] However, it fails to indicate the nature of this 'scientific' proof, nor do the authors provide any reference to any publications by Professor Linney, who is in fact an ear surgeon. This is hearsay (in other words, the authors report what Professor Linney said but do not provide any evidence that he said it or indeed even quote him directly). Asked by Roger Clark about Williams's claim, Linney replied that 'some of the remarks you report the authors as making are certainly wide of the truth'.[50] Similarly, they claim that Hitler's brother-in-law Hermann Fegelein escaped the bunker with Hitler, but again the evidence is not only hearsay, and third-party at that, but also postwar – the claim allegedly was made by Fegelein's father to an interviewing officer in September 1945, though in fact there is direct contemporary evidence from eyewitnesses to show that Fegelein was shot on 28 April 1945 on the personal orders of Hitler – for trying to leave the bunker without permission.[51]

Captain Peter Baumgart, the pilot who *Grey Wolf* claims flew Hitler and his group out of Berlin, presented this story at his trial for unspecified war crimes (presumably committed in Poland) in Warsaw on 17 December 1947; he repeated it later. The trial was delayed while he was given psychiatric tests, whether because of his claim about Hitler is unclear; he was declared sane, but again, whether this was because the Polish authorities wanted to bring him to justice or because he really was sane remains unclear. He was apparently sentenced to five years in prison by the Polish court. Baumgart's boast that he had shot down 128 Allied planes during his career as a pilot was clearly bogus. Nor was it credible that a converted bomber could have landed in Berlin at this late date, least of all close to the Reich Chancellery building, which was surrounded by rubble. Neither could it have carried enough fuel to make a return journey when almost all other German planes were grounded because fuel supplies had run out.[52] Baumgart also said that he had landed at Magdeburg on the way, but Magdeburg had already fallen to the Americans on 19 April. The book describes him as belonging to a secret air force squadron numbered 200, but the standard work on this unit makes no mention of him.[53]

The narrative continues with the group flying on to the Baltic resort of Travemünde. Here, *Grey Wolf* tells its readers, 'Eva Braun now bade her sister Ilse a fond farewell . . . Fegelein also embraced her.'[54] The passage is not in italics and so not, presumably, the outcome of 'deductive reasoning', but no source is given, and the narrative has to be judged purely speculative on several counts, not least the fact that Fegelein was already dead. Further testimony is supplied by another pilot, Werner Baumbach, who was indeed head of special mission squadron 200 in the Luftwaffe, but his diaries made no mention of Hitler being in Travemünde.[55] From there, the narrative, unsupported by any evidence, has Hitler's party being flown to Reus, near Barcelona, and thence to Fuerteventura, in the Canary Islands.[56] Dunstan

and Williams reject the usual suspect, U-530, as the means of trans-
port to Argentina and plump instead for a group of three U-boats
known to have gone missing from an Atlantic 'wolf-pack' of submarines, U-518, U-880 and U-1235. In fact, according to the website
uboat.net, U-518 was sunk by American destroyers on 22 April 1945
with the loss of all hands; U-880 met the same fate on 16 April 1945;
and U-1235 on 15 April 1945, so they were missing because they had
been lost in action, not because they had been detached from their
unit in order to ferry Hitler to Argentina.[57] However, *Grey Wolf*
asserts: 'Special orders must have been delivered to the commanders
of U-1235, U-880 and U-518 before they sailed in March 1945, with
instructions for them to be opened at a specified longitude. Drafted
in Berlin on Bormann's instructions, these contents of these orders
would be known only to a select few.'[58] So secret were they, in fact,
that they do not even appear to have been known to Dunstan or Williams. Their account, in other words, is pure speculation.

With a great deal of circumstantial detail, all of it presented in
italics to denote the fact that it is pure invention (or based on 'deductive reasoning'), the book describes the party's journey to Argentina
on the three submarines, all of which were scuttled after their
arrival.[59] Then they were taken to the Nazi-built ranch near Bariloche, far to the south-west, in the foothills of the Andes, where they
were joined in September by Ursula, Eva Braun's daughter by Hitler,
born in San Remo in 1938 (she was in fact the daughter of Eva
Braun's friend Gitta Schneider; photographs of her with Hitler and
Eva Braun appear frequently in the survival literature). The story
continues with Eva Braun giving birth to a second daughter, con-
ceived in Munich in March 1945 (how, is not made clear; Hitler had
not left Berlin since 16 January 1945 except once, on a brief visit to
the now nearby front line at Wriezen on 3 March).[60] It is worth noting that the film of the book, also entitled *Grey Wolf*, mentions only
one daughter, Ursula or 'Uschi'.[61] However many daughters she had,
Eva apparently became bored with life on the ranch, and eventually
moved away to another town, 230 miles away to the north-east,
effectively ending her marriage to Hitler.[62]

What is the evidence for these stories? Aside from second-hand
reports in early postwar US Intelligence files, the authors include

extracts of an interview with one Catalina Gomero, who remembered a secret visitor to a German house where she worked, and was
told by the owner that it was Hitler. She had to leave his meals on a
tray outside his bedroom door (the documentary has her going into
the room, played, of course, necessarily, like every other character, by
an actor, though she made it clear in another, separate interview, that
she never set eyes on the mysterious guest).[63] He 'ate the same food as
everyone else in the house – typical German meals – sausage, ham,
vegetables', she remembered. In the film, the actress playing her also
takes sausages into the room. Williams asserted that this was 'confirmation from a real human being that Adolf Hitler didn't die in the
bunker in 1945'.[64] But the unseen man in the hotel cannot have been
Hitler, if for no other reason than the fact that the Nazi dictator was
a lifelong vegetarian. Because his teeth were in bad shape, he ate a
poor diet consisting mostly of mashed beans, food that was in no way
identifiable as German.[65]

Apart from Catalina Gomero, *Grey Wolf* also cites an FBI informer
who reported an unidentified Frenchman as having seen a man 'having numerous characteristics of Hitler' at a restaurant chatting
amiably with the other guests; again, this was extremely unlikely to
have been Hitler, since Hitler did not chat with other people at mealtimes in a friendly or any other manner but subjected them to endless
monologues, as recorded for posterity during the war in the so-called
'table-talk'. In any case, like the other supposed reports of sightings
of the former dictator, this was hearsay evidence. Another unidentified witness cited in *Grey Wolf*, known only as 'Schmidt', recalled living
as a child in a German (or, the book says, Nazi) colony at Bariloche in
Patagonia run by former senior SS officer Ludolf von Alvensleben.
Alvensleben was certainly a real person, a Nazi war criminal who came
to play a major role in the activities of the circle of diehard Nazi exiles
who met in Buenos Aires for secret discussions with Adolf Eichmann in
the 1950s. He was recorded in them as alienating his interlocutors
by criticizing the Holocaust as 'ignoble' and 'un-Germanic' instead of
glorifying it, as the others did. But 'Schmidt' did not mention seeing
Hitler, and although there were several old Nazis living in Bariloche,
including Erich Priebke, an SS officer eventually extradited to Italy to
stand trial for war crimes committed there, Alvensleben was not

among them: he lived in Córdoba, many hundreds of miles to the north of Bariloche.[66]

The bank manager Jorge Batinic is shown in *Grey Wolf* remembering his mother telling him she had seen Hitler in Argentina and that he had been identified as Hitler by one of his companions. Again, this is no more than hearsay evidence – invented, embellished or misremembered.[67] Though Hitler was closely guarded, he apparently travelled a great deal, because another interviewee, a carpenter called Hernán Ancín, recalled meeting him several times on a building site at the coastal town of Mar del Plata in the early 1950s – white-haired, frail, and accompanied by a 'large, well-fed' Eva Braun. Was this the ex-Führer? Nobody, not even Hitler's alleged host in Mar del Plata, the former Croatian fascist dictator Ante Pavelić (who did indeed work as a builder in Argentina), identified him in evidence as the former Nazi leader, although Pavelić is shown meeting him in the *Grey Wolf* movie, both characters, of course, being played by actors (Eva is not plump here but normal size and 'worried').[68] Ancín's uncorroborated statement must therefore be discounted.

The lawyer Alicia Oliveira, during an interview, recalled meeting a woman in 1985 who told her she was Hitler's daughter 'Uschi'; but Oliveira refused to reveal the woman's full name on the grounds of 'lawyer–client confidentiality'[69] – again, second-hand hearsay evidence without identification or corroboration (*Grey Wolf* simply shows an interview with an actress playing 'Uschi'). In another interview, the eighty-seven-year-old Jorge Colotto, the head of President Perón's personal bodyguard, recalled visits by Bormann in the 1950s, but, again, his testimony is uncorroborated by any written or oral evidence from anyone else who worked for Perón. Araceli Méndez worked as a translator and bookkeeper for a 'senior Nazi' around the same time, but the Nazi never revealed his real name to her (despite the fact that they became friends) and she knew him only as 'Ricardo Bauer'.[70] Finally, the authors make extensive use of a 1987 book by Manuel Monasterio, a self-proclaimed 'gnosticist' and astrologer – once again, the occult wormed its way into the paranoid imagination. The book, *Hitler murió en la Argentina*, which the author himself admitted was partly made up, contains a mishmash of 'strange ramblings' and occultist speculation, and cannot really be regarded as reliable in any respect, not least since the documents on which it is based were supposedly lost during a house move.[71] According to this source, Hitler died in Argentina in 1972; Eva Braun disappeared from view; the supposed daughters have never been located. One of them, it is rumoured on the Internet, is actually Angela Merkel, who became German Federal Chancellor in 2005: the claim appears on the website *The Pizzagate Files*, founded to uphold the notorious fake news story, spread around during the 2016 US Presidential election campaign, that leading Democrats kept a paedophile den in a cellar beneath a pizza parlour in Washington D.C.[72]

One of the journalists who has demolished the Hitler-in-Argentina myth is, as we have seen, Mike King, of the *Tomatobubble* website. Though not directed specifically at *Grey Wolf*, his strictures undermine every assumption behind the book and the film. King notes that Hitler's last will and testament declared his intention of choosing death when it was clear he was no longer able to carry out his duties as Leader; that all the bunker witnesses who survived stuck to their account of his suicide; and that his dental bridge records were matched to the physical remains located in the Reich Chancellery garden and examined by the Russians in 1945. Consequently, King says, the proponents of the survival myth are asking us to believe

that Hitler *(a thrice-decorated, twice-wounded war hero who volunteered for dangerous duty)* turned into a deceiving coward who faked his Final Testament, tricked his inner circle, and then abandoned ship as his city was being destroyed;

that witnesses such as Rattenhuber, Schenck, Junge, and Misch all kept the secret until their dying day *(even though Hitler had abandoned them to the Soviets)*, or had somehow been duped while innocent body doubles were killed and then thrown into the cremation fire;

that the Russians somehow created fake dental records that forensic dentists *30 years later* would be able to match-up to American-obtained dental records, or, that Dr. Sognnaes & Dr. Strom became co-conspirators 30 years after the fact [King's emphasis].

King points out that the supposed documentary evidence presented by the 'Argentinianists' turns out on closer inspection to be hearsay, unconfirmed, uncorroborated or anonymous second-hand testimony, some of which was filed by the FBI (who filed all such documents sent to them, however erroneous or deranged), some of which was deliberately misleading material put out by the Soviets and the Russians. A widely circulated image of an elderly Hitler in exile turns out to be a digitally altered image of Bruno Ganz, the actor playing the Nazi leader in the movie *Downfall*. Nowhere in the photographic record is there an authentic image of Hitler taken after the end of April 1945. Neither is there any direct, independently corroborated evidence of Hitler's survival in either the interview material or the documentary record.[73]

The survival story almost always portrays Hitler as cheating both death and justice, triumphing over history and cocking a snook at the world. It has Hitler living with Eva Braun in domestic bliss in, usually, an Argentinian hideaway, reaching a peaceful old age and doing nobody any harm, sunning himself perhaps on a South American beach, or enjoying a promenade in the tropics with his henchmen. Indeed, the movie *Grey Wolf* closes with a scene in which Hitler, aged ninety-six, is pushed along in a wheelchair, by his granddaughter both grandfather and granddaughter being played, it scarcely needs saying, by actors.[74] This was certainly not the case with Adolf Eichmann and other old Nazis, who spent much of their time in exile living in a political fantasy-world, plotting their return to Germany. If they retained their ideological commitment, it is hard to believe Hitler would have abandoned his. According to the film *Grey Wolf*, indeed, he continued plotting his comeback, aided by Martin Bormann, until Perón was overthrown in a coup in 1954, after which Bormann gave up the struggle and devoted himself to his business interests, aided by the huge fortune he had supposedly smuggled out of Germany in 1945. In another version, Hitler ends his days in 1972 a tragic figure, old, ill, decrepit, demented, betrayed by Bormann and weeping uncontrollably as he is plagued by demonic visions of the people he has sent to the gas chambers: a retrospective portrait of conscience's final return and the triumph, away from the public eye, of history's revenge on the monster's psyche. Which of these pictures – the guilt-ridden eighty-three-year-old or the serene ninety-six-year-old – is the true one, we are not told: both are fantasies.

V

Both book and film were widely hyped when they appeared.[75] Galloping Films Australia, distributors of the *Grey Wolf* programme, claimed that the film presented 'a story that will change everything we have ever been taught about Adolf Hitler and make it impossible to believe the official story about anything, ever again'.[76] Overall, the film, which was released straight to DVD, earned a five-star rating from 41 per cent of viewers on amazon.co.uk and 67 per cent of viewers on amazon.com. Reviews on amazon.co.uk described it as 'excellent' and 'brilliant'. 'There are no facts to dispute the evidence in this DVD,' wrote one: 'It's about time the mainstream historians removed their head's [*sic*] from the sand' and admitted that Hitler 'escaped to South America'. 'Most of what we have been told is a lie,' said another: 'Hitler's alleged death in Berlin is no exception.'[77] But others were more critical: a quarter or slightly over of viewers in both countries awarded the film only one star. The *Sun* newspaper sent its intrepid reporter Oliver Harvey to Argentina to investigate. Filing his copy on 4 March 2012, Harvey told his readers that he had visited the houses where Hitler was supposed to have lived, and talked to many people, but found nothing: no reports of sightings, no DNA evidence from possible gravesites, no living Hitler relatives.[78] Reviewing the book on amazon.co.uk on 7 June 2012, Donald McKale noted that its stories were mostly rehashes of claims made many decades earlier, and continued:

> Like the predecessors – cited above – of their story, Dunstan and Williams are masters at the 'claim by association' or 'claim by implication' technique of journalism. That is, they allege or imply something else that happened in actual fact, but [was] only remotely related ... When one has no factual or otherwise reliable proof, one resorts to associating one's claims with something else or to using hearsay and other dubious evidence, including unnamed or

unidentified sources. The FBI files kept on Hitler sightings, also used in *Grey Wolf*, produced not a single credible instance of the dictator's survival.[79]

Then there are the arguments from silence – the missing evidence one would expect to find if the claims advanced by *Grey Wolf* were true. It stretches credulity beyond breaking point to believe that Eva Braun, a professional photographer who was constantly filming and taking snaps during her years on the Obersalzberg, left no photographic evidence of any kind of her alleged decades in Argentina, not even of her supposed daughter or daughters (indeed, the film invents scenes showing her on more than one occasion taking ciné-films of Hitler, his friends and their child, though no such films have ever been found).[80] Nothing survives of any of Hitler's possessions of the time, though plenty does from his years in Germany. Huge swathes of the book's narrative are unfootnoted and unsupported by any evidence at all, not even evidence by association. The authors' rhetoric turns speculation into supposition and supposition into fact. Thus on page 185 we are told that 'Hitler's escape from Berlin, as can be seen from the preceding chapters, is remarkably well documented', when a careful reading of the chapters shows that in fact it is no such thing.

Although the film *Grey Wolf* was not a success, the book continued to sell and to be debated long after it appeared. Even before it was published, however, Dunstan and Williams began to run into trouble. 'We have ruffled some very big feathers,' Williams commented of his theory in October 2011: 'Traditional historians don't like it and certain governments don't like it. We have had some death threats already.'[81] But the problems were not so much with homicidal historians as with Williams's financial backer, Magnus Peterson, founder of Weavering Capital – 'my benefactor, supporter, and convivial companion throughout the trials and tribulations of this project', as Williams describes him in the Acknowledgements to the book, or the producer, as he appears in the credits to the film. The movie was well made and involved a lot of expenditure. 'The credits,' as Roger Clark points out, 'list over 50 actors, 15 voice over artists and 60 people on the production side', as well as a composer thanked for the score and the artists employed on the slick cover and slipcase for the DVD.[82] But the global financial crisis that broke in 2008, coupled with the film's failure to achieve commercial success, soon led to money problems. Cameramen and others who worked on the film were never paid. Peterson was unable to repay his investors. His hedge fund collapsed in 2009, leading to a raid by the Serious Fraud Office on his house in Kent. A succession of companies involved in financing the film collapsed: one of them, Gerbil Films, was wound up in August 2012, followed by another, Lobos Gris (Spanish for 'Grey Wolf'), and then Grey Wolf Media, which was compulsorily wound up after failing to file reports in two successive years. In January 2015 Peterson was sentenced to thirteen years in prison for fraud, forgery, false accounting and fraudulent trading. The funds lost by investors came to nearly £350 million. The UK authorities said he had 'rewarded himself handsomely from investors' monies' to the tune of £5.8 million. He was banned from working in the financial services industry. Another investigative journalist, Laurence de Mello, alleged that over £2 million from Weavering Capital had been used to back *Grey Wolf*.[83] 'Of course,' as Roger Clark adds, 'there is no suggestion that Gerrard Williams was aware of Mr Peterson's fraudulent activities, and it must be assumed he accepted the financing of his film in good faith.' But there remain many unanswered questions about Peterson's role in the making of the film.[84]

Worse was to follow. On 15 October 2007 Williams's production company, Gerbil Films Ltd, had signed a contract with an Argentinian writer based in Bariloche, Abel Basti, for exclusive use of his research in return for a substantial sum of money. Basti had already published a book on Hitler in Argentina and went on to publish several more, including *El exilio de Hitler* (2010), *Los secretos de Hitler* (2011) and *Tras los pasos de Hitler* (2014). None of these was listed in the Bibliography or footnotes of *Grey Wolf*. These works were summed up in 2012 in a German edition, *Hitler überlebte in Argentinien*, co-edited by Stefan Erdmann and Jan van Helsing (actually Jan Udo Holey, an author who drew his pen-name from the vampire-hunter hero of Bram Stoker's *Dracula*). Son of a self-styled clairvoyant, van Helsing was noted for having published two books banned in Germany for spreading racial hatred, along with other publications drawing on conspiracy theories involving the Illuminati, the Rothschilds, the Freemasons and the 'New

World Order' (the conspiracist fantasy of a world government). His works on secret societies had sold a hundred thousand copies by 2005. He has also published on 9/11, Rudolf Hess, vaccination, the Egyptian Pyramids, and many other subjects. Erdmann was also described by the Federal Office for the Protection of the Constitution as a propagandist for *The Protocols of the Elders of Zion* in the esoteric milieu.[85]

Basti may or may not have shared such views, though by allowing his work to be published by Erdmann and van Helsing he was implicitly endorsing them. In his Preface to the German edition he warned of dark powers who were preparing a new world war and suppressing the truth about Hitler's survival.[86] The Americans and the British, he maintained, had kept Hitler in power, helped him escape at the end of the war and spread the myth of his death to avoid being compromised; and indeed a strong element of anti-Americanism characterizes some passages of the book.[87] Basti's views on Hitler's escape were formed in the 1990s, when he conducted a series of interviews beginning in Bariloche and soon extending to other parts of Argentina. None of his interviewees provided direct, corroborated evidence of having actually met and talked to Hitler, and some of their statements seemed, to put it mildly, unlikely, for example that of Alberto Vitale, who claimed to have seen the ex-dictator often in 1953 'wearing huge boots and riding a black ladies' bicycle from house to house selling herbs'.[88]

Basti's interviews with Catalina Gomero, Jorge Batinic, Manuel Monasterio, Mar Chiquita, Araceli Méndez, Ingeborg Schaeffer, Jorge Colotto and Hernán Ancín, along with statements, videos, photographs, and copies of his newspaper articles and two of his books, *Hitler en Argentina* and *Bariloche Nazi*, were handed over to Gerrard Williams as part of the deal. But once Williams's financial backer had fallen by the wayside, leaving debts of US$98,929 owed to Basti unpaid and, as Williams confessed, unpayable, Basti considered the contract no longer valid and formally notified Williams on 12 August 2009 that he was withdrawing his permission to use the material he had made available to him. Williams ignored Basti's request to send the material back to him, so Basti consulted his lawyer at the British Association of Journalists, who wrote to his publishers on 7 May 2013 demanding compensation for plagiarism, breach of copyright, and losses of US$130,450 incurred by the cancellation of a six-part

television series on which Basti had spent this sum of money in pre-
production because its contents had been made public in Dunstan's and
Williams's book and film and so its claim to originality and thus its
marketability had been destroyed. It is noticeable that in the credits
that follow the end of the movie Basti's name is not mentioned. Basti's
lawyer made reference to the statement in the Preface to *Grey
Wolf* – 'The authors have spent the last five years researching this
subject – travelling the globe, interviewing eyewitnesses, unearthing
documents' – and commented: 'That is, of course, a grossly misleading statement.' Dunstan and Williams were 'passing off what are
mainly the efforts of Mr Basti as their own'.[89]

After the production company Grey Wolf Media was wound up,
Williams managed to secure US$16 million from the History Chan-
nel for a television series devoted to an exploration of the idea that
Hitler had survived the war in Argentina. As far as the circumstances
surrounding Hitler's death were concerned, the History Channel
claimed, this investigation was 'the most in-depth and revealing the
world has ever seen'.[90] Production values were high, and the whole
series looked slick and professional. Produced by Karga Seven Pictures, *Hunting Hitler* ran on television's History Channel for three
seasons of eight episodes each, from 10 November 2015 to 20 February 2018, after which it was cancelled, despite averaging some three
million viewers per episode. Fronted by a retired UN war crimes
investigator, Dr John Cencich, who had worked on the Yugoslav
War Crimes Tribunal; actor, reality TV star and private investigator
Lenny DePaul; ex-CIA agent Bob Baer; martial arts practitioner Tim
Kennedy; the historian James Holland; and, last but not least, Gerrard Williams himself, the programmes moved around Europe and
Latin America, brandishing 'declassified intelligence files' and uncovering hidden tunnels through which Hitler 'may have' escaped,
locations where he 'may have' stayed, and places that 'could have
housed nuclear facilities with Nazi ties after the war'. *Variety* magazine commented in its review of the series: 'If viewers were to take a
shot of alcohol every time someone uses a phrase like, "There could
have been . . ." or, "There's a chance that Hitler might have come
here . . ." or, "If there was in fact a bunker," they would be plastered
by the second or third commercial break.'[91]

'All these stories we've been told about Hitler's bunker,' says Baer, the former CIA agent, on camera: 'there's nothing to back it up. It's the biggest mystery of the twentieth century.' The entire historical profession, governments, journalists, people who lived through the war itself, have, the History Channel asserts, been involved in 'what could be the biggest cover-up in history'. Williams himself asks rhetorically: 'Why aren't we being told the truth?' 'The narrative the government gives us,' Baer says, 'is a lie.'[92] This is language typical of conspiracy theorists: they alone know the truth, they alone have penetrated the veil of 'official' knowledge. It makes for good entertainment, but not one single concrete finding is presented in any of the twenty-four episodes.[93] When Baer says, 'There is no evidence that Hitler died in the bunker,' he is simply confessing his own ignorance. Serious historians and biographers have gone over the evidence countless times. What *Hunting Hitler* presents is not real evidence at all. Any factual material there is, as Roger Clark has pointed out, is constantly over-interpreted in the series, subjected to unwarranted conclusions, or used as the basis for pure speculation. The discovery that a skull fragment allegedly from Hitler, kept in Moscow, was not that of Hitler at all, is presented to viewers as a decisive revelation: the skull is shown on camera in the first episode of *Hunting Hitler*, followed by Baer's voice telling us that 'the forensics we do have make it look as if Hitler got away'. In fact, the scientist who subjected the skull to a DNA test, Nicholas Bellantoni, actually said that Hitler 'clearly died in the bunker'. Hitler was a sick man in April 1945, too ill to have managed a daring escape. 'Because the skull plate was not him doesn't mean he didn't die in the bunker, it simply means what they recovered was not him.' But Bellantoni, for good reason, does not appear at all in *Hunting Hitler*.[94]

When the series does break new ground, its investigations quickly reveal themselves to be built on sand. Much is made, for example, in episode 7 of the team's military-style investigation of the Inalco House, in the southern Andes; a 'secret' location, 'where Hitler could have stayed'. It is extremely isolated, they say, and may be protected by armed guards. It is in fact only 250 metres away from a national trunk road, but, they claim, can only be accessed across a nearby lake, so members of the team wearing wet-suits swim across, and though they encounter no armed guards, they go on to claim that there were 'underground steel-lined chambers beneath the offices', where the 'most important and sinister documents of that century', the twentieth, were kept. But *Hunting Hitler* contains no footage showing the interior of the house and offices, either above ground or below, and, in fact, visitors can enter the house by the front door, and frequently do. Once more, all is innuendo, suggestion and invention. Not only is there no evidence that Hitler was ever there, there is no evidence that the house is either secret or remote.[95]

In one of the episodes of *Hunting Hitler*, the team claim to have discovered a report that Hitler went to a ballet performance in the Brazilian town of Cassino, known to have been a place where a number of ex-Nazis lived, in 1947. They leaf through contemporary local newspapers in the town's archive and discover that a ballet was performed there on two evenings. There's no reference to Hitler. But Gerrard Williams concludes he must have been at a third, unreported performance. His evidence? The existence of a French poem praising the ballet, dated differently from reports about the two public performances. 'I feel quite blown away,' Williams says: 'He was here.' As Hitler looked around the wealthy members of the audience, he must have been thinking: 'Who amongst these people may be able to help us get back?' This, as Clark points out, is an unadulterated 'flight of fancy'. There is not one shred of evidence that even hints that Hitler was there.[96] The series descends even further into fantasizing, mixed with sensational speculation, when it suggests that Hitler flew to Colombia in 1948 with two physicists who 'carried with them secret plans for the V-3 Sky Rocket bomb and the complete record of the German nuclear investigations'. They follow up a lead that brings us to a swamp where the aircraft is said to have been ditched. But they fail to find anything on a number of dives. 'It's a major disappointment,' confesses Baer as he emerges from the water. But it was a wild-goose chase from the very beginning. There is absolutely no evidence to support the claim that Hitler flew to Colombia from Argentina, let alone that he was ever in Argentina in the first place. The V-3 was not a rocket but a huge gun designed to fire on London from the Channel coast; it was destroyed by Allied bombers before it could become operational. The Nazis' nuclear programme never got anywhere near practicality, nor could it ever have done so, given its inability to acquire the necessary raw materials – a problem that would have faced Hitler in South America to an almost infinitely greater degree than it had back in Germany.[97]

VI

As Roger Clark has noted, '*Grey Wolf* and *Hunting Hitler* are part of a flourishing Hitler survival industry.' *Grey Wolf* is one of a number of similar, though less ambitious, books that have appeared in recent years putting forward the survival thesis, though it is unique in having spawned a major television series. There has been a notable revival of survivalist theories following a long period of relative inactivity, and it may be that the example of Dunstan's and Williams's book, together with the film and TV series, has played a role in encouraging this. All of these theories claim to be true, in contrast to obvious and outright fictions of one kind and another. Yet, as Clark points out, 'all Hitler survival theories cannot be true since they contradict one another. But all Hitler survival theories can be untrue – and are. Their advocates can produce only rumor and hearsay. They disagree about how and when Hitler escaped from Berlin, how he traveled abroad, where he lived, what he did, and how, when and where he died.' Moreover, nobody has ever produced any photographs of Hitler after 30 April 1945, or for that matter of Eva Braun or of any of their supposed offspring. Nor has anyone on the Allied or German side who allegedly facilitated their escape ever been tracked down and interrogated.[98] But this has not stopped the conspiracy theorists from continuing to exercise their paranoid imagination, whatever their motives might be. And time and again, gullible media outlets report new 'discoveries' that 'prove' Hitler escaped from the bunker, despite the fact that in reality they do no such thing.[99]

Writings about Hitler's escape are shot through with obvious errors, there on the page for everybody to see. While many conspiracy theorists – for example those writing about Rudolf Hess – cite each other, the survivalists each tend to present their discoveries as exclusively their own work, so that it does not seem to matter that they contradict each other on many key issues. Simoni Renee Guerreiro Dias, for example, is the author of a book claiming that Hitler fled to Latin America at the end of the war, but not to Bariloche: he apparently went via Paraguay to Brazil, where he settled in the Mato Grosso town of Nossa Senhora do Livramento, near Cuiabá, where he hunted for buried treasure with a map given to him by allies in the Vatican. He had a black girlfriend to disguise his Nazi background and lived to the age of ninety-five under the name of Adolf Leipzig – Leipzig, Dias asserts, was the birthplace of Hitler's favourite composer, J. S. Bach (in fact his favourite composers were Wagner and, during the war, Bruckner – he does not seem to have liked Bach at all; and Bach was born in Eisenach, not Leipzig). 'An unidentified Polish nun recognized an elderly man due to have an op at a hospital in Cuiabá in the early eighties as Hitler and demanded he leave – but was reprimanded by a superior who claimed he was there on Vatican orders.' The author's 'suspicions about Adolf Leipzig increased after she photoshopped a moustache on to the grainy picture she obtained of him and compared it to photos of the Nazi leader'.[100]

From the frequent references to the Vatican's supposed role in all this, it seems that the author is motivated at least in part by a strong hostility to the Catholic Church. This is, in a sense, a version of the survival myth emanating from the milieu of Catholic anticlericalism. And indeed, what is striking about the new wave of Hitler survival claims is how many of them have emerged from organizations, groups and individuals who decry mainstream religion, science and scholarship and promote alternative knowledge of one kind and another. Some of the survivalist conspiracy theorists, for instance, have emanated from the occultist milieu, from students of the supernatural and the paranormal. While this form of alternative knowledge has obtruded, if somewhat marginally, into the other conspiracy theories examined in this book, it has taken a far more central position in conspiracy theories about the survival of Adolf Hitler. Thus, for example, the hypothesis of Hitler's escape to Indonesia has been put forward by Peter Levenda, an American author whose previous works include *Unholy Alliance: A History of Nazi Involvement with the Occult* (1994) and several books on 'American political witchcraft'. After two decades of writing on Freemasons, Kabbalists and similar subjects, he came to the topic of Hitler's alleged survival in 2012 with *Ratline: Soviet Spies, Nazi Priests, and the Disappearance of Adolf Hitler*, returning to it two years later, after publishing a book on the destruction of the twin towers of the World Trade Center in New York in 2001 – a favourite topic for conspiracists – with *The Hitler Legacy: The Nazi Cult in Diaspora, How It was Organized, How It was Funded, and Why It Remains a Threat to Global Security in the Age of Terrorism* (2014). In *Ratline*, Levenda identified Hitler with a German doctor who had been working in Indonesia after the war. The man went under the name of Georg Anton Pöch. 'Regardless of who Pöch really was – the Chief Medical Officer of the Salzburg Gau, or the leader of the Third Reich – he was definitely a Nazi who made it to Indonesia', Levenda wrote. Here, it seems, Hitler (or Pöch) converted to Islam and married a young local woman.[101] *Ratline* is vague on almost every detail, and is written obviously to appeal to the occultist community; it makes no attempt at coherent argument and does not baulk at presenting hearsay or even obviously spurious evidence.

More detailed is the lengthy essay by Giordan Smith, 'Fabricating the Death of Adolf Hitler', published on the occultist website *Nexus Illuminati*, which focuses, like the former Spandau doctor Hugh Thomas's book, on exposing minute differences of detail in the evidence and eyewitness testimony to argue that Hitler's and Eva Braun's bodies were never found. Like Thomas, Smith, an independent Australian writer, did not go any further than this, but it is clear that his basic objection was to the fact that Hitler's suicide cast the Nazi leader in a less than heroic light. Trevor-Roper, Smith declared, ventriloquized his interlocutors, some of whom, like the aviatrix Hanna Reitsch, later rejected his account and insisted that Hitler had 'died with dignity'. His investigation was part of a British conspiracy 'to enshrine anti-Nazi propaganda as historical fact'. 'The suicide theory was also a weapon of psychological warfare on the German population' by trying to persuade them that Hitler was a coward and that they should submit meekly to Allied occupation.[102] The contents of the magazine *Nexus*, founded in Australia in 1986, and the *Nexus Illuminati* website, are described by a recent authoritative survey of the extreme right in Europe as 'a mixture of esoteric, conspiratorial and neo-Nazi matters'.[103] Not all esoteric or occultist websites can be described as ultra-right-wing or neo-Nazi, of course, but on the margins the two clearly overlap.

Here, occultism merges into the alternative political milieu of the ultra right. With the rise of populism in recent years, this milieu has begun to exert an influence on what used to be regarded as more mainstream conservatism. Perhaps the most interesting of the new wave of survivalist literature in this regard is the right-wing American politician Jerome Corsi's *Hunting Hitler* (2014). This slim volume is based not on original research but mainly on Dunstan and Williams, on the earlier book by Bezymenski, and on reports by what the author described (somewhat inaccurately) as 'respected military historian and journalist Ladislas Farago'.[104] Like other conspiracists, Corsi made extensive use of American Intelligence and other reports from the immediate aftermath of the war. He argued in what was by now the customary fashion that a double replaced Hitler in the bunker on 22 April 1945. The real Hitler fled by helicopter to Austria and thence by plane to Barcelona, from where he took a U-boat to Argentina (though, in fact, getting through the British naval blockade of the Straits of Gibraltar would by this time have been more or less impossible).[105] Corsi followed Dunstan and Williams in locating Hitler's hideaway on a lakeside retreat near Bariloche, where he lived out his days with Eva Braun in a Bavarian-style mansion built for them two years before (implying, somewhat implausibly, that already in 1943 Hitler was anticipating defeat in the war). 'When Hitler arrived in Argentina,' he noted, 'he found an enthusiastic German community ready to welcome his presence' (strange, then, that no records of the community's welcome for him have ever been found).[106]

What is the significance of these hypotheses for Corsi? Hitler, he says, escaped justice because he was protected by Allen Dulles, head of the CIA, and Juan Perón. Both had close ties with German capitalism, because Bormann in 1943 had 'implemented a plan to invest billions of dollars of stolen wealth in . . . business enterprises in the United States and Argentina'.[107] Dulles recognized that National Socialism was the way of the future in the struggle against Communism, imported Nazi experts like the rocketeer Wernher von Braun to the United States, and co-opted the Nazi Intelligence Service into the

CIA. But these Nazis also brought their ideology with them and (how and why is not clear) encouraged free trade agreements (of a kind) that privileged global organizations like the World Trade Organization and the United Nations, which threatened to destroy American sovereignty. The degree of government surveillance of US citizens that was put in place as a result would, says Corsi, have been 'unimaginable even to the Nazis at the height of their power', while critics of the government and advocates of American freedoms were ridiculed instead of being recognized as 'the Tea Party Patriots they truly are . . . Just as Hitler was allowed to escape Berlin and permitted to enter Argentina by submarine, national socialism has thrived in what is arguably the Fourth Reich that we ourselves have unwittingly become.'[108]

Thus in Corsi's confused vision, the escape of Hitler to Argentina becomes a kind of symbol for the links between the American Establishment, including that of both Democratic and Republican parties, and German Nazism, whose legacy lives on in big government. A financial services marketing specialist, Corsi had won fame in 2004 with his book *Unfit for Command: Swift Boat Veterans Speak Out against John Kerry* (2004), an attack on Democratic Presidential candidate John Kerry's Vietnam war record, subsequently strongly criticized by veterans who had actively served with Kerry.[109] The book sold over a million copies and was followed by a string of others, alleging among other things that the Democratic Party had been corrupted by Iranian oil money. In 2005 Corsi published (with Craig Smith) *Black Gold Stranglehold: The Myth of Scarcity and the Politics of Oil*, in which, according to the flap text:

> Jerome R. Corsi and Craig R. Smith expose the fraudulent science that has been sold to the American people in order to enslave them – the belief that oil is a fossil fuel and a finite resource. On the contrary, this book presents authoritative research, currently known mostly in the scientific community, that oil is not a product of decaying dinosaurs and prehistoric forests. Rather, it is a natural product of the Earth. The scientific evidence cited by Corsi and Smith suggests that oil is constantly being produced by the Earth, far below the planet's surface, and that it is brought to attainable depths by the centrifugal forces of the Earth's rotation.

In another book, *The Late Great USA – The Coming Merger with Canada and Mexico* (2007), Corsi alleged a bureaucratic plot to destroy American sovereignty and create a transatlantic version of the European Union.

Another Corsi bestseller, *The Obama Nation: Leftist Politics and the Cult of Personality* (2008), alleged that Democratic Presidential candidate Barack Obama was a far-left political figure with links to black-liberation ideology and connections to Islam who was working to undermine US foreign policy and military strength – the title has to be pronounced with an American accent to get the full effect of the intended pun. In response, the Obama campaign issued a forty-page rebuttal, querying many of the details of the book, under the title 'Unfit for Publication', and declared:

> His book is nothing but a series of lies that were long ago discredited, written by an individual who was discredited after he wrote a similar book to help George Bush and Dick Cheney get re-elected four years ago ... The reality is that there are many lie-filled books like this in the works cobbled together from the Internet to make money off of a presidential campaign.[110]

In 2008, Corsi lent his support to the 9/11 truth movement, which propagates the conspiracy theory that the twin towers were destroyed by elements within the US government to provide an excuse for the invasion of Iraq.[111] Not surprisingly, Corsi is also a 'birther': in 2011 he published *Where's the Birth Certificate? The Case that Barack Obama is not Eligible to be President*, a book whose impact was somewhat dented by Obama's release of his long-form birth certificate three weeks before it was published; the birther movement was aimed at discrediting the black Democratic politician, who was, notwithstanding, re-elected US President in 2012. Corsi is a vigorous self-publicist: his biography on the website of the Tea Party, a right-wing populist organization within the Republican Party, named after the rebels of 1773 who campaigned against taxes imposed by the British colonial power in the run-up to the War of American Independence, reports that: 'For the past 5 years, Dr Corsi has averaged 100 radio shows per month.' If true, this must mean he makes on average at least three broadcasts a day.[112] A number of his broadcasts are available online. In one of them he claims somewhat incoherently that 'in both my books on Kennedy – because who really killed Kennedy? – and "Hunting Hitler" – because I'm developing themes and going back and looking at disinformation – the murder of Kennedy and the escape of Hitler. And the events tie together. The same names show up – the Dulles, the CIA, the OSS and the Bushes.'[113] Hitler, in Corsi's view, was an extreme leftist who developed universal healthcare, just as Obama did later with the Affordable Care Act ('Obamacare'); the parallels were, he claimed, inescapable. In the end, therefore, all Corsi really wanted to do was to brand Obama a Nazi and draw a continuity of conspiratorial manipulation by the American Establishment back to 1945. He was not interested at all in what happened to Hitler after he reached Argentina.

It should not surprise anybody that Corsi became an impassioned supporter of Donald Trump in his successful campaign for the Presidency of the United States in 2016, and, as Alex Nichols, a hostile critic, has pointed out, 'hopped aboard Pizzagate, the debunked rumor that Clinton campaign manager John Podesta ran a child-sex ring underneath a D.C. pizza restaurant, and joined the effort to diagnose Hillary Clinton with everything from Parkinson's disease to autism'. Following Trump's victory, Corsi was appointed to an editorial position in *InfoWars*, becoming its Washington bureau chief in 2017, though he subsequently left the organization. *InfoWars* is a far-right, fake news website owned by conspiracy theorist Alex Jones. It has been banned from several social media platforms for spreading disinformation that in some cases has been alleged to have led to the serious harassment of its victims: 'Pizzagate' is an example, since the pizza parlour owner began to receive death threats and, eventually, on 4 December 2016, a twenty-eight-year-old man, Edgar Welch, entered the parlour armed with a rifle and started firing shots in the belief that he was rescuing the children confined in the (non-existent) cellar – fortunately, nobody was injured. Despite the theory having been exposed as a hoax, the harassment continued, including a failed arson attack on 25 January 2019. Conspiracy theories can have real consequences.[114] Most recently, Corsi has published a book, *Killing the Deep State*, which presents criminal investigations into President Trump by prosecutor Robert Mueller as part of a widespread conspiracy to remove him from office and stage a *coup d'état* in order to bring in what right-wing conspiracy theorists in the United States call 'The New World Order'.[115]

This has taken us a very long way from the Hitler survival myth.[116] But Corsi's anti-Establishment use of the myth can also be found in what must be the most outlandish of all the survival theories, that which takes its starting point in the Nazi 'New Swabia' expedition to Antarctica in 1938–9. Here we are entering the imaginative world of another community of alternative knowledge, the world of 'Ufologists', or people and groups who study Unidentified Flying Objects (UFOs). Drawing on the fact that the Nazis had also been researching rocket propulsion, jet fighters and other types of advanced military technology during the war, including a jet-powered flying wing, US military investigators of Unidentified Flying Objects supposedly linked them to a purported Nazi flying machine using anti-gravity technology, and speculated that they might be emanating from secret Nazi bases under the Antarctic, where Hitler had apparently fled at the end of the war, and later died and was buried. These flying machines had been manufactured by the Vril Society of Berlin, according to some accounts; an occultist group of Nazis who took their name from the Victorian writer Edward Bulwer-Lytton's novel *Vril: The Power of the Coming Race* (originally published in 1871 as *The Coming Race*), which was taken to be at least in part a description of empirical fact by theosophists such as Madame Blavatsky and Rudolf Steiner. 'Vril' is the term, obviously a shortened version of 'virile', used by Bulwer-Lytton to describe the mysterious source of power, both destructive and healing, used by the Vril-ya, a race dwelling beneath the earth and preparing to take it over. In their 1960 book *Morning of the Magicians*, Louis Pauwels (a disciple of the Russian magus George Gurdjieff) and Jacques Bergier, a Russian exile (whose last words, spoken on his deathbed, were reportedly, 'I am not a legend'), connected Vril with nuclear physics and Nazis with UFOs. The book became a cult classic in the 1960s and spawned a number of other fantasies linking Nazism, science and the occult.[117]

These ideas were part of a fascination in the alternative culture with the links between Nazism and occultism, links for which there was very little evidence in reality, not even on the wilder pseudo-religious and pseudo-scientific fringes of the SS.[118] Along with many other forms of alternative knowledge, the worlds of Ufology and occultism manage to coincide and overlap in the books of Maximillien De Lafayette, author of *Chronology of World War Two: Hitler in Berlin and Argentina and Nazis 1945–2013* (2014), *Hitler's Doubles: Photos, Proofs, Testimonies, Facts, Eyewitnesses* (2018) and *Hitler's Visitors in Argentina from 1945 to 1985* (2 vols., 2018–20). Among his other works – the list of them extends to over a hundred pages on amazon.co.uk, and he is listed online as author of more than 2,000 books – are publications about extraterrestrials on Earth such as *1921, Germany: Birth of the First Man-Made UFO, Extraterrestrials Messages to Maria Orsic in Ana'kh Aldebaran Script to Build the Vril* (2014), and books on UFOs and the supernatural, sorcery, witchcraft and the occult. A brief entry on *RationalWiki* claims that

> Maximillien De Lafayette is an alleged 'UFO researcher' and ancient astronauts advocate who has appeared on *UFO Hunters* and *Ancient Aliens* [American television series]. According to a woman who claims to be his former girlfriend, he was actually a scam artist who republished text and photos gathered from around the Internet as books.[119]

Whatever the truth or otherwise of this claim, Lafayette, though he seems to operate independently of any particular group or organization (indeed, it seems unlikely he would have the time even to sign up to one, given the fact that he must surely spend every minute of the day writing), is interesting precisely for his appeal, such as it is, to readers who consume a wide variety of unofficial kinds of knowledge, in much the same way as people who propagate one conspiracy theory are likely to believe in others as well.

Here we have entered a strange literary underworld inhabited by self-published or online authors whom nobody much appears to take seriously, though they seem at least to make a kind of living from their work. There are other figures comparable to Lafayette, though none is anywhere near as productive. Perhaps the most prominent was Ernst Zündel (1939–2017), a German Holocaust denier who was jailed several times for inciting racial hatred and deported from the USA and Canada for his activities. Zündel not only published a book, *UFOs: Nazi Secret Weapons?* (1974, writing as Christof Friedrich), arguing that flying saucers (*fliegende Untertassen*) were spy-craft sent from the subterranean Nazi bases of New Swabia, but also in 1978 invited the public to participate in an expedition to find them, at $9,999 a ticket. Ticket holders would be issued with an official UFO investigator pass and a chart with instructions on how to find UFOs. Zündel was reported to have confessed in a telephone interview:

> 'I realized that North Americans were not interested in being educated. They want to be entertained. The book was for fun. With a picture of the Führer on the cover and flying saucers coming out of Antarctica, it was a chance to get on radio and TV talk shows. For about fifteen minutes of an hour program I'd talk about that esoteric stuff . . . And that was my chance to talk about what I wanted to talk about.' 'In that case,' I asked him, 'do you still stand by what you wrote in the UFO book?' 'Look,' he replied, 'it has a question mark at the end of the title.'[120]

For Zündel, therefore, the flying saucer story was a way to get media time for antisemitism and Holocaust denial. More sinister still was Richard Chase, the so-called Vampire of Sacramento, a paranoid schizophrenic who killed six victims in the space of a month in 1977, drank their blood and ate their corpses. Chase claimed he had been told to do so by men speaking to him from Nazi UFOs, and asked the investigating officer for a radar gun so he could shoot them down and have them put on trial instead of himself.[121]

It's only a short step from here to imagining that Hitler and Nazis, who after all through Wernher von Braun developed the V-2 rocket, escaped not to Antarctica but to the moon or even Mars. In 1992, celebrating half a century of the German moon base, the Bulgarian Ufologist Vladimir Terziski, President of the American Academy of Dissident Sciences (an institution whose only member appears to be himself), claimed to have proved that the moon had an atmosphere. To survive, 'a pair of jeans, a pullover and sneakers are just about enough'. The first man on the moon was a German; the Americans, of course, never got there in 1969, but faked it in a studio.[122] These ideas were taken up in the 2012 movie *Iron Sky*, which portrayed in pulp-fiction style a whole Nazi community on the far side of the moon, accidentally discovered by US astronauts in 2018. Intended as political satire, the movie undermines Nazi racial stereotypes, draws parallels between Nazi ideas and those of the Tea Party and the Republican Right, and pleads implicitly for tolerance, peace and love in a world where Nazi values have become dominant. The movie was not a success. The German weekly *Die Zeit* commented: 'There is practically nothing good about this film, not the plot, the gags, the casting, the digs, and certainly not the desire to break taboos.'[123] Nevertheless, a crowd-funded sequel appeared in 2019.

VII

'There's a wealth of difference,' Roger Clark points out, 'between bad, but entertaining, war movies labelled works of fiction, and war movies that claim they are historically accurate and rubbish the truth.'[124] It is clear that the Hitler survival myth is attractive to a wide variety of writers with widely varying motives. All of them, however, in one way or another, belong to communities of alternative knowledge. As Michael Butter observes, we are dealing here not with the public sphere, in which people in general share a common understanding of what is true and what is not, but with 'partial publics with differing concepts of the truth'.[125] The one thing almost all of them have in common is a contempt for what they call 'official knowledge'. They all believe that the global media, historians, journalists and almost everyone who has ever written about Hitler have been hoodwinked by a clever plot into believing that he is dead when in fact he is not. Occultists, UFO and U-boat enthusiasts, birthers, truthers, JFK and 9/11 conspiracy theorists, antisemites and Holocaust deniers, neo-Nazis and many more constitute communities of the like-minded who reinforce their identity and sense of worth by the accretion of fresh detail to bolster their reputation with their fellow-members. These communities of alternative knowledge are in some cases well organized, like Holocaust deniers, in other cases barely organized at all; they may overlap to a degree, with believers in UFOs sharing a fascination with the occult, or birthers going along with 9/11 conspiracy theories, but essentially each one is a separate entity with its own websites, publications, conferences and conventions. Some may genuinely believe in the ideas they propagate; others may merely regard them as a chance to suspend disbelief in the interests of entertainment; others yet again may be cynically exploiting them for the purposes of financial gain or political propaganda. For some it's a chance to enter alternate or parallel worlds where they can mould and control reality rather than having to confront its intractable complexities. Disappointing historical outcomes can be made right, complex tangles of evidence can be straightened out, fantasy worlds and virtual realms of the imagination can be created that provide compensations for the difficulties and frustrations of everyday life. It is hardly surprising that virtual realities, from the simple good and evil of Tolkien's Middle-earth to the rational patterns of deduction of Sherlock Holmes's Victorian and Edwardian London, have become popular in the politically and culturally uncertain world of today.[126]

In this world of moral anxiety, Hitler and Nazism have become icons of evil, signifiers of malefaction and malignity beyond any kind of moral rescue, unlike even Stalin, who still has those who defend him by pointing out that he industrialized Russia and defeated the Third Reich. Alternative knowledge communities zero in on Hitler because he is an instantly recognizable cultural figure who will attract widespread attention, especially if some new claim is advanced that seemingly revises the universally known and therefore 'official' facts about his life. The story the survival myth presents is simple and easily grasped if we strip away its many different variants and outliers: Hitler did not die in the bunker but escaped by submarine to Argentina – a story, it might be argued, well suited for propagation by the Internet. The American science journalist Nicholas Carr has recently argued that by chopping up information into small chunks the Internet encourages 'cursory reading ... distracted thinking, and superficial learning'. Thus it encourages the propagation of misinformation and discourages users from viewing it critically, as they move every half a minute or so from one website to the next.[127] Certainly, some of the reader reviews on the amazon.co.uk website are lengthy, detailed and devastatingly critical. But of some 480 reader reviews on the website, 83 per cent give a rating of 4 or 5 out of 5 (87 per cent of over 500 reader reviews on amazon. com also give the same rating). Critical and sceptical readers are clearly in the minority.

Some of the many different communities of alternative knowledge that have espoused the theory of Hitler's survival clearly belong to a broadly far-right political milieu and are inspired by a belief that Hitler was not the kind of man to die in an underground bunker in a shabby suicide pact. This desire to rescue him from the ignominy of his real death has lent the bulk of the survivalist presentations a distinctive character that makes them differ markedly from many other conspiracy theories. If one takes for a moment the idea of Hitler's escape from the bunker seriously, it's clear that there must have been a conspiracy of considerable dimensions involving Hitler's entire entourage in the bunker, significant parts of what little remained of the German army, navy and air force, substantial elements in the Argentine Establishment and most likely the FBI and CIA as well – though if there was indeed an elaborate conspiracy to escape from the bunker, then why did so many of those involved, starting with Joseph and Magda Goebbels, who must have been in on the plot, kill themselves rather than trying to avail themselves of the opportunity to escape along with Hitler?

Whoever was involved, the escape would have had to be prepared meticulously with the knowledge of senior figures in the armed forces, and Hitler's lengthy residency in Argentina would have required the absolute and lifelong silence of all those directly involved in sustaining and concealing it, just as his escape from the bunker would have done. Other leading Nazis living in postwar exile in South America, such as Adolf Eichmann or Franz Stangl, were traced, located and apprehended after all. However, none of those who would have been part of the conspiracy either in Germany or in Spain or in Argentina has ever spoken up about what they are supposed to have done. But then the survivalist literature hardly mentions any of those directly involved, let alone printing interviews with them or recollections or conversations of others who were supposedly with them. It is repeatedly claimed in the literature that Hitler and Eva Braun were substituted by doubles in the bunker, yet nobody is even named who might have organized or carried out the deception, let alone traced and interviewed. At most, Martin Bormann, despite the proven fact of his death in Berlin in the final days of the war, is credited, especially in *Grey Wolf*, with organizing Hitler's escape and going with him to South America to live a life of agreeable retirement. The accomplices remain shadowy figures; a few, like the airplane pilot Captain Baumgart, are named, but nothing is said about who recruited them or how: they simply appear. Particularly surprising is the absence of Hitler's closest aides, his adjutants, assistants and secretaries, who must surely have been instrumental in the plot to help him escape, if there was one. This is, in the end, a conspiracy without conspirators.[128]

The reason for this is obvious: Hitler has to retain his charisma; he cannot be seen to be the witting or unwitting tool of an elaborate plot; the escape has to have been his work and his alone. As Donald McKale puts it:

> Almost singlehandedly, Hitler had been responsible for the war. From the Western viewpoint, the war had been a death struggle against the human incarnation of Satan, Good against Evil, Right against Wrong. As his Nazi followers had zealously worshipped him as their godlike Fuehrer, so his enemies had attributed to him demonic and super-human powers. Might not such qualities, so the reasoning went, have ensured his survival?[129]

Despite the occasional gestures of moral disapproval made by some of the survivalists, Hitler emerges from the story as the genius who, by unknown and unfathomable means, engineered his own survival and escape. Abel Basti's Hitler, for example, appears throughout his life to have enjoyed powers far greater than those of normal mortal men. During his years in power, Basti says, 'he welcomed to his bed unknown young women, actresses, sportswomen and other celebrity women'. Unity Mitford bore a child by him; so did Magda Goebbels; and so, too, did the Olympic javelin champion Tilly Fleischer, whose daughter Gisela's supposed memoirs were published in Paris under the title *Adolf Hitler mon père*, although Gisela and her mother both denied publicly in 1966 that she, Gisela, had written the book and asserted that she was most definitely not Hitler's child.[130] The occultist literature endows him with occult powers; UFO enthusiasts depict him in command of technology of staggering sophistication; neo-Nazis attribute to him a breathtaking ability to avoid detection and apprehension. Hitler emerges from this literature as a man who fooled the world into believing he was dead in 1945 and continued to do so for many years after. It is significant that Dunstan and Williams are almost the only advocates of the idea of Hitler's escape from the bunker who do not appear to have political motives or admire the Nazi leader in some way, and their book, and Cooper's, are the only ones that names someone other than Hitler as the organizer of the conspiracy.

Sightings of Hitler belong also to a long-established tradition of sensationalism in the popular press. News-stand tabloids like the *National Enquirer* and the *Police Gazette* thrived on 'scoops' that other newspapers failed, or refused, to publish. Whether or not people actually believe these stories is immaterial; they are published as a form of entertainment in a tradition that goes back not merely to the heyday of the *Police Gazette* in the 1950s, but further, to the yellow press of the 1890s, when Pulitzer and Hearst fought a circulation war through carrying ever more sensational stories in their newspapers; to the 'penny dreadful' stories of blood and gore in the Victorian era; or the products of 'Grub Street' in the eighteenth century; even as far back as the sixteenth century, when the recently invented printing press produced broadsheets telling of extraordinary events. Miracles, ghosts, all aspects of the supernatural and the inexplicable have been the stuff of popular literature and folk tales over the centuries, and the story of Hitler's escape from the bunker can be seen as an updated version of this tradition, kitted out with the footnotes, source references and witness statements that are today's signifiers of veracity. Like the Internet, the mass popular press in the age of the telegraph and telephone transcended linguistic boundaries as news agencies syndicated stories across the globe, and Hitler, a globally recognizable figure, provided fodder for sensationalist reporting all over the world.

In a democratic political culture, the story has taken on for some a political significance that is linked to neo-Nazism and antisemitism because it dovetails with a wider belief that the post-1945 world of 'official' knowledge has suppressed the truth about the war, the

Holocaust, the Nazi Party and its leader. The proponents of the Hitler survival myth are often disempowered figures, eking out a living on or even beyond the margins of the world of journalism, art collecting, politics or academia, looking for a way in. In this sense, they too continue a tradition of heresy and alternative knowledge that has a very long pedigree indeed. The Internet may have allowed this world of subterranean pseudo-information to spread further and faster than it was previously able to do, but in terms of content it does not really represent anything very new. Indeed, it fits rather neatly into a context that is very old – that of the great leader who supposedly cheats death and lives on in secret as an inspiration to his followers, like the ancient British King Arthur, the medieval German Emperor Frederick Barbarossa, or even the French Emperor Napoleon, who has been reportedly sighted recently in a Corsican restaurant.[131]

As Roger Clark concludes, the myth of Hitler's survival has persuaded thousands – even, through its dissemination over a lengthy and well-produced television series, millions – that it is right to dismiss reputable and scholarly historians as liars and deceivers, despite the scorn and derision poured on it by people who really do know what they are talking about. He continues:

Conspiracy theorists pollute the wells of knowledge – exploiting and patronising the poorly educated and intensifying their ignorance. They encourage people to disbelieve works of scholarship and drag down the reputations of legitimate historians ... If we damage the credibility of properly researched books and films then we substitute myths for reality. If serious historians are wrong about Hitler's death – and he really did survive for years after 1945 – then perhaps they're wrong about everything else, including the Holocaust. It's disturbing to see how many Hitler survivalists are also antisemitic and Holocaust deniers. Bogus history does harm. It offends war veterans and millions of victims of the Nazis. To suggest Hitler retired to some hideaway with the connivance of the western allies is insulting. It trivialises and negates the hard-won victory over the Nazis. It depicts Hitler and his henchmen as shrewd and skilful supermen outwitting their enemies. The Fuehrer, we are led to believe, was never defeated.[132]

In some versions, conspiracy theories, even those alleging Hitler's survival beyond 1945, may appear relatively harmless. Certainly, not all of them are motivated by malign political purposes. But all of them have in common a radical yet in some ways naïve scepticism that casts doubt not only on the truth of the conclusions reached by painstaking and objective historical research, but on the very idea of truth itself. And once this is discredited, the possibility of organizing society on rational lines and on the basis of reasoned and informed decisions is thrown into question.

Conclusion

Conspiracy theories have existed since time immemorial, but only in the last few centuries, and above all since the Enlightenment and the French Revolution, have they taken on the features with which we have become all too familiar in recent years, as they have spread relentlessly across the news media, and then the Internet, and the fictional worlds of television series and Hollywood movies. They are in many ways the product of modern science and scholarship, appearing to share their most common structures and modes of argument while at the same time radically challenging them. They present to their consumers a world of black and white, of individual heroes, usually outsiders, who strive against overwhelming odds to uncover the truth, and of collective villains, usually in positions of power, who do everything to conceal it. Against the moral ambiguities of real life, they paint a picture of moral absolutes, of good and evil, a picture that is both easier to understand and, because of this, more interesting and exciting to portray than the grey complexity of documented reality. The reader, television viewer or movie-goer can gain satisfaction from identifying with the intrepid hero as he, or less commonly she, penetrates the veil of secrecy drawn by officialdom to unmask the plotters and conspirators who are manipulating events to their own advantage.[1]

For the compilers and consumers of *The Protocols of the Elders of Zion*, an underlying truth is revealed about the evil force behind the tragedies and disasters of world history: the Jews. For the proponents of the stab-in-the-back myth, the heroic German troops fighting valiantly on the Western Front are betrayed by socialist revolutionaries at home, whose secret treachery is at last unmasked. For the conspiracy theorists of the Reichstag Fire, the Nazi perpetrators are finally

brought to book after decades in which their supporters have successfully persuaded historians that they were not responsible for the
burning down of the German legislature, with all that followed. For
the proponents of the idea that Rudolf Hess was carrying an offer to
the British that could have ended history's most destructive war, the
machinations of the Establishment, led by Churchill, are at last
exposed. For most of the exponents of the theory that Hitler escaped
the Berlin bunker, to live and eventually die peacefully in Argentina,
the Nazi leader's reputation as a genius, sullied by the Allied claim
that he died a miserable death by suicide as the Red Army was closing
in, is triumphantly restored.

Common to many conspiracy theories is a counterfactual suggestion amounting in the minds of at least some of those who purvey
them to a degree of wishful thinking: *if only* the Jews had not been
conspiring behind the scenes, then, according to conservative antisemites, the modern evils of liberalism, equality, free-thinking and
secularization would not be with us; *if only* the German army had
not been stabbed in the back, according to German nationalists, it
would have won the First World War, or at the very least forced the
Allies to agree to reasonable peace terms; *if only* the Reichstag had
not been burned down by the Nazis, according to the Communists
and their left-wing successors, then Weimar democracy would have
survived and the Holocaust would not have happened; *if only* Hess's
peace mission had succeeded, according to British nationalists, nostalgic imperialists and retrospective Appeasers, then the Second
World War would have been brought to an end, millions of lives
saved, the British Empire preserved, and, again, the Holocaust
averted; *if only* the world had realized that Hitler had fooled his
enemies and escaped from the bunker, then, according to his admirers,
we would know how great a genius, how brave and heroic he truly
was – or alternatively, for a minority, we would have been able to
bring him to justice for his crimes. Conspiracy theorists' claims to
have discovered unrecognized truths are often accompanied by
claims to have realized unconsidered possibilities.[2]

Conspiracy theories, as Michael Butter has remarked, always start
at the end of an event. They begin by asking the question *cui bono?* –
whom does the event benefit? Whoever benefited must have brought

the event to pass. The French Revolution benefited the Jews, the Free-masons, the Illuminati, so they must have started it; the rise of liberalism in nineteenth-century Europe led to the emancipation of the Jews, so they must have been behind it. In many cases, this way of thinking has opened the floodgates of fantasy and misrepresenta-tion, in the drive to provide apparent empirical backing to unexamined racial, religious or political prejudice; thus the presence in the leader-ship of Communist and socialist movements in the late nineteenth and early twentieth century of some people of Jewish origin is exag-gerated and distorted until these movements are portrayed as wholly Jewish in inspiration, the expression of a global conspiracy to under-mine the traditional order of things. Instead of being forced to engage with ideas such as socialism or communism, antisemites are enabled by conspiracy theories to dismiss them as the produce of the evil machinations of a subversive Jewish plot. Where evidence is lacking, invention steps in: right-wing nationalists in Germany before 1914, for instance, claimed that the leaders of the feminist movement, which they accused of undermining the German family, subverting patri-archy and lowering the birth rate, were all Jewish, although almost none of them actually was.[3] Hard-working peasant farmers in Ger-many, made bankrupt by crises in the economy, whether in the 1870s or the 1920s, that they were unable to comprehend, grasped with relief the claim advanced by antisemitic politicians that the malign manipulations of Jewish bankers in the cities were to blame. In this manner, the puzzling complexities of politics and society are reduced to a simple formula that everyone can understand.

In a similar way, it seemed obvious that the real beneficiaries of Germany's defeat in the First World War were German liberals, demo-crats and socialists, who took over the reins of power in the Revolution of 1918 and led the democratic Weimar Republic that followed it: so they must have been responsible for the defeat themselves. There could be no doubt about who benefited from the Reichstag Fire. Hitler and the Nazis were so obviously the beneficiaries, since it allowed them to take the first, crucial step towards establishing their dictatorship on a quasi-legal basis, that it seemed beyond doubt that they started the fire. Marxist ideology taught Communists to look for hidden truths – to capitalist self-interest behind liberal democratic politics, for instance – and Stalin, as the leader of world Communism, was a conspiracy theorist on the grand scale, so it is not surprising that Stalin can be found behind the claims that the Nazis started the Reichstag Fire, Rudolf Hess flew to England at Hitler's behest to conclude a separate peace, and Hitler survived the bunker, however far these conspiracy theories moved on from their Russian origins. Just as Allied propaganda benefited from its dismissal of Hess as a lunatic, so too the postwar order established by the Allies benefited from its defamation of Hitler as a coward and a loser whose suicide in the bunker was anything but admirable. In cases such as these, the 'real' facts, for so long suppressed, were uncovered by the conspiracists to undermine the credibility of the 'Establishment' and point to a different reading of history that would rehabilitate those like Hess or Hitler, whom the 'official' record has discredited.

Conspiracy theories exhibit a strong obsession with detail, often taking the form of highlighting a tiny piece of evidence and blowing it up out of all proportion, and buttressing their claims with a display of pseudo-scholarship, quasi-academic documentary editions and endless footnotes. When they examine the real evidence, conspiracy theorists do not accept that minor inconsistencies come from mistakes in reporting, or small faults (such as watches and clocks being set to slightly diverging times): such inconsistencies must, in the conspiracy theorist's mind, be deliberate, designed to deceive. A conspiracy theory therefore must be superior to the 'official' version of an event because it reconciles such inconsistencies. If witnesses support the 'official version', it must be because they are lying, either because they are involved in the conspiracy themselves and want to avoid exposure, or – a common theme in conspiracy theories – because they are being blackmailed. In many cases, the witnesses who could tell the truth (as the conspiracists see it) have died or been murdered or, like Martin Bormann or Heinrich Müller, simply disappeared. If the documents supporting the conspiracy theory don't exist, then they must be invented – and falsification is a factor that crops up in one conspiracy theory after another, as we have seen, beginning with *The Protocols of the Elders of Zion*. Or they have mysteriously disappeared, or been deliberately suppressed or destroyed. The theory itself never changes, no matter how much new alleged evidence is added to it. Any new discovery is taken into account only if it supports a conspiratorial explanation of an event. Real evidence that tells against a conspiracy theory is usually ignored or bypassed.[4] If it is not, the conspiracists frequently try to discredit it by alleging underhand motives or self-interest on the part of those who have generated or supplied it.

The current proliferation and, in some cases, revival of conspiracy theories involving Hitler is part of a much wider trend, in which a number of influences have come together increasingly to blur the boundaries between truth and fiction; or rather, perhaps, to present alternative 'truths', each of which claims to correspond to reality and presents its own panoply of quasi-evidential support to back up its claims. Each community of alternative knowledge has its own truth; sometimes, as with the propagators of conspiracy theories about Hitler's survival or the Hess flight or the Reichstag Fire or the stab-in-the-back legend, there are many differing claims within the overall conspiracist paradigm, though the conspiracy theorists seldom argue with each other, preferring instead to concentrate their fire on what they call 'official knowledge' or 'traditionalist' historians. But there cannot be different and opposing true statements about something; there can only be one truth, even if it can sometimes be very hard to ascertain. Among the most alarming features of some conspiracy theories is the apparent belief that whether they are true or not doesn't really matter. Yet it does matter. Working out what really happened in history is difficult: it requires a great deal of hard work, it demands direct examination of the evidence, it presupposes a willingness to change one's mind, it involves the abandonment of one's prejudices and preconceptions in the face of evidence that tells against them. But it can be done, even in an age like our own, where the gatekeepers of opinion formation have been bypassed through the Internet and anyone can put out their views into the public sphere, no matter how bizarre they might be. Social media companies have begun to wake up to the problem, but in the end, the only way to establish what is true and what is false is by painstaking research. The case studies presented in this book are a modest contribution towards that end.

Acknowledgements

This book owes its existence in the first place to the Leverhulme Trust, which generously supported my research with a Programme Grant on *Conspiracy and Democracy*, on which I was the Principal Investigator from 2013 to 2018. I am extremely grateful to the Trustees and their administrative staff, and to the Trust's Director Professor Gordon Marshall, for putting their faith in the project. I owe a debt of gratitude to the research grants administration staff at Cambridge University, and the Centre for Research in the Arts, Humanities and Social Sciences at Cambridge and especially its then Director, Professor Simon Goldhill, for their invaluable help in organizing and running the programme. My co-investigators, Professor David Runciman and Professor John Naughton, and the postdoctoral researchers on the programme, Dr Hugo Drochon, Dr Tanya Filer, Dr Rolf Fredheim, Dr Rachel Hoffman, Dr Hugo Leal, Dr Nayanika Mathur, Dr Andrew McKenzie-McHarg and Dr Alfred Moore, were a source of constant stimulation; I learned a great deal from their contributions to our multidisciplinary Wednesday-morning workshops, which provided repeated moments of great intellectual excitement. I owe a lot to them all and hope they find this contribution to the discussion of interest. The many visiting lecturers and fellows on the project put forward a huge variety of ideas, many of which have found their way into this book. I am deeply indebted to them all, but especially to Michael Hagemeister, Michael Butter and Claus Oberhauser. Hugo Drochon and Andrew McKenzie-McHarg read an earlier draft of the book and made many suggestions for improvement. Roger Cook kindly kept me supplied with information about *Hunting Hitler*. The staff at *The Times* (News UK) archive made the papers of Philip Graves available and helpfully guided me through them. Cambridge University Library, as always, proved a treasure trove of obscure literature on many of the topics covered in this book, and I owe a great deal to the helpfulness of the staff. In the early stages of the project, Wolfson College, Cambridge, provided the space and the facilities for writing. My agent, Andrew Wylie, and the head of his London office, James Pullen, found publishers for this book in a number of countries. My editor at Penguin, Simon Winder, was generous with his encouragement and advice. Sarah Day was a meticulous copy-editor, and Cecilia Mackay helped with the illustrations. Ruth Pietroni oversaw the production process, Pat Rush and Kit Shepherd were sharp-eyed proofreaders, and Marian Aird compiled the Index. Christine Corton kindly read the proofs and spotted errors that had escaped my attention, as well as sustaining me during the writing process and pushing me over the finishing line. I am grateful to them all.

The Bodleian Library (Oxford) supplied a copy of the otherwise unobtainable work of James Murphy. Parts of Chapter 3 originally appeared in the *London Review of Books* Vol. 36, No. 9 (8 May 2014), pp. 3–9, and I am grateful for permission to reproduce them here.

Richard J. Evans
Barkway
Hertfordshire
June 2020

List of Illustrations
and Photographic Credits

1. p.12. *Protokolle der Weisen von Zion: Die größte Fälschung des Jahrhunderts! (The Protocols of the Elders of Zion: The Greatest Falsehood of the Century!)* edited by Johann Baptist Rusch from a manuscript probably written by the prominent Swiss Zionist Saly Brauschweig , published in Switzerland, 1933. *Private collection.*

2. p.46. *Der Dolchstoss (The Stab in the Back)*: front cover of the right-wing German nationalist magazine *Süddeutsche Monatshefte*, published in Munich, April 1924. *akg-images/Alamy.*

3. p.84. Tract published in 1933 by Adolf Ehrt, presenting the Reichstag Fire as the product of a conspiracy to establish the rule of 'Jewish Bolshevism' in Germany. Ehrt ran the office for 'defence against the Marxist-Communist atheist movement' in the press service of the German Evangelical Church. The man in the cloth cap on the right of the illustration is Marinus van der Lubbe, who was arrested at the scene of the fire. *Private collection.*

4. p.120. Debris of Rudolf Hess's Messerschmitt ME-110 at Floors Farm, Eaglesham, East Renfrewshire, Scotland, May 1941. The aircraft crashed after Hess had bailed out. *Hulton Archive/Getty Images.*

5. p.164. Likenesses of Adolf Hitler produced in June 1944 by Eddie Senz, a make-up artist, for the US Office of Strategic Services, to show how Hitler might be disguised in order to escape. *UIP/Getty Images.*

Notes

INTRODUCTION

1. Michael Butter, '*Nichts ist, wie es scheint*'. *Über Verschwörungstheorien* (Frankfurt am Main, 2018), pp. 22–9. See also Michael Barkun, *A Culture of Conspiracy: Apocalyptic Visions in Contemporary America* (Berkeley, CA, 2003).
2. Joseph E. Uscinski, 'Down the Rabbit Hole We Go!' in *idem* (ed.), *Conspiracy Theories and the People Who Believe Them* (New York, 2019), pp. 1–32, at p. 1.
3. Quoted in Luke Daly-Groves, *Hitler's Death: The Case against Conspiracy* (Oxford, 2019), p. 25.
4. Alec Ryrie, *Unbelievers: An Emotional History of Doubt* (London, 2019), p. 203.
5. Barkun, *A Culture of Conspiracy*. Barkun's proposition that, when the two types of conspiracy theory are merged into one, they constitute a third type, the 'super conspiracy theory', seems to me unnecessarily confusing.
6. Linda von Keyserlingk-Rehbein, *Nur eine 'ganz kleine Clique'? Die NS-Ermittlungen über das Netzwerk vom 20. Juli 1944* (Berlin, 2018).
7. For this approach, see David Welch, *The Hitler Conspiracies: Secrets and Lies behind the Rise and Fall of the Nazi Party* (New York, 2013).

1. WERE THE *PROTOCOLS* A 'WARRANT FOR GENOCIDE'?

1. Butter, '*Nichts ist, wie es scheint*'. pp. 164, 166.
2. Norman Cohn, *Warrant for Genocide: The Myth of the Jewish World-Conspiracy and the Protocols of the Elders of Zion* (London, 1967); quote on p. 13. Cohn's pioneering investigation, though overhauled by

more recent research in many respects, remains the classic work on the subject.

3. Alex Grobman, *License to Murder: The Enduring Threat of the Protocols of the Elders of Zion* (New York, 2011).

4. Eva Horn and Michael Hagemeister, 'Ein Stoff für Bestseller', in *idem* (eds.), *Die Fiktion von der jüdischen Weltverschwörung. Zu Text und Kontext der 'Protokolle der Weisen von Zion'* (Göttingen, 2012), p. xviii, Hannah Arendt, *The Origins of Totalitarianism* (London, 2017), p. xix; Robert Wistrich, *A Lethal Obsession. Anti-Semitism from Antiquity to the Global Jihad* (New York, 2010), p. 158.

5. Alexander Stein, *Adolf Hitler – Schüler der 'Weisen von Zion'* (ed. Lynn Ciminski and Martin Schmitt, 2011 [1936]), pp. 32, 289.

6. Walter Laqueur, *Russia and Germany: A Century of Conflict* (London, 1965), p. 103.

7. David Redles, 'The Turning Point: *The Protocols of the Elders of Zion* and the Eschatological War between Aryans and Jews', in Richard Landes and Steven T. Katz (eds.), *The Paranoid Apocalypse: A Hundred-Year Retrospective on* The Protocols of the Elders of Zion (New York, 2012), pp. 112–31, at p. 118.

8. Klaus Fischer, *Nazi Germany: A New History* (London, 1995), p. 168.

9. Jovan Byford, *Conspiracy Theories: A Critical Introduction* (London, 2011), p. 55.

10. Umberto Eco, *The Prague Cemetery* (London, 2012). See also *idem*, 'Eine Fiktion, die zum Albtraum wird. Die Protokolle der Weisen von Zion und ihre Entstehung', *Frankfurter Allgemeine Zeitung*, 2 July 1994, p. B2.

11. Wolfgang Wippermann, *Agenten des Bösen. Die grossen Verschwörungstheorien und was dahinter steckt* (Berlin, 2007), pp. 67–77. See also Wolfram Meyer zu Uptrup, *Kampf gegen die 'jüdische Weltverschwörung'. Propaganda und Antisemitismus der Nationalsozialisten 1919–1945* (Berlin, 2003); Armin Pfahl-Traughber, *Der antisemitisch-antifreimaurerische Verschwörungsmythos in der Weimarer Republik und im NS-Staat* (Vienna, 1993).

12. Svetlana Boym, 'Conspiracy Theories and Literary Ethics: Umberto Eco, Danilo Kiš and *The Protocols of Zion*', *Comparative Literature* 512 (1999), 9 pp. 97–122, at p. 97. See also Esther Webman (ed.), *The Global Impact of the 'Protocols of the Elders of Zion': A Century-Old Myth* (New York, 2011).

13. Stephen Bronner, *A Rumor about the Jews. Reflections on Antisemitism and the* Protocols of the Elders of Zion (New York, 2000), p. 7.

14. Nora Levin, *The Holocaust: The Destruction of European Jewry, 1939–1945* (New York, 1968).

15. Walter Laqueur, *A History of Zionism* (New York, 2003); Michael Hagemeister, 'Die "Protokolle der Weisen von Zion" und der Basler Zionistenkongress von 1897', in Heiko Haumann (ed.), *Der Traum von Israel. Die Ursprünge des modernen Zionismus* (Weinheim, 1998), pp. 250–73.

16. Jeffrey L. Sammons (ed.), *Die Protokolle der Weisen von Zion. Die Grundlage des modernen Antisemitismus – eine Fälschung. Text und Kommentar* (Göttingen, 1998), pp. 27–55.

17. Ibid, pp. 56–113.

18. Ibid, 9th session, paragraph 11, p. 58.

19. Michael Hagemeister, 'Die Protokolle der Weisen von Zion – eine Anti-Utopie oder der Grosse Plan in der Geschichte?' in Helmut Reinalter (ed.), *Verschwörungstheorien. Theorie – Geschichte – Wirkung* (Innsbruck, 2002), pp. 45–57.

20. Bronner, *A Rumor about the Jews*, p. 1, fails to grasp this point when he asserts that the document 'incorporates many of the most vicious myths about the Jews handed down over the centuries'.

21. Ibid, p. 102.

22. Horn and Hagemeister, 'Ein Stoff', pp. vii–xxii, at p. xv.

23. For a point-by-point refutation (a rather quixotic undertaking, in many respects), see Steven Leonard Jacobs and Mark Weitzman, *Dismantling the Big Lie: The Protocols of the Elders of Zion* (Los Angeles, 2003). As Hannah Arendt pointed out in *The Origins of Totalitarianism* (p. 8), what is more important in the end is not to unmask the *Protocols* as a forgery or to dismantle its various claims and pretensions but to explain why they were accepted as essentially true by fascists and antisemites, despite the fact that they had been widely discredited.

24. Pierre-André Taguieff, *Les Protocoles des Sages de Sion* (2 vols., Paris, 1992).

25. Stefan Pennartz, 'Die Protokolle der Weisen von Zion', in Ute Caumanns et al. (eds.), *Wer zog die Drähte? Verschwörungstheorien im Bild* (Düsseldorf, 2012), pp. 23–46, at p. 33.

26. Claus Oberhauser, *Die verschwörungstheoretische Trias: Barruel – Robison – Starck* (Innsbruck, 2013), shows that Barruel obtained his information about the Bavarian Illuminati from the German Freemason Johann August Starck, whose aim was to defend the Freemasons by blaming the Illuminati instead. However, Starck's writings were neither

strictly comparable to those of Barruel and Robison nor nearly as influential (ibid, p. 289).

27. Cohn, *Warrant for Genocide*, pp. 25–36, also for the following. Wolfgang Benz, *Die Protokolle der Weisen von Zion. Die Legende von der
jüdischen Weltverschwöring* (Munich, 2007), is a brief introduction,
now in need of updating in the light of recent research. Cohn's claims
that Barruel and Robison met in London and that the former plagiarized
the latter do not stand up to close scrutiny. See also Michael Hagemeister,
'Der Mythos der "Protokolle der Weisen von Zion"', in Ute Caumanns
and Mathias Niendorf (eds.), *Verschwörungstheorien: Anthropologis-
che Konstanten – historische Varianten* (Osnabrück, 2001), pp. 89–101.

28. Oberhauser, *Die verschwörungstheoretische Trias*, pp. 268–77, presents
archival findings demonstrating that Simonini was a real person, not, as
some have suspected, an invention of Barruel or the French police (for
this view, see Cohn, loc. cit., and Pierre-André Taguieff, *La Judéophobie
des Modernes. Dès Lumières au jihad mondial* (Paris, 2008,), p. 329).
See also Reinhard Markner, 'Giovanni Battista Simonini. Shards from
the Disputed Life of an Italian Anti-Semite', Marina Ciccarini, Nicoletta
Marcialis and Giorgio Ziffer (eds.), *Kesarevo Kesarju. Scritti in onore di
Cesare G. De Michelis,* eds. (Florence 2014).

29. Volker Neuhaus, *Der zeitgeschichtliche Sensationsroman in Deutschland
1855–1878. 'Sir John Retcliffe' und seine Schule* (Berlin, 1980), esp.
pp. 110–18, and Volker Klotz, *Abenteuer-Romane: Sue, Dumas, Ferry,
Retcliffe, May, Verne* (Munich, 1979). An extract from the scene in the
cemetery is reprinted in Sammons (ed.), *Die Protokolle*, pp. 121–7. The
scene provides the title for the imaginative reconstruction of the origins of
the *Protocols* in Eco, *The Prague Cemetery*. There is a further treatment
in Ralf-Peter Märtin, *Wunschpotentiale. Geschichte und Gesellschaft in
Abenteuerromanen von Retcliffe, Armand, May* (Königstein im Taunus,
1983), esp. pp. 21–47.

30. Cohn, *Warrant for Genocide*, pp. 37–45. The document is reprinted by
Cohn on pp. 300–305.

31. Ibid, pp. 46–57. See also Jeffrey Mehlman, '*Protocols of the Elders of
Zion*: Thoughts on the French Connection', in Landes and Katz (eds.),
The Paranoid Apocalypse, pp. 92–9, and Carlo Ginzburg, 'Vergegen-
wärtigung des Feindes. Zur Mehrdeutigkeit historischer Evidenz',
Trajekte 16 (2008), pp. 7–17.

32. The claim, advanced by Cohn and others, that Krushevan distributed
copies of the *Protocols* in Kishinev in order to provoke the pogrom,
appears to originate with the earliest biography of Hitler: Konrad Heiden,

Der Führer: Hitler's Rise to Power (Boston, MA, 1944), p. 11. It does not hold water, however: the pogrom occurred in April 1903, some months *before* the publication of the *Protocols* (see Richard S. Levy, 'Die "Protokolle der Weisen von Zion" und ihre Entlarvung. Ein vergebliches Unterfangen', in Horn and Hagemeister (eds.), *Die Fiktion*, pp. 208–30, at pp. 216–7). Indeed, Krushevan may well have published the *Protocols* in an attempt to provide retrospective justification for the pogrom, which he had been instrumental in provoking: see Steven J. Zipperstein, *Pogrom: Kishinev and the Tilt of History* (New York, 2018), pp. 97–9. The document in any case was ill suited as a means of provoking the illiterate Russian masses to commit acts of violence against Jews. Nor is there any evidence to support the claim that 'The *Protocols* retained its ability to incite the masses during the reign of Hitler' (Bronner, *A Rumor about the Jews*, p. 123).

33. Cesare G. De Michelis, 'Die inexistente Manuskript. Die Geschichte und die Archive', in Horn and Hagemeister (eds.), *Die Fiktion*, pp. 123–39. See also Michael Hagemeister, 'Sergej Nilus und die "Protokolle der Weisen von Zion". Überlegungen zur Forschungslage', *Jahrbuch für Antisemitismusforschung* 5 (1996), pp. 127–47; idem, 'Zur Frühgeschichte', in Horn and Hagemeister (eds.), *Die Fiktion*, pp. 143–50; idem, 'Trilogie der Apokalypse – Vladimir Solov'ev, Serafim von Sarov und Sergej Nilus über das Kommen des Antichrist und das Ende der Weltgeschichte', in Wolfram Brandes and Felicitas Schmieder (eds.), *Antichrist. Konstruktion von Feindbildern* (Berlin, 2010), pp. 255–75; idem, 'Wer war Sergej Nilus? Versuch einer bio-bibliographischen Skizze', *Ostkirchliche Studien* 40 (1991), pp. 49–63; and idem, 'Die "Weisen von Zion" als Agenten des Antichrist', in Bodo Zelinsky (ed.), *Das Böse in der russischen Kultur* (Cologne, 2008), pp. 76–90.

34. Cohn, *Warrant for Genocide*, pp. 73–83. Umberto Eco suggested that Joly in turn adapted the 'Jewish Plan' for the conquest of the world from a 'Jesuit plan' outlined by the pulp-fiction writer Eugène Sue in his *Le Juif errant* (Paris, 1844–5) and *Les Mystères du peuple* (Paris, 1849–57): see Umberto Eco, 'Introduction', in Will Eisner, *The Plot: The Secret Story of the Protocols of the Elders of Zion* (New York, 2005), pp. v–vii (a remarkable graphic novel version of the story). There is a revealing juxtaposition of the Joly text and the *Protocols* on pp. 73–89 of Eisner, *The Plot*.

35. Cesare G. De Michelis, *The Non-Existent Manuscript: A Study of the 'Protocols of the Sages of Zion'* (London, 2004). The widespread supposition that, as Umberto Eco put it, the document was 'produced by

secret services and police of at least three countries', is not supported by the evidence (Umberto Eco, *Six Walks in the Fictional World* (Cambridge, MA, 1994), Chapter 6).

36. See also Michael Hagemeister, '"The Antichrist as an Imminent Political Possibility": Sergei Nilus and the Apocalyptical Reading of *The Protocols of the Elders of Zion*', in Landes and Katz (eds.), *The Paranoid Apocalypse*, pp. 79–91. The Russian secret police does not, however, seem to have been officially involved, and its oft-alleged part in the wave of pogroms that swept across Russia in the early twentieth century has been persuasively doubted: see for example Hans Rogger, *Jewish Policies and Right-Wing Politics in Imperial Russia* (London, 1986).

37. Zipperstein, *Pogrom*, pp. 146–50, 167–71. The story that Tsar Nicholas II enthusiastically embraced the *Protocols*, only to reject their use as a 'dirty method' in the struggle against Jewish subversion when he was told by his Prime Minister Stolypin that they were a forgery (Cohn, *Warrant for Genocide*, pp. 118–26), has been discredited as a subsequent invention (Hagemeister, 'Zur Frühgeschichte', pp. 153–6).

38. Cohn, *Warrant for Genocide*, pp. 138–47. For pogroms and antisemitic actions during the Russian Revolution and Civil War, and in particular the Bolsheviks' attempts to combat them, see Brendan McGeever, *Antisemitism and the Russian Revolution* (Cambridge, 2019). More generally, see Michael Kellogg, *The Russian Roots of Nazism: White Émigrés and the Making of National Socialism, 1917–1945* (Cambridge, 2005).

39. Cohn, *Warrant for Genocide*, pp. 148–55.

40. Volker Ullrich, *Hitler: Ascent 1889–1939* (London, 2016), p. 103. For the ex-Kaiser's rabid antisemitism, in which the *Protocols* played a role, though not the main one, see John C. G. Röhl, *Wilhelm II. Der Weg in den Abgrund, 1900–1941* (Munich, 2008), pp. 1,291–7.

41. Gottfried zur Beek, *Die Geheimnisse der Weisen von Zion* (Berlin-Charlottenburg, 1923), p. 17. See also (anon.), *Der jüdische Kriegsplan zur Aufrichtung der Judenweltherrschaft im Jahre des Heils 1925. Nach den Richtlinien der Weisen von Zion* (Lorch, Württemberg, 1925), for another example, largely consisting of quotes from the *Protocols* linked to recent and contemporary events.

42. Erich Ludendorff, *Kriegführung und Politik* (Berlin, 1922), p. 322.

43. Cohn, *Warrant for Genocide*, pp. 157–63, citing Karl Brammer, *Das politische Ergebnis des Rathenau-Prozesses* (Berlin, 1922), which includes the stenographic reports of the trial proceedings; see also Heinrich

Hannover and Elisabeth Hannover-Druck, *Politische Justiz 1918–1933* (Frankfurt am Main, 1966), pp. 212–24.

44. Cohn, *Warrant for Genocide*, pp. 187–99; George L. Mosse, *The Crisis of German Ideology: Intellectual Origins of the Third Reich* (London, 1966), p. 142.

45. Richard J. Evans, *The Coming of the Third Reich* (London, 2003), Chapter 1.

46. Peter Longerich, *Hitler: Biographie* (Munich, 2015), pp. 62–72.

47. Eberhard Jäckel (ed.), *Hitler. Sämtliche Aufzeichnungen 1905–1924* (Stuttgart, 1980), pp. 458–9.

48. Timothy W. Ryback, *Hitler's Private Library: The Books that Shaped his Life* (London, 2009), pp. 70–71; Christian Hartmann *et al.* (eds.), *Hitler, Mein Kampf. Eine kritische Edition* (2 vols., Munich, 2016), Vol. I, p. 226, n. 219. Ford withdrew his antisemitic claims when threatened with a libel suit by a Jewish journalist, Herman Bernstein: see Eisner, *The Plot*, pp. 104–5; Herman Bernstein, *The History of a Lie: The Protocols of the Wise Men of Zion* (New York, 1921); and Victoria Saker Woeste, *Henry Ford's War on Jews and the Legal Battle against Hate Speech* (Stanford, CA, 2012), pp. 114–18. Bernstein returned to his critique in *The Truth about 'The Protocols of Zion': A Complete Exposure* (New York, 1935, reprinted with an introduction by Norman Cohn, New York, 1971).

49. Elke Fröhlich (ed.), *Die Tagebücher von Joseph Goebbels* (Munich, 2004), Part I, Vol. 1/I, p. 120 (8 April 1924).

50. Ernst Boepple (ed.), *Adolf Hitlers Reden* (Munich, 1934), p. 71.

51. Michael Hagemeister, 'The Protocols of the Elders of Zion: A Forgery?', in Gabriella Catalano, Marina Ciccarini and Nicoletta Marcialis (eds.), *La verità del falso. Studi in onore di Cesare G. De Michelis* (Rome, 2015), pp. 163–72, argues that it is not a forgery because 'we call an object a forgery when its origin is different from what we are led to believe', and we do not know what the origin of the *Protocols* is. But the document clearly is a forgery, since it was a document intended to deceive and falsely claiming to be genuine.

52. Times Newspapers Ltd Archive [TNL Archive], News UK and Ireland Ltd: Subject Boxes: *Protocols of the Elders of Zion* – Correspondence 12/7/21–2/2/22: Graves to Wickham Steed, 13 July 1921.

53. TNL Archive: Subject Boxes: *Protocols of the Elders of Zion* – Correspondence 12/7/21–2/2/22: Raslovlev to Graves, 12 and 13 July 1921; Graves to Steed, 13 July 1921; Memorandum of Agreement, made

this 2nd day of August 1921; TNL Archive: Subject Boxes: *Protocols of the Elders of Zion* – Correspondence 24/1/1924–13/9/45: V. Barker to Lintz Smith, 24 January 1924; Raslovlev to *The Times*, Paris, 4 February 1927; TNL Archive: Basil Long Papers, TT/FE/BKL/1: Correspondence between Basil Long and Philip Graves: Graves to Long, 15 August 1921. The story of Graves's discovery was first told on the basis of this archival material by Colin Holmes, 'New Light on the "Protocols of Zion"', *Patterns of Prejudice*, 11/6 (1977), pp. 13–21, and *idem*, 'The *Protocols* of the Britons', *Patterns of Prejudice*, 12/6 (1978), pp. 13–18; see also Gisela Lebeltzer, 'The *Protocols* in England', *Wiener Library Bulletin*, 47–8 (1978), pp. 111–17.

54. Eisner, *The Plot*, pp. 67–91, reproducing extracts from the articles; see also Keith M. Wilson, 'The *Protocols of Zion* and the *Morning Post*, 1919–1920', *Patterns of Prejudice* 19/2 (1985), pp. 5–15; and *idem*, 'Hail and Farewell? The Reception in the British Press of the First Publication in English of the *Protocols of Zion*, 1920–1922', *Immigrants and Minorities* 11/2 (1992), pp. 171–86. A widely used English translation was produced by Victor Marsden, Russian correspondent of the London *Morning Post*; it is reproduced in full in Lucien Wolf, *The Myth of the Jewish Menace in World Affairs, or The Truth about the Forged Protocols of the Elders of Zion* (London, 1920), pp. 71–140. The first English translation to appear was by George Shanks, another employee of the *Morning Post*. Shanks had grown up in Russia, where his father was a businessman forced to leave by the Bolshevik Revolution. He called his version *The Jewish Peril: Protocols of the Learned Elders of Zion* (London, 1920). The second edition was published by an extreme right-wing organization, The Britons, as was the first edition of Marsden's work: see Sharman Kadish, *Bolsheviks and British Jews: The Anglo-Jewish Community, Britain, and the Russian Revolution* (London, 1992), and Robert Singerman, 'The American Career of the "Protocols of the Elders of Zion"', *American Jewish History* 71 (1981), pp. 48–78.

55. Philipp Theisohn, 'Die "Protokolle der Weisen von Zion" oder Das Plagiat im Denkraum des Faschismus', in Horn and Hagemeister (eds.), *Die Fiktion*, pp. 190–207, at p. 192.

56. Wolf, *The Myth*.

57. Bernstein, *The History of a Lie*.

58. TNL Archive: Subject Boxes: *Protocols of the Elders of Zion* – Correspondence 12/7/21–2/2/22: Graves to Foreign Editor, *The Times*, 25 July 1921, 1 August 1921; Foreign Department note, 9 August 1921; *The Times* telegram to Graves, 18 August 1921; reprint order 22 August

1921; Foreign Department to Graves, 31 August 1921; B. Barker to Foreign Editor, 1 October 1921; Philip Graves, *The Truth about the Protocols: A Literary Forgery. From The Times of August 16, 17, and 18 1921* (London, 1921).

59. Binjamin Segel, *Die Protokolle der Weisen von Zion kritisch beleuchtet. Eine Erledigung* (Berlin, 1924); and *idem, A Lie and a Libel: The History of the* Protocols of the Elders of Zion (1926, ed. and transl. Richard S. Levy, Lincoln, NE, 1995).

60. Cohn, *Warrant for Genocide*, pp. 200–201, citing Hitler, *Mein Kampf*, Vol. I, p. 325. See also Randall L. Bytwerk, 'Believing in "Inner Truth": The *Protocols of the Elders of Zion* in Nazi Propaganda, 1933–1945', *Holocaust and Genocide Studies* 29/2 (2015), pp. 212–29, at p. 213. For the original, with commentary, see Hartmann *et al.* (eds.), *Hitler, Mein Kampf*, Vol. I, pp. 799–803. Cohn goes on to cite further alleged statements by Hitler in Hermann Rauschning's book *Hitler Speaks* (London, 1939), but this is an unreliable source, since Rauschning's claim to have spoken with Hitler on innumerable occasions is demonstrably false: see Wolfgang Hänel, *Hermann Rauschnings 'Gespräche mit Hitler'. Eine Geschichtsfälschung* (Ingolstadt, 1984).

61. Goebbels diaries, 10 April 1924, quoted and translated in Bytwerk, 'Believing', p. 213.

62. Alfred Rosenberg, *Die Protokolle der Weisen von Zion und die jüdische Weltpolitik* (Munich, 1923), p. 147, and new edition, 1933, cited in Cohn, pp. 215–18. See also Ernst Piper, *Alfred Rosenberg. Hitlers Chefideologe* (Munich, 2005), pp. 69–75.

63. Cohn, *Warrant for Genocide*, pp. 218–24, citing *Völkischer Beobachter*, 31 March 1933; Bytwerk, 'Believing', for further details.

64. *Jewish Telegraphic Agency*, 16 July 1934 (online).

65. TNL Archive: Subject Boxes: Protocols of the Elders of Zion – Correspondence 24.1.24–13/9/45: Graves to Editor, *The Times*, 28 February 1934; Urs Lüthi, *Der Mythos von der Weltverschwörung. Die Hetze der Schweizer Frontisten gegen Juden und Freimaurer, am Beispiel des Berner Prozesses um die 'Protokolle der Weisen von Zion'* (Basel, 1992), pp. 65–7.

66. Ibid, pp. 81–5; and Catherine Nicault, 'Le Procès des Protocoles des Sages de Sion. Une tentative de riposte juive à l'antisémitisme dans les années 1930', *Vingtième siècle. Revue historique* 55 (1979), pp. 68–84. For the Bern trials, see Michael Hagemeister, '*The Protocols of the Elders of Zion* in Court: The Bern Trials, 1933–1937', in Webman (ed.), *The Global Impact,* pp. 241–3. A comprehensive collection of docu-

ments relating to the trial has been published by Michael Hagemeister, *Die 'Protokolle der Weisen von Zion' vor Gericht. Der Berner Prozess 1933–1937 und die 'Antisemitische Internationale'* (Veröffentlichungen des Archivs für Zeitgeschichte des Instituts für Geschichte der ETH Zürich, Vol. 10, Zürich, 2017). For legal aspects, see Sibylle Hofer, *Richter zwischen den Fronten. Die Urteile des Berner Prozesses um die 'Protokolle der Weisen von Zion', 1933–1937* (Basel, 2011). More recently, the story of the trial has been recounted by the Israeli judge Hadassa Ben-Itto, *The Lie that Wouldn't Die: The Protocols of the Elders of Zion* (Edgware, 2005), which is partly based on the relevant documents, including those in the TNL Archive; but the book includes so many fictitious elements (such as the imagined thoughts of the participants) that one reviewer thought it would have been better served if the author had presented it as an historical novel: see Hagemeister, *Die 'Protokolle der Weisen von Zion' vor Gericht*, p. 19; and Michael Brenner, 'Verleumdungen vom Fliessband', *Frankfurter Allgemeine Zeitung*, 17 February 1999, p. 52. Among many other distortions, for example, Ben-Itto (p. 97) presents Raslovlev's letters to Graves of 12–13 July 1921 as a conversation between the two men in an Istanbul club, inventing a good deal of it (' "Walls have ears," he whispered. Throughout lunch he cast nervous looks in all directions,' etc.).

67. TNL Archive: Subject Boxes: *Protocols of the Elders of Zion –* Correspondence 24/1/1924–13/9/45: Graves to Dawson, 18 February 1939.

68. Ibid: 14 September 1939 Memorandum from the Assistant Manager, 14 September 1939. See also Gordon Martel (ed.), *The Times and Appeasement: The Journals of A. L. Kennedy, 1932–1939* (Camden Fifth Series, Vol. 16, Royal Historical Society, Cambridge, 2000).

69. Bytwerk, 'Believing', also for these quotations.

70. *Der Parteitag der Arbeit vom 6. bis 13. September 1937. Offizieller Bericht über den Verlauf des Reichsparteitages mit sämtlichen Kongressreden* (Munich, 1938), p. 15.

71. Jeremy Noakes and Geoffrey Pridham (eds.), *Nazism 1919–1945* (Exeter, 2001), Vol. 3, p. 441.

72. Max Weinreich, *Hitler's Professors: The Part of Scholarship in Germany's Crimes against the Jewish People* (New York, 1946), pp. 144–5.

73. Quoted in Peter Longerich, *Goebbels: A Biography* (London, 2015), p. 585.

74. Cohn, *Warrant for Genocide*, p. 230, quoting *Politischer Dienst (Arbeitsmaterial für Presse und Publizistik)*, p. 370. *Morning Post*

correspondent Victor Marsden identified the Elders of Zion as 'the three hundred' in the introduction to his 1920 edition of the *Protocols*, reprinted in 1931 (Victor E. Marsden, *Protocols of the Meetings of the Learned Elders of Zion* (London, 1931), p. 7.

75. Meyer zu Uptrup, *Kampf gegen die 'jüdische Weltverschwörung'*, makes this assumption throughout (pp. 91–131, 150–62); also Pfahl-Traughber, *Der antisemitisch-antifreimaurerische Verschwörungsmythos*, p. 110 and elsewhere. See more generally Bytwerk, 'Believing'.

76. Pfahl-Traughber, *passim*. The fantasy of the secret international Jewish conspiracy to gain economic and political power can be found for example in *The Local and Universal Jewish Brotherhoods* by Jacob Brafman (1825–79, a Jewish convert to Orthodoxy), published in 1868 (discussed in Webman (ed.), *The Global Impact*), and *The Conquest of the World by the Jews* (Basel, 1878) by Osman Bey (James Milligan, a Christian convert to Islam and officer in the Ottoman army). A common target of such conspiratorial fantasies was the Alliance Israélite Universelle, founded in Paris in 1860 with the aim of protecting Jews from persecution across the world. For visual representations, see Pennartz, 'Die Protokolle', and Olga Hartmann et al., 'Jüdischer Bolschewismus', both in Caumanns *et al.* (eds.), *Wer zog die Drähte?*, pp. 23–46 and 47–76.

77. Quoted in Raul Hilberg, *The Destruction of the European Jews* (London, 1985), p. 294.

78. Cohn, *Warrant for Genocide*, p. 284.

79. Daniel Pipes, *Conspiracy: How the Paranoid Style Flourishes and Where it Comes From* (New York, 1997), p. 85.

80. Butter, *'Nichts ist, wie es scheint'*, p. 165; Hagemeister, 'The Protocols of the Elders of Zion: A Forgery?', p. 164.

81. Oberhauser, *Die verschwörungstheoretische Trias*, pp. 279–80.

82. John Gwyer, *Portraits of Mean Men: A Short History of the Protocols of the Elders of Zion* (London, 1938), pp. 9–10.

83. Ibid, pp. 11–12.

84. Ibid, pp. 13–15.

85. Ibid, p. 129.

86. Cited in Weinreich, *Hitler's Professors*, p. 24 (from Alfred Bäumler, *Alfred Rosenberg und der Mythus des 20. Jahrhunderts* (Munich, 1943), p. 19). The exposure as a forgery of another, similar document, 'The Manifesto of Adolphe Crémieux' (Crémieux was a major figure in the Alliance Israelite Universelle), prompted the statement by its editor: 'This has been pronounced a forgery, and something much less committed – especially written for Gentile consumption [i.e. the genu-

ine document] – has been proclaimed as the "real" thing. The unfortunate part of the business is that the "forgery" corresponds infinitely more closely with the *facts* of history than that which is claimed to be genuine!' (*4 Protocols of Zion (not the Protocols of Nilus)* (London, 1921), p. 4.)

87. Horn and Hagemeister, 'Ein Stoff', p. xi.
88. Byford, *Conspiracy Theories*, p. 55.
89. Nesta Webster, *Secret Societies and Subversive Movements* (London, 1924), pp. 408–9.
90. Boym, 'Conspiracy Theories', p. 99.
91. Brian Bennett, 'Hermetic Histories: Divine Providence and Conspiracy Theories', *Numen* 54 (2007), pp. 174–209.
92. Butter, *'Nichts ist, wie es scheint'*, pp. 160–69, though it is doubtful whether this effect was intended by the compilers of the *Protocols*, as Butter claims, otherwise they would have incorporated explicitly contemporary references themselves.
93. Eva Horn, 'Das Gespenst der Arkana. Verschwörungsfiktion und Textstruktur der "Protokolle der Weisen von Zion"', in Horn and Hagemeister (eds.), *Die Fiktion*, pp. 1–25; Butter, *'Nichts ist, wie es scheint'*, pp. 164–5.
94. Sammons (ed.), *Die Protokolle, passim*.
95. Quoted in Johann Chapoutot, *The Law of Blood: Thinking and Acting as a Nazi* (Cambridge, MA, 2018), p. 179.
96. Elke Fröhlich (ed.), *Die Tagebücher von Joseph Goebbels*, Part II, Vol. 8 (Munich, 1993), p. 287. Goebbels had previously considered using the *Protocols* in propaganda, particularly against France shortly after the outbreak of war in 1939 (ibid, pp. 180 (3 November 1939), 181 (4 November 1939)). He also mentioned the *Protocols* briefly in a speech a few weeks later (Helmut Heiber (ed.), *Goebbels-Reden 1932–1945* (Düsseldorf, 1971), Vol. II, pp. 234–5). This passage is usually heavily redacted when quoted by students of the *Protocols* (for instance, Eisner, *The Plot*, p. 110). Walter Laqueur thought that 'Hitler was shrewd enough to realize the enormous propagandist potential of the basic ideas of the *Protocols*,' but did not provide any evidence for this assertion (Laqueur, *Russia and Germany*, p. 103). See also Bytwerk, 'Believing', p. 213.
97. Ibid. Parts of this passage have been quoted by other writers on the Nazi understanding of the *Protocols*, but without the final sentences (e.g. Pfahl-Traughber, *Der antisemitisch-antifreimaurerische Verschwörungsmythos*, p. 109).
98. Butter, *'Nichts ist, wie es scheint'*, p. 165, though it is questionable whether, as Butter asserts, the vagueness of the document was a deliberate

ploy by its compilers to gain as wide a reception as possible, given the haste and lack of forethought with which it was put together.

99. Ibid, p. 166.

100. This is the procedure used by Alexander Stein, in his book *Adolf Hitler – Schüler der 'Weisen von Zion'*, pp. 56–134.

2. WAS THE GERMAN ARMY 'STABBED IN THE BACK' IN 1918?

1. Ulrich Heinemann, *Die verdrängte Niederlage. Politische Öffentlichkeit und Kriegsschuldfrage in der Weimarer Republik* (Göttingen, 1983); Boris Barth, *Dolchstosslegenden und politische Desintegration. Das Trauma der deutschen Niederlage im Ersten Weltkrieg 1914–1933* (Düsseldorf, 2003), p. 3.

2. Richard Bessel, *Germany after the First World War* (Oxford, 1993), esp. Chapter 9.

3. The literature on these events is too vast to cite here. For a sober and judicious analysis, see David Stevenson, *With Our Backs to the Wall: Victory and Defeat in 1918* (London, 2011); for Germany, see Alexander Watson, *Ring of Steel: Germany and Austria-Hungary in World War I: The People's War* (London, 2014). For the peace negotiations and the treaties, see Margaret MacMillan, *Peacemakers: The Paris Peace Conference of 1919 and Its Attempt to End War* (London, 2001), and Jörn Leonhard, *Der überforderte Frieden. Versailles und die Welt, 1918–1923* (Munich, 2018).

4. David Welch, *Germany: Propaganda and Total War 1914–1918* (London, 2000); Dirk Stegmann, 'Die deutsche Inlandspropaganda 1917/18. Zum innenpolitischen Machtkampf zwischen OHL und ziviler Reichsleitung in der Endphase des Kaiserreiches', *Militärgeschichtliche Mitteilungen* 2 (1972), pp. 785–816; Christian Lüdtke, *Hans Delbrück und Weimar. Für eine konservative Republik – gegen Kriegsschuldlüge und Dolchstosslegende* (Göttingen, 2018), pp. 317–18; Rainer Sammet, *'Dolchstoss'. Deutschland und die Auseinandersetzung mit der Niederlage im Ersten Weltkrieg (1918–1933)* (Berlin, 2001), pp. 21–49, with numerous examples of newspapers and civilian politicians as well as leading military figures who believed in the certainty of a German victory well into the second half of 1918.

5. Wilhelm Deist, 'The Military Collapse of the German Empire: The Reality behind the Stab-in-the-Back Myth', *War in History* 5/2, (1996), pp. 186–223, at pp. 188–90, translated by Edgar Feuchtwanger from

Wilhelm Deist, 'Der militärische Zusammenbruch des Kaiserreichs. Zur Realität der "Dolchstosslegende"', in Ursula Büttner (ed.), *Das Unrechtsregime. Internationale Forschung über den Nationalsozialismus. Festschrift für Werner Jochmann zum 65. Geburtstag* (2 vols., Hamburg, 1986), Vol. 1: *Ideologie – Herrschaftssystem – Wirkung in Europa*, pp. 101–29.

6. See especially Stevenson, *With Our Backs to the Wall*, for the course of events.

7. Ibid, and Sammet, '*Dolchstoss*', pp. 31–41.

8. Deist, 'The Military Collapse', pp. 191–200.

9. Hartmann *et al.* (eds.) *Hitler, Mein Kampf*, Vol. I, p. 545; Deist, 'The Military Collapse', pp. 201-4.

10. Joachim Petzold, *Die Dolchstosslegende. Eine Geschichtsfälschung im Dienst des deutschen Imperialismus und Militarismus* (East Berlin, 1963), p. 33, with discussion of the source for this statement, the diaries of the staff officer Albrecht von Thaer, in note 19. Petzold concluded that although Thaer later edited his diaries before publication, his report of Ludendorff's statement is likely to have been accurate, since he would not have introduced damaging material such as this retrospectively, given its politically explosive implications.

11. Petzold, *Die Dolchstosslegende*, p. 33.

12. Sammet, '*Dolchstoss*', pp. 25–31, 50–66.

13. Alan Kramer, 'The Poisonous Myth: Democratic Germany's "Stab in the Back" Legend', *Irish Times*, 1 January 2019.

14. Richard J. Crampton, *Bulgaria* (Oxford, 2007), pp. 210–19.

15. *Amtliche Urkunden zur Vorgeschichte des Waffenstillstandes 1918. Auf Grund der Akten der Reichskanzlei, des Auswärtigen Amtes und des Reichsarchiv herausgegeben vom Auswärtigen Amt und vom Reichsministerium des Innern* (2nd edn, Berlin, 1924), Document number 9a, p. 31 (my translation).

16. *Papers Relating to the Foreign Relations of the United States, 1918: Supplement I: The World War* (Publications of the Department of State, Washington DC, 1933), Vol. I, p. 338.

17. *Amtliche Urkunden*, Document number 83, p. 205 (my translation).

18. Kramer, 'The Poisonous Myth'; see also Alexander Watson, 'Stabbed at the Front', in *History Today* 58/11 (2008).

19. Wilhelm Deist (ed.), *Militär und Innenpolitik im Weltkrieg 1914–1918* (Quellen zur Geschichte des Parlamentarismus und der politischen Parteien, Zweite Reihe: Militär und Politik, Vol. 1, Düsseldorf, 1970).

20. The classic work on the subject is Fritz Fischer, *Germany's Aims in the First World War* (London, 1967).

21. Friedrich Freiherr Hiller von Gaertringen, ' "Dolchstoss-Diskussion" und "Dolchstosslegende" im Wandel von vier Jahrzenhten', in *idem* and Waldemar Besson (eds.), *Geschichte und Gegenwartsbewusstsein. Historische Betrachtungen und Untersuchungen, Festschrift für Hans Rothfels zum 70. Geburtstag dargebracht von Kollegen, Freunden und Schülern* (Göttingen, 1963), pp. 122–60, at pp. 124–5.

22. Barth, *Dolchstosslegenden*, pp. 11–380, *passim*.

23. Ludendorff, *Kriegführung und Politik*, p. 298.

24. Barth, *Dolchstosslegenden*, pp. 324–41.

25. Explicitly referred to by the far-right politician Albrecht von Graefe in a debate in the National Assembly on 29 October 1919: see Hiller von Gaertringen, ' "Dolchstoss-Diskussion" ', pp. 137–8, and Barth, *Dolchstosslegenden*, p. 325.

26. Quoted in Deist, 'Der miltärische Zusammenbruch', p. 121.

27. Barth, *Dolchstosslegenden*, pp. 324–341.

28. Petzold, *Die Dolchstosslegende*, pp. 35–41; Ernst Müller-Meiningen, *Aus Bayerns schwersten Tagen. Erinnerungen und Betrachtungen aus der Revolutionszeit* (Berlin, 1923), pp. 27–8; Hiller von Gaertringen, ' "Dolchstoss-Diskussion" ', p. 131.

29. Petzold, *Die Dolchstosslegende*, p. 43.

30. Ibid, pp. 125–30, 134–6, with further examples. Beck later joined the resistance movement, whose failure to overthrow Hitler on 20 July 1944 caused him to attempt suicide, unsuccessfully, before he was shot.

31. Ibid, p. 129.

32. *The Times*, 17 November 1919, p. 12, cited in George S. Vascik and Mark R. Sadler, *The Stab-in-the-Back Myth and the Fall of the Weimar Republic: A History in Documents and Visual Sources* (London, 2016), p. 120, doc. 8.9; Petzold, *Die Dolchstosslegende*, pp. 43–46.

33. John W. Wheeler-Bennett, *Hindenburg: The Wooden Titan* (London, 1939), p. 244; Anna von der Goltz, *Hindenburg: Power, Myth, and the Rise of the Nazis* (Oxford, 2009), pp. 67–9.

34. Quoted in Jesko von Hoegen, *Der Held von Tannenberg. Genese und Funktion des Hindenburg-Mythos* (Cologne, 2007), p. 250.

35. Hiller von Gaertringen, 'Dolchstoss-Diskussion', pp. 137–8.

36. Reported in *Deutsche Tageszeitung*, 18 December 1918, p. 1, translated and printed in Vascik and Sadler, *The Stab-in-the-Back Myth*, pp. 96–7.

37. Frederick Maurice, *The Last Four Months: The End of the War in the West* (London, 1919), pp. 216–32, excerpted in Vascik and Sadler, *The Stab-in-the-Back Myth*, pp. 100–102. See also Sammet, 'Dolchstoss', pp. 86–93, and Petzold, *Die Dolchstosslegende*, pp. 25–8, pointing out the repetition of the claims about Maurice or Malcolm in older standard works such as Walter Görlitz, *Der deutsche Generalstab* (Frankfurt am Main, 1953) and Karl Dietrich Erdmann, *Die Zeit der Weltkriege* (*Handbuch der deutschen Geschichte*, Vol. 4, Stuttgart, 1959), p. 115.

38. Erich Kuttner, *Der Sieg war zum greifen Nahe!* (Berlin, 1921), pp. 5–6, excerpted and translated in Vascik and Sadler, *The Stab-in-the-Back Myth*, p. 103, doc. 7.5. See also Barth, *Dolchstosslegenden*, pp. 324–41.

39. D. J. Goodspeed, *Ludendorff: Genius of World War I* (Boston, MA, 1966), pp. 279–80, excerpted in Vascik and Sadler, *The Stab-in-the-Back Myth*, pp. 105–6 (doc. 7.8).

40. See the comprehensive demolition of Ludendorff's testimony in Hiller von Gaertringen, ' "Dolchstoss-Diskussion" ', pp. 127–8, n. 20.

41. *Die Ursachen des deutschen Zusammenbruchs im Jahre 1918* (Berlin, 1928), Vol. 4, pp. 3, 33–5, 78–80, excerpted and translated in Vascik and Sadler, *The Stab-in-the-Back Myth*, pp. 104–5 (docs. 7.6, 7.8).

42. Petzold, *Die Dolchstosslegende*, pp. 53–5.

43. Generalfeldmarschall [Paul] von Hindenburg, *Aus meinem Leben* (3rd edn, Leipzig, 1920), p. 403. The memoirs were written by a team: see Andreas Dorpalen, *Hindenburg and the Weimar Republic* (Princeton, PA, 1964), pp. 44–5; Hoegen, *Der Held von Tannenberg*, pp. 251–9; Wolfram Pyta, *Hindenburg. Herrschaft zwischen Hohenzollern und Hitler* (Berlin, 2007), pp. 405–9; Goltz, *Hindenburg*, pp. 67–9.

44. Gerd Krumeich, *Die unbewältigte Niederlage. Das Trauma des Ersten Weltkriegs und die Weimarer Republik* (Freiburg in Breisgau, 2018), pp. 189–91.

45. Petzold, *Die Dolchstosslegende*, p. 59.

46. Max Bauer, *Konnten wir den Krieg vermeiden, gewinnen, abbrechen? Drei Fragen* (Berlin, 1919), p. 62, cited in Tim Grady, *A Deadly Legacy: German Jews and the Great War* (London, 2017), p. 209. See also Petzold, *Die Dolchstosslegende*, pp. 51–3. For Bauer's attack on feminism, see Richard J. Evans, *The Feminist Movement in Germany 1894–1933* (London, 1976), pp. 183–4.

47. *Die Ursachen* Vol. 3, pp. 213–15; translation in Ralph H. Lutz (ed.), *The Causes of the German Collapse in 1918: Sections of the Officially Authorized Report of the Commission of the German Constituent*

Assembly and of the German Reichstag, 1919–1928 (Palo Alto, CA, 1934), pp. 86–8; printed in Vascik and Sadler, *The Stab-in-the-Back Myth*, pp. 63–76.

48. Ludendorff, *Kriegführung und Politik*, pp. 300–303, 314.
49. Barth, *Dolchstosslegenden*, pp. 340–431.
50. Quoted in Petzold, *Die Dolchstosslegende*, p. 43.
51. *Die Ursachen*, Vol. 3, pp. 6–16, and Lutz, *Causes*, pp. 113–31; Vascik and Sadler, *The Stab-in-the-Back Myth*, doc. 6.4, pp. 4–5.
52. Petzold, *Die Dolchstosslegende*, pp. 28–9.
53. *Stenographische Berichte über die Verhandlungen des deutschen Reichstags*, 134 (26 February 1918), pp. 4, 162–4, 171, in Vascik and Sadler, *The Stab-in-the-Back Myth*, doc. 4.10, pp. 60–61.
54. Vascik and Sadler, *The Stab-in-the-Back Myth*, pp. 9–62; Petzold, *Die Dolchstosslegende*, pp. 42–3.
55. Friedrich Ebert, *Schriften, Aufzeichnungen, Reden* (Dresden, 1926), Vol. 2, p. 127, translated and printed in Vascik and Sadler, *The Stab-in-the-Back Myth*, pp. 89–90, as doc. 6.7.
56. Vascik and Sadler, *The Stab-in-the-Back Myth*, p. 86.
57. Quoted in Petzold, *Die Dolchstosslegende*, p. 42.
58. Quoted in Hoegen, *Der Held von Tannenberg*, p. 242.
59. Cited in ibid, pp. 244–5, n. 92.
60. Sammet, 'Dolchstoss', pp. 67–72.
61. Hiller von Gaertringen, ' "Dolchstoss-Diskussion" ', pp. 136–7; Sammet, 'Dolchstoss', pp. 71–5.
62. Bessel, *Germany after the First World War*, pp. 78, 263–4; Deist, 'The Military Collapse', p. 205; more generally, see Alexander Watson, *Enduring the Great War: Combat, Morale and Collapse in the German and British Armies, 1914–1918* (Cambridge, 2008).
63. Hiller von Gaertringen, ' "Dolchstoss-Diskussion" ', pp. 139–41.
64. Petzold, *Die Dolchstosslegende*, pp. 63–5.
65. Vascik and Sadler, *The Stab-in-the-Back Myth*, pp. 129–58; Bernhard Fulda, *Press and Politics in the Weimar Republic* (Oxford, 2009), pp. 80–89 (for the distortions of the nationalist press reporting the trial); Krumeich, *Die unbewältigte Niederlage*, pp. 204–8.
66. Ibid, pp. 202–4; Vascik and Sadler, *The Stab-in-the-Back Myth*, pp. 159–76.
67. Ibid, pp. 179–207; see also Sammet, 'Dolchstoss', pp. 84–6 and 211–31; Petzold, *Die Dolchstosslegende*, pp. 101–10 (from the East German Communist perspective); and Krumeich, *Die unbewältigte Niederlage*, pp. 189–202.

68. Lüdtke, *Hans Delbrück und Weimar*, pp. 307–91, also for the following; see also Sammet, '*Dolchstoss*', pp. 76–84.

69. Roger Chickering, *We Men Who Feel Most German: A Cultural Study of the Pan-German League, 1886–1914* (London, 1984); Peter Pulzer, *The Rise of Political Anti-Semitism in Germany and Austria* (New York, 1964).

70. Evans, *The Feminist Movement in Germany*, pp. 175–205.

71. For the wider context, see Egmont Zechlin, *Die deutsche Politik und die Juden im Ersten Weltkrieg* (Göttingen, 1969).

72. Jacob Rosenthal, '*Die Ehre des jüdischen Soldaten*'. *Die Judenzählung im Ersten Weltkrieg und ihre Folgen* (Frankfurt am Main, 2007); Grady, *A Deadly Legacy*, pp. 137–47.

73. Quoted in Alfred Niemann, *Revolution von oben – Umsturz von unten. Entwicklung und Verlauf der Staatsumwälzung in Deutschland 1914–1918. Mit einem Dokumentenanhang* (4th edn, Berlin, 1928), p. 321.

74. Quoted in Sammet, '*Dolchstoss*', p. 121.

75. Albrecht von Thaer, *Generalstabsdienst an der Front und in der OHL. Aus Briefen und Tagebuchaufzeichnungen 1915–1919* (ed. Siegfried Kähler, Göttingen, 1958), p. 256.

76. Grady, *A Deadly Legacy*, pp. 208–11; Sammet, '*Dolchstoss*', p. 119.

77. Ernst von Wrisberg, 'Über die Angriffe gegen den Offiziersstande', *Militär-Wochenschrift für die deutsche Wehrmacht*, 25 March 1919, p. 262, cited in Rosenthal, *Die Ehre*, p. 131.

78. Ernst von Wrisberg, *Heer und Heimat* (Leipzig, 1921), p. 95, cited in Rosenthal, *Die Ehre*, p. 132.

79. Max Bauer, *Der grosse Krieg in Feld und Heimat* (Tübingen, 1921), p. 259–60, cited in Rosenthal, *Die Ehre*, p. 133. See also Adolf Vogt, *Oberst Max Bauer. Generalstabsoffizier im Zwielicht* (Osnabrück, 1974), pp. 171–98.

80. Hans Blüher, *Secessio judaica, philosophische Grundlegung der historischen Situation des Judentums und der antisemitische Bewegung* (Berlin, 1922), p. 48, cited in Rosenthal, *Die Ehre*, p. 134. For Blüher's anti-feminism, see Evans, *The Feminist Movement in Germany*, pp. 182–4. Weininger was Jewish, and in perhaps the most extreme of all instances of Jewish self-hatred, took the logical consequences of his antisemitism and committed suicide at the age of twenty-three: see Chandak Sengoopta, *Otto Weininger: Sex, Science and Self in Imperial Vienna* (Chicago, 2000).

81. Max Voss, *Enthüllungen über den Zusammenbruch. Eine Betrachtung über die Ursachen, dass es so gekommen ist* (Halle, 1919), p. 43, cited in Sammet, 'Dolchstoss', p. 116.

82. Arthur Hoffmann-Kutsche, *Der Dolchstoss durch das Judentum. Materialien zur deutschen Geschichte und zur jüdischen Politik* (Halle, 1922), cited in Sammet, 'Dolchstoss', pp. 115–16.

83. Ludendorff, *Kriegführung und Politik*, p. 133; Sammet, 'Dolchstoss', p. 118.

84. Ernst Rademacher, later on a Nazi Party member and SS officer, cited in Sammet, 'Dolchstoss', p. 117.

85. Sammet, 'Dolchstoss', p. 118, citing Wilhelm Meister, *Judas Schuldbuch. Eine deutsche Abrechnung* (3rd edn, Munich 1919), p. 154.

86. Sammet, 'Dolchstoss', p. 116.

87. Jäckel (ed.), *Hitler*, indexes the term on only 16 pages out of a total of 1,231; similarly Max Domarus (ed.), *Hitler. Reden und Proklamationen 1932–1945* (4 vols., Wiesbaden, 1973); and Bärbel Dusik *et al.* (eds.), *Hitler. Reden, Schriften, Anordnungen Februar 1925 bis Januar 1933* (6 vols., Munich, 1992–8).

88. Quoted in Sammet, 'Dolchstoss', p. 251 (*Mein Kampf*, Vol. 1, Chapter 10).

89. Hiller von Gaertringen, '"Dolchstoss-Diskussion"', pp. 142–3.

90. Wolfgang Schivelbusch, *Die Kultur der Niederlage. Der amerikanische Süden 1865, Frankreich 1871, Deutschland 1918* (Berlin, 2001), pp. 254–5.

91. Gerhard Hirschfeld, 'Der Führer spricht vom Krieg. Der Erste Weltkrieg in den Reden Adolf Hitlers', in Gerd Krumeich (ed.), *Nationalsozialismus und Erster Weltkrieg* (Essen, 2010), pp. 35–51. See also Bernd Sösemann, 'Der Erste Weltkrieg im propagandistischen Kalkül von Joseph Goebbels', in ibid, pp. 53–75.

92. Barth, *Dolchstosslegenden*, pp. 540–45.

93. All quoted in Sammet, 'Dolchstoss', pp. 116–18.

94. For the relatively few, scattered mentions during the 1920s and early 1930s, see ibid, pp. 250–55.

95. Petzold, *Die Dolchstosslegende*, pp. 74–7, does not convince when he equates 'November criminals' with the supposed agents of the stab in the back. For Nazi views, see also Gerd Krumeich, 'Die Dolchstoss-Legende', in Étienne François and Hagen Schulze (eds.), *Deutsche Erinnerungsorte* (Munich, 2001), Vol. I, pp. 575–99, at p. 598.

96. Sammet, 'Dolchstoss', pp. 119–24, quoting Gustav Andersen, *Unsere Stellung zur Sozialdemokratie nach Weltkrieg und Umsturz*, Vol. II: *Ihr*

Versagen nach dem Zusammenbruch. Aus den Tatsachen ermittelt (Hamburg, 1924), p. 138.

97. Richard Bessel, *Nazism and War* (London, 2004).

98. Ian Kershaw, 'Vorwort', in Krumeich (ed.), *Nationalsozialismus und Erster Weltkrieg*, pp. 7–10.

99. Ulrich Herbert, 'Was haben die Nationalsozialisten aus dem Ersten Weltkrieg gelernt?', in Krumeich (ed.), *Nationalsozialismus und Erster Weltkrieg*, pp. 21–32.

100. Quoted in Joachim Schröder, 'Der Erste Weltkrieg und der "jüdische Bolschewismus"', in Krumeich (ed.), *Nationalsozialismus und Erster Weltkrieg*, pp. 77–96, at p. 79.

101. Hiller von Gaertringen, 'Dolchstoss-Diskussion', pp. 145–6.

102. Petzold, *Die Dolchstosslegende*, pp. 69–73.

103. Krumeich, *Die unbewältigte Niederlage*, Chapter III/2: 'Dolchstoss. Lüge, Legende oder doch ein wenig wahr?' pp. 183, 199, 209.

104. Richard M. Hunt, 'Myths, Guilt, and Shame in Pre-Nazi Germany', *Virginia Quarterly Review* 34 (1958), pp. 355–71, exaggerates the spread and influence of the myth.

3. WHO BURNED DOWN THE REICHSTAG?

1. For the sequence of events, see Alfred Berndt, 'Zur Entstehung des Reichstagsbrandes. Eine Untersuching über den Zeitablauf', *Vierteljahrshefte für Zeitgeschichte* 23 (1975), pp. 77–90, and Hersch Fischler, 'Zum Zeitablauf der Reichstagsbrandstiftung. Korrekturen der Untersuching Alfred Berndts', *Vierteljahrshefte für Zeitgeschichte* 55 (2005), pp. 617–32. These two differing accounts already point to the division of opinion about the origins of the fire.

2. Sefton Delmer, *Trail Sinister* (London, 1981), pp. 185–200. The 'presidential palace' was the official residence of the President, or Speaker, of the Reichstag, an office Göring held as the formal leader of the largest parliamentary delegation in the legislature.

3. Ian Kershaw, *Hitler, 1889–1936: Hubris* (London, 1999), p. 457.

4. Hans Mommsen, 'Der Reichstagsbrand und seine politischen Folgen', *Vierteljahrshefte für Zeitgeschichte* 12 (1964), pp. 351–413.

5. Taken from http://spartacus-educational.com/GERreichstagF.htm

6. Alfons Sack (ed.), *Der Reichstagsbrand-Prozess* (Berlin, 1934). Sack, a conservative, was the lawyer assigned to Torgler's defence, but declared

that he was only interested in whether his client was innocent or guilty, not in the political imperatives behind the trial. He was arrested by the Nazis in 1934 but released, and died in an air raid ten years later.

8. The verdict was quashed retrospectively in 2007 in accordance with a 1998 law on Nazi injustice: see Marcus Giebeler, *Die Kontroverse um den Reichstagsbrand. Quellenprobleme und historiographische Paradigmen* (Munich, 2010), pp. 44–5.

9. *The Brown Book of the Hitler Terror and the Burning of the Reichstag, Prepared by the World Committee for the Victims of German Fascism, with an Introduction by Lord Marley* (London, 1933).

10. Ibid, p. 138.

11. Richard Wolff, 'Der Reichstagsbrand 1933. Ein Forschungsbericht', *Aus Politik und Zeitgeschichte* 3/56, 18 January 1956, pp. 25–56.

12. Fritz Tobias, *Der Reichstagsbrand. Legende und Wirklichkeit* (Rastatt, 1962). The English translation, *The Reichstag Fire* (New York, 1964), is heavily abridged.

13. Tobias, *Reichstagsbrand*, pp. 171–205 (Oberfohren), 446.

14. Ibid, pp. 420–56.

15. Ibid, pp. 101–4.

16. Mommsen, 'Der Reichstagsbrand'. Giebeler, *Die Kontroverse*, esp. pp. 74–80, reduces the controversy to a by-product of this wider debate.

17. Sean McMeekin, *The Red Millionaire: A Political Biography of Willi Münzenberg, Moscow's Secret Propaganda Tsar in the West, 1917–1940* (New Haven, CT, 2004).

18. Edouard Calic, *Le Reichstag brûle!* (Paris, 1969); idem, *Reinhard Heydrich* (New York, 1982), pp. 85–96.

19. Edouard Calic (ed.), *Unmasked: Two Confidential Interviews with Hitler in 1931* (London, 1971; original German edition *Ohne Maske. Hitler-Breiting Geheimgespräche* (Frankfurt am Main, 1968)).

20. Ibid, p. 56.

21. When I taught a course on the Third Reich at the University of East Anglia in the 1980s I used to ask the students to work out whether it was genuine; they had no difficulty in concluding that it was not.

22. Walther Hofer, Friedrich Zipfel and Christoph Graf (eds.), *Der Reichstagsbrand. Eine wissenschaftliche Dokumentation* (2 vols., Berlin 1972 and 1978). See especially Vol. I, pp. 257–78.

23. See the contribution by Henning Köhler in *idem* et al., *Reichstagsbrand: Aufklärung einer historischen Legende*, p. 167.

24. Sven Felix Kellerhoff, *Der Reichstagsbrand; Die Karriere eines Kriminalfalls* (Berlin, 2008), p. 11.

25. Ibid, p. 112.

26. Fritz Thyssen, *I Paid Hitler* (London, 1941).

27. Hans-Joachim Bernhard and David Elazar (eds.), *Reichstagsbrandprozess und Georgi Dimitroff. Dokumente* (Berlin, 1982 and 1989).

28. Klaus Drobisch, *Reichstag in Flammen* (Illustrierte historische Hefte 29, Berlin, 1983), p. 30 ('Cui bono? Wem nützt es?').

29. Alexander Bahar and Wilfried Kugel (eds.), *Der Reichstagsbrand. Wie Geschichte gemacht wird* (Berlin, 2001).

30. *Frankfurter Allgemeine Zeitung*, 22 February 2001, p. 8; *Neue Zürcher Zeitung*, 25 April 2001.

31. http://blog.globale-gleichheit.de/?author=1

32. http://www.parapsych.org/users/wkugel/profile.aspx. The Parapsychological Association's website says it is dedicated to the study of phenomena such as 'telepathy, clairvoyance, psychokinesis, psychic healing, and precognition'.

33. See also the revelations about Kugel in http://www.welt.de/print-welt/article627231/Wir-erhalten-Informationen-aus-der-Zukunft.html

34. Dieter Deiseroth (ed.), *Der Reichstagsbrand und der Prozess vor dem Reichsgericht* (Berlin, 2006).

35. Kellerhoff, p. 125.

36. Ibid, pp. 128–9; Hans Schneider (ed.), *Neues vom Reichstagsbrand? Eine Dokumentation. Bei Versäumnis der deutschen Geschichtsschreibung, mit einem Geleitwort von Iring Fetscher und Beiträgen von Dieter Deiseroth, Hersch Fischler, Wolf-Dieter Narr* (Berlin, 2004). The additional contributions were by well-known left-wing German political scientists.

37. At this point, a dissertation appeared that attempted to sum up the controversy (Giebeler, *Die Kontroverse*), but while it contains useful summaries of the numerous contributions to the debate, it fails to address the main issues directly and does not take contextual political factors into consideration. Its conclusion that the debate is still unresolved is little more than a confession of intellectual helplessness in the face of the mountain of argument and evidence, claims and counter-claims presented by the participants.

38. Benjamin Carter Hett, *Burning the Reichstag. An Investigation into the Third Reich's Most Enduring Mystery* (New York, 2014).

39. Ibid, p. 17.

40. Tobias, *Reichstagsbrand*, pp. 527–49.

41. Hett, *Burning the Reichstag*, p. 272.

42. Ibid, p. 73. For an instance of the far-right Druffel-Verlag publishing a book (on the Third Reich and the Palestine Question) without the author's consent, see Francis Nicosia, 'Scholars and Publishers: A New Twist to an Old Story?', *German History* 8/1 (1990), pp. 217–22.

43. Tobias, *Reichstagsbrand*, p. 3.

44. Ibid, p. 4.

45. Hett, *Burning the Reichstag*, pp. 262–3; *idem*, 'Who Burned the Reichstag?' (letter to the *London Review of Books*, 19 May 2014).

46. Helmut Krausnick and Hans-Heinrich Wilhelm, *Die Truppe des Weltanschauungskrieges. Die Einsatzgruppen der Sicherheitspolizei und des SD 1938–1942* (Stuttgart, 1981); Helmut Krausnick et al., *Anatomy of the SS State* (London, 1968); Horst Möller and Udo Wengst (eds.), *50 Jahre Institut für Zeitgeschichte. Eine Bilanz* (Munich, 1999).

47. Hett, *Burning the Reichstag*, p. 317.

48. *Idem*, p. 289.

49. Hett, 'Who Burned the Reichstag?'

50. Hett, *Burning the Reichstag*, p. 92.

51. Ibid, p. 323.

52. Tobias, *Reichstagsbrand*, pp. 257–69.

53. Kershaw, *Hitler: Hubris*, p. 457; Delmer, *Trail Sinister*, pp. 185–200.

54. Kellerhoff, *Der Reichstagsbrand* pp. 135–6.

55. Hett, *Burning the Reichstag*, pp. 320–21.

56. Horst Karasek, *Der Brandstifter:Lehr- und Wanderjahre des Maurergeselle Marinus van der Lubbe, der 1933 auszog, den Reichstag anzuzünden* (Berlin, 1984); see also the discussion in Tobias, *Reichstagsbrand* pp. 23–75 and 470–501.

57. Hett, *Burning the Reichstag*, p. 269.

58. Ibid, p. 20.

59. Tobias, *Reichstagsbrand*, p. 592.

60. Hett, *Burning the Reichstag*, p. 251.

61. Conrad Meding, 'Wer war der wahre Brandstifter?', *Hannoversche Allgemeine Zeitung*, 26 July 2019, pp. 2–3.

62. 'Dokument aufgetaucht. SA-Mann Hans-Martin Lennings will am Reichstagsbrand beteiligt gewesen sein', *Frankfurter Rundschau*, 26 July 2019; 'Archivfund in Hannover. Erklärung von SA-Mann erschüttert Einzeltäterthese zum Reichstagsbrand', *Süddeutsche Zeitung*, 26 July 2019; 'Reichstagsbrand Erklärung von SA-Mann legt NS-Beteiligung nahe', *Berliner Zeitung*, 26 July 2019; 'Newly Uncovered Testimony Casts Doubt on Reichstag Fire Claims', *Times of Israel*, 27 July 2019; Alex Winston, 'Newly Discovered Account of 1933 Reichs-

tag Fire Casts Doubt on Nazi Narrative', *Jerusalem Post*, 28 July 2019.

63. Sven Felix Kellerhoff, 'Was die neue Eidesstattliche Erklärung eines SA-Mannes bedeutet', *Die Welt*, 26 July 2019; *idem*, 'Der Kronzeuge gegen die Nazis war ein "lügnerischer Mensch"', *Die Welt*, 29 November 2019.

64. Tony Paterson, 'Historians Find "Proof" that Nazis Burned Reichstag', *Daily Telegraph*, 15 April 2001.

4. WHY DID RUDOLF HESS FLY TO BRITAIN?

1. Fictionalized reconstruction in James Leasor, *Rudolf Hess: The Uninvited Envoy* (London, 1962); Roy Conyers Nesbit and Georges Van Acker, *The Flight of Rudolf Hess: Myths and Reality* (Stroud, 1999). The pilot Adolf Galland's claim (*The First and the Last*, London, 1955, pp. 108-9), that Göring ordered him to intercept Hess, who had gone mad and was flying to England, is uncorroborated.

2. Nesbit and Van Acker, *The Flight*, pp. 49–74. The principal source for this account is Hess's subsequent letter to his son, now in the National Archives at Kew in file FO 1093/I (facsimile of first page of the letter in Nesbit and Van Acker, *The Flight*, p. 160); also Hess's maps, with course marking, found after he landed, now on display at the present Duke of Hamilton's home at Lennoxlove, in East Lothian (ibid, p. 58).

3. Nesbit and Van Acker, *The Flight*, pp. 74–7, citing further documents in the National Archives; Sir John Colville, *The Fringes of Power* (London, 1985), p. 386.

4. Leasor, *Rudolf Hess*, p. 11, quoting documents presented to the Nuremberg War Crimes Trials; Ivone Kirkpatrick, *The Inner Circle: Memoirs* (London, 1959), pp. 173–85; James Douglas-Hamilton, *Motive for a Mission: The Story behind Hess's Flight to Britain* (London, 1971), following the standard accounts. For the full text of the reported 'peace offer' and other documents, see Peter Raina, *A Daring Venture: Rudolf Hess and the Ill-Fated Peace Mission of 1941* (Frankfurt am Main, 2014).

5. Gabriel Gorodetsky (ed.), *The Maisky Diaries: Red Ambassador to the Court of St James's 1932–1943* (London, 2015), p. 359 (10 June 1941).

6. See Richard J. Evans, *Altered Pasts: Counterfactuals in History* (London, 2014), pp. 73–8.

7. Nesbit and Van Acker, *The Flight*, pp. 1–13; Ilse Hess, *Ein Schicksal in Briefen* (Leoni am Starnberger See, 1984), a collection of Hess's letters.

8. Nesbit and Van Acker, *The Flight*, pp. 13–21.

9. Ibid, pp. 21–31.

10. Peter Longerich, 'Hitler's Deputy: The Role of Rudolf Hess in the Nazi Regime', in David Stafford (ed.), *Flight from Reality: Rudolf Hess and His Mission to Scotland, 1941* (London, 2002), pp. 104–20.

11. Nesbit and Van Acker, *The Flight*, pp. 32–4.

12. Longerich, 'Hitler's Deputy', argues for his continuing importance. However, in *Hitler: A Life* (Oxford, 2019), p. 730, Longerich admits that Hess had been experiencing a 'growing isolation within the Reich leadership' in the years up to his flight.

13. Kurt Pätzold and Manfred Weissbecker, *Rudolf Hess. Der Mann an Hitlers Seite* (Leipzig, 1999), pp. 235–60.

14. Joachim C. Fest, *The Face of the Third Reich* (London, 1970), pp. 290–91; Rainer F. Schmidt, *Rudolf Hess. 'Botengang eines Toren'. Der Flug nach Grossbritannien vom 10. Mai 1941* (Düsseldorf, 1997), pp. 273–4.

15. Quoted in Jürgen Matthäus and Frank Bajohr (eds.), *Alfred Rosenberg. Die Tagebücher von 1934 bis 1944* (Frankfurt am Main, 2015), p. 288 (24 Sept. 1939) and pp. 384–7 (14 May 1941).

16. Peter Longerich, *Hitlers Stellvertreter. Führung der Partei und Kontrolle des Staatsapparates durch den Stab Hess und die Partei-Kanzlei Bormann* (Munich, 1992), pp. 109–18; Armin Nolzen, 'Der Hess-Flug und die öffentliche Meinung im NS-Staat', in Martin Sabrow (ed.), *Skandal und Diktatur. Formen öffentlicher Empörung im NS-Staat und in der DDR* (Göttingen, 2004), pp. 130–56, at p. 131.

17. Wulf Schwarzwäller, *Rudolf Hess. Der Stellvertreter* (Munich, 1987), p. 160.

18. Eugene K. Bird, *The Loneliest Man in the World: The Inside Story of the 30-Year Imprisonment of Rudolf Hess* (London, 1974), pp. 260–61.

19. Ian Kershaw, *Hitler, 1936–1945: Nemesis* (London, 2000), pp. 369–70, p. 940 n. 220; Rainer F. Schmidt, 'Der Hess-Flug und das Kabinett Churchill', *Vierteljahrshefte für Zeitgeschichte* 42 (1994), pp. 1–28, at p. 28.

20. Nesbit and Van Acker, *The Flight*, pp. 34–5.

21. Hans-Adolf Jacobsen, *Karl Haushofer. Leben und Werk* (Boppard am Rhein, 1979), Vol. 2, pp. 452–5; James Douglas-Hamilton, *The Truth about Rudolf Hess* (Edinburgh, 1993), pp. 125–33; Haushofer correspondence printed in Appendix I to Leasor, *Rudolf Hess*, pp. 219–26.

22. Nesbit and Van Acker, *The Flight*, p. 151, for a facsimile.

23. Longerich, *Hitlers Stellvertreter*, p 146; Schwarzwäller, *Rudolf Hess*, p. 177.

24. Ibid, pp. 173–5.

25. Wolf Rüdiger Hess, *Rudolf Hess. 'Ich bereue nichts'* (Graz, 1994), pp. 65–72.

26. John Costello, *Ten Days that Saved the West* (London, 1991), p. xiv. Costello unfortunately supplied no details to support his claim that this was proved by recently declassified 'top-secret' files in the UK, USA and USSR (ibid, pp. 15–20), except a summary of a document full of KGB disinformation.

27. J. Bernard Hutton, *Hess: The Man and His Mission* (London, 1970), pp. 21, 70–73.

28. Ibid, pp. 30–33.

29. Ibid, p. 23.

30. Peter Padfield, *Hess: Flight for the Führer* (London, 1991), pp. 138–41.

31. See for example Bird, *The Loneliest Man in the World*, p. 252 (affidavit from Hess 'to be handed to the world Press').

32. Ilse Hess, *Prisoner of Peace* (London, 1954).

33. Transcript in Pätzold and Weissbecker, *Rudolf Hess*, pp. 451–4.

34. Schmidt, *Rudolf Hess*, pp. 280–81.

35. Volker Ullrich, *Adolf Hitler. Biografie. Die Jahre des Untergangs* (Frankfurt am Main, 2018), pp. 192–202, citing Bodenschatz on p. 195.

36. Schwarzwäller, *Rudolf Hess*, p. 185, claims Hess adhered for the rest of his life to a 'pact' of silence with Hitler but does not produce any evidence for the existence of such a pact.

37. Hutton, *Hess*, pp. 57–9; Schwarzwäller, *Rudolf Hess*, p. 200.

38. Albert Speer, *Inside the Third Reich* (London, 1975 edn), p. 250, also for the following. Speer was wrong to claim that Pintsch was accompanied by another of Hess's adjutants: see Kershaw, *Hitler: Nemesis*, p. 937, n. 178. See also the account prepared for Stalin in 1949 and based on the eyewitness testimony of Hitler's valet Heinz Linge and his adjutant Otto Günsche, who had fallen into Soviet hands at the end of the war: Henrik Eberle and Matthias Uhl (eds.), *The Hitler Book: The Secret Dossier Prepared for Stalin* (London, 2005), pp. 70–72.

39. Paul Schmidt, *Hitler's Interpreter* (London, 1951), p. 233.

40. Matthäus and Bajohr (eds.), *Alfred Rosenberg: Die Tagebücher*, p. 387 (14 May 1941).

41. Fröhlich (ed.), *Die Tagebücher*, Part I, vol. 4, pp. 638 (13 May 1941), 640 (14 May 1941).

42. Nolzen, 'Der Hess-Flug', pp. 130–56.

43. Kershaw, *Hitler: Nemesis*, p. 375.

44. As claimed by Edouard Calic, *Reinhard Heydrich* (New York, 1982), p. 233.

45. Leasor, *Rudolf Hess*, pp. 172–4. A. J. P. Taylor, *Beaverbrook* (London 1972), p. 624, n.1, after recounting an inconclusive interview with the imprisoned Hess by the newspaper magnate and aircraft production minister, notes that 'it is conceivable that Hitler knew of Hess's intention', but leaves it at that.

46. Robert Gellately, *The Gestapo and German Society: Enforcing Racial Policy, 1933–1945* (Oxford, 1990); Eric A. Johnson, *Nazi Terror: The Gestapo and Ordinary Germans* (New York, 1999); and Klaus-Michael Mallmann and Gerhard Paul, 'Omniscient, Omnipotent, Omnipresent? Gestapo, Society and Resistance', in David F. Crew (ed.), *Nazism and German Society 1933–1945* (London, 1994), pp. 166–96; superseding Edward Crankshaw, *Gestapo: Instrument of Tyranny* (London, 1956).

47. Eberle and Uhl (eds.), *The Hitler Book*, pp. 70–72.

48. Nesbit and Van Acker, *The Flight*, p. 125.

49. Lothar Kettenacker, 'Mishandling a Spectacular Event: The Rudolf Hess Affair', in Stafford (ed.), *Flight from Reality*, pp. 19–37, at pp. 19–20.

50. Kershaw, *Hitler: Nemesis*, pp. 369–81, the best brief account.

51. John Harris and M. J. Trow, *Hess: The British Conspiracy* (London, 2011), pp. 8–10.

52. Peter Padfield, *Hess, Hitler and Churchill: The Real Turning Point of the Second World War: A Secret History* (London, 2013), p. 20.

53. Harris and Trow, *Hess,* p. 21.

54. Padfield, *Hess: Flight for the Führer*, pp. 346–51; similarly in Louis C. Kilzer, *Churchill's Deception: The Dark Secret that destroyed Nazi Germany* (New York, 1994), pp. 271–4.

55. Ulrich von Hassell, *The von Hassell Diaries, 1938–1944: The Story of the Forces against Hitler inside Germany as recorded by Ambassador Ulrich von Hassell, a Leader of the Movement* (London, 1948), pp. 179–80.

56. Ibid, p. 194.

57. Harris and Trow, *Hess*, p. 170. Allegations of the suppression of documentary evidence have even been accepted by otherwise sensible historians: see for example Neal Ascherson, 'Secrets are Like Sex', *London Review of Books*, 2 April 2020, p. 20.

58. Pätzold and Weissbecker, *Rudolf Hess*, pp. 281–3.

59. Ibid, pp. 5 and 254, n. 7.

60. Padfield, *Hess, Hitler and Churchill*, p. 363.

61. Leasor, *Rudolf Hess*, pp. 73–81.

62. Calic, *Reinhard Heydrich*, p. 233.

63. Nesbit and Van Acker, *The Flight*, pp. 126–7, and technical Appendices.

64. Ibid, pp. 126–31.
65. David Stafford, 'Introduction', in *idem* (ed.), *Flight from Reality,* p. 2. A useful brief guide and assessment can be found in John Kirkpatrick, *10 May 1941: Rudolf Hess's Flight to Scotland, a Bibliographical Study* (Glasgow 2008). Conspiracy theories surrounding the flight have also inspired a number of works of fiction, including Brian Moffatt, *Fallen Angels, Lost Highways (The Long Fall of Rudolf Hess)* (Hawick, 2012); Philip S. Jacobs, *Hess: The Camouflaged Emissary* (Oxford, 1993); and, most recently, Graham Hurley, *Raid 42* (London, 2019).
66. James J. Barnes and Patience P. Barnes, *Hitler's* Mein Kampf *in Britain and America: A Publishing History 1930–1939* (Cambridge, 1980), for details of Murphy's life and career; see also *idem, James Vincent Murphy: Translator and Interpreter of Fascist Europe 1880–1946* (Langham, MD, 1987).
67. James Murphy, *Adolf Hitler: The Drama of His Career* (London, 1934), p. viii.
68. Ibid, p. x.
69. Ibid, pp. 15–16.
70. Ibid, pp. 124–7, 138–9; Werner E. Mosse, *Jews in the German Economy: The German-Jewish Elite 1820–1935* (Oxford, 1987); *idem, The German-Jewish Elite 1820–1935: A Socio-Cultural Profile* (Oxford, 1989).
71. Barnes and Barnes, *James Vincent Murphy,* pp. 164–6.
72. Richard Griffiths, *Fellow Travellers of the Right: British Enthusiasts for Nazi Germany 1933–1939* (Oxford, 1983), p. 128; Barnes and Barnes, *Hitler's* Mein Kampf, pp. 56–7; Shareen Blair Brysac, *Resisting Hitler: Mildred Harnack and the Red Orchestra: The Life and Death of an American Woman in Nazi Germany* (New York, 2000), pp. 57–8. Murphy's grandson John Murphy attempted to dissociate his grandfather from support for Nazism many years later: https://www.mhpbooks.com/the-remarkable-story-of-mein-kampfs-translation-into-english/ and https://www.bbc.co.uk/news/magazine-30697262
73. Greta Kuckhoff, *Vom Rosenkranz zur Roten Kapelle* (East Berlin, 1973), pp. 180–81, 197–8.
74. Barnes and Barnes, *Hitler's* Mein Kampf, pp. 51–72, 235.
75. Quotes and summary in ibid, pp. 26–8.
76. James Murphy, *Who Sent Rudolf Hess?* (London, 1941), pp. 1, 4. I am grateful to the Bodleian Library, Oxford, for supplying a copy of this rare pamphlet.
77. Vidkun Quisling was a Norwegian fascist installed as Prime Minister following the German conquest of Norway in 1940. The term 'fifth column'

derived from the Spanish Civil War (1936–9), in which the four columns of the Nationalist armies were supposedly joined by a fifth, carrying out acts of subversion behind the Republican lines.

78. Murphy, *Who Sent Rudolf Hess?* pp. 8–9.

79. Ibid, pp. 10–14.

80. Ibid, pp. 15–23.

81. Ibid, pp. 24–34. Svengali was a manipulative Jew who, in George du Maurier's antisemitic novel *Trilby*, published in 1894, uses hypnosis to turn an innocent young woman into a talented singer; the idea of Hitler as a 'somnambulist' derives from his statement on 15 March 1936 that 'I go the way that Providence dictates with the certainty of a sleepwalker.'

82. Ibid, pp. 34–5, 42–3. Murphy invoked another conspiracy theory when he declared that Fritsch, who was sacked in February 1938, allegedly because he was being blackmailed by a rent-boy, in reality because he was too sceptical about Germany's ability to fight a European war in the near future, was murdered by the Nazis shortly after the outbreak of war. Eyewitnesses in fact reported that Fritsch, who had volunteered for active service on the Eastern Front in an attempt to restore his reputation, was killed by a stray bullet during the invasion of Poland (see the report in the news magazine *Der Spiegel* 34/1948 (21 August 1948), p. 18).

83. Murphy, *Who Sent Rudolf Hess?* pp. 44–5.

84. Ibid, Foreword.

85. Andrew Thorpe, *The British Communist Party and Moscow 1920–1943* (Manchester, 2000), pp. 265–7.

86. Gorodetsky (ed.), *The Maisky Diaries*, p. 356 (3 June 1941).

87. Ibid, pp. 119–20, citing the report of the case in *The Times*, 19 February 1942.

88. Ibid, p. 121.

89. Nesbit and Van Acker, *The Flight*, p. 122.

90. Ibid, pp. 122–3; Stafford (ed.), *Flight from Reality*, pp. 4–6. See also Padfield, *Hess, Hitler and Churchill*, p. 299.

91. Nesbit and Van Acker, *The Flight*, p. 122.

92. E.g. Costello, *Ten Days*, pp. 5–6.

93. Nesbit and Van Acker, *The Flight*, pp. 131–7.

94. Ibid, pp. 60–69. The official RAF report on the progress of Hess's Messerschmitt is given on pp. 157–9.

95. Alfred Smith, *Rudolf Hess and Germany's Reluctant War 1939–41* (Lewes, Sussex, 2001), p. xix.

96. Padfield, *Hess: Flight for the Führer,* p. 348. The release of the files provided no support for the theory of a conspiracy to invite Hess to Britain.

97. Smith, *Rudolf Hess,* p. xix, suggests that the Secret Services were involved because they were themselves part of the 'peace party', though there is no evidence to back up this hypothesis.

98. Harris and Trow, *Hess,* pp. 125, 131. They concede, however, that McCormick 'is not regarded today as particularly faithful to the facts' (p. 131). McCormick was the author of *The Master Book of Spies* (London, 1973) and *The Life of Ian Fleming* (London, 1993).

99. Harris and Trow, *Hess,* pp. 248–52.

100. Smith, *Rudolf Hess,* p. 387.

101. Kilzer, *Churchill's Deception,* (1994), p. 276.

102. Ibid.

103. Schmidt, *Hess,* pp. 278–80 (relying on the well-known Haushofer letters, together with postwar testimony); also Harris and Trow, *Rudolf Hess,* pp. 243–5. The theory that Ernest Bevin, Minister of Labour in Churchill's coalition Cabinet, was forewarned about Hess's flight by a coded message, turns out to rest on a newspaper article published in 1969 by a man whose many lapses of memory in other parts of the article render his testimony completely unreliable (Schmidt, *Hess,* p. 32, n. 69).

104. Ted Harrison, ' ". . . wir wurden schon viel zu oft hereingelegt." Mai 1941: Rudolf Hess in englischer Sicht', in Pätzold and Weissbecker, *Rudolf Hess,* pp. 368–92.

105. Stafford (ed.), *Flight from Reality,* p. 11.

106. Martin Allen, *The Hitler/Hess Deception: British Intelligence's Best-Kept Secret of the Second World War* (London, 2003), esp. p. 283.

107. As reported by Edmund A. Walsh, 'The Mystery of Haushofer', *Life,* 16 September 1946, pp. 106–20; see also Jacobsen, *Karl Haushofer,* and Daniel Wosnitzka, 'Karl Haushofer, 1869–1946' (on the website of the Deutsches Historisches Museum).

108. Martin Allen, *Himmler's Secret War: The Covert Peace Negotiations of Heinrich Himmler* (New York, 2005).

109. Paul Lewis, 'The 29 Fakes behind a Rewriting of History', *Guardian,* 5 May 2008.

110. Martin Allen, *'Lieber Herr Hitler . . .' 1939/40. So wollte der Herzog von Windsor den Frieden retten* (Inning, 2001); *idem, Churchills Friedensfalle. Das Geheimnis des Hess-Fluges 1941* (Stegen, 2003); *idem, Das Himmler-Komplott 1943–1945* (Stegen, 2005).

111. Harris and Trow, *Hess*, p. 264, n. 2.

112. Ibid, pp. 6 and 255, n. 10.

113. Ibid, p. 8.

114. Peter Allen, *The Crown and the Swastika: Hitler, Hess and the Duke of Windsor* (London, 1983), p. 188.

115. Ibid, p. 239.

116. Ernst Haiger, 'Fiction, Facts, and Forgeries: The "Revelations" of Peter and Martin Allen about the History of the Second World War', *Journal of Intelligence History*, 6/1 (2006), pp. 105-18.

117. Stafford, *Flight from Reality*, p. 5.

118. Padfield, *Hess, Hitler and Churchill*, p. 355.

119. Smith, *Rudolf Hess*, esp. pp. 398-401. It is worth noting that Smith's bibliography contains no items in German.

120. Hess, *Prisoner of Peace*; Victor E. Marsden (trans.), *Protocols of the Meetings of the Learned Elders of Zion* (London, 1920); see also Gisela Lebeltzer, 'Henry Hamilton Beamish and the Britons: Champions of Anti-Semitism', in Kenneth Lunn and Richard Thurlow (eds.), *British Fascism: Essays on the Radical Right in Interwar Britain* (London, 1980).

121. Lynn Picknett, Clive Prince and Stephen Prior, *Double Standards: The Rudolf Hess Cover-Up* (London, 2001), pp. 493-4. This book's bibliography contains not a single item in German.

122. Pätzold and Weissbecker, *Rudolf Hess*, pp. 275-81.

123. See Daniel Pick, *The Pursuit of the Nazi Mind: Hitler, Hess, and the Analysts* (Oxford University Press, 2012).

124. Nesbit and Van Acker, *The Flight*, pp. 100-114.

125. Edmund Mezger, *Kriminalpolitik auf kriminologischer Grundlage* (Stuttgart, 1934), pp. 18-25.

126. Gert Heidenreich, 'Freiheit im Freistaat. Polizeiaktion gegen Münchner Verlage – die Vergangenheit des bayerischen Innenministers Alfred Seidl', *Die Zeit*, 20 October 1978.

127. Anton Maegerle, ' "Club der Revisionisten". Seit nunmehr 25 Jahren ist die "Zeitgeschichtliche Forschungsstelle Ingolstadt" damit beschäftigt, historische Fakten zu verdrehen', *Blick nach Rechts* 25 (11 December 2006).

128. Richard J. Evans, *Telling Lies About Hitler* (London, 2002), pp. 10-12, 233-72.

129. Ibid, p. 39.

130. David Irving, *Hess: The Missing Years 1941-1945* (London, 1987), pp. 4, 41.

131. Albert Speer, *Spandau: The Secret Diaries* (Glasgow, 1976), pp. 449, 466.

132. Tony Le Tissier, *Farewell to Spandau* (Leatherhead, 1994), p. 71. Le Tissier was the last governor of Spandau. For a detailed account of Hess's time in confinement from 1941 to 1946, see Stephen McGinty, *Camp Z: How British Intelligence Broke Hitler's Deputy* (London, 2013).

133. Nesbit and Van Acker, *The Flight*, pp. 111–18; the letter is reproduced and translated in Le Tissier, *Farewell to Spandau*, p. 77. The coded reference to 'Freiburg' was to Hildegard Fath, his secretary, not a hint that the entire document was a deceit, as suggested by some conspiracists (e.g. Padfield, *Hess, Hitler and Churchill* p. 17).

134. Wolf-Rüdiger Hess, *Mord an Rudolf Hess? Der geheimnisvolle Tod meines Vaters in Spandau* (Leoni am Starnberger See, 1990), pp. 51, 151–3, 156, 163. See also Smith, *Rudolf Hess*, p. 386 ('a most convenient death').

135. Cahal Milmo, 'Adolf Hitler's Nazi Deputy Rudolf Hess "Murdered by British Agents to Stop him Spilling Wartime Secrets"', *Independent*, 6 September 2013. See also Harris and Trow, *Hess*, pp. 171–99.

136. John Greenwald and Clive Freeman, 'Germany: The Inmate of Spandau's Last Wish', *Time*, 6 December 2009.

137. Padfield, *Hess, Hitler and Churchill*, p. 17.

138. Ibid, p. 323; Abdullah Melaouhi, *Rudolf Hess: His Betrayal and Murder* (Washington DC, 2013); Le Tissier, *Farewell to Spandau*, pp. 102–4. Le Tissier hinted that the orderly was short of money after the closure of Spandau and had been paid to provide his testimony by people who deliberately put ideas into his head. Melaouhi's book was published by the *Barnes Review*, a magazine named after the 'revisionist' historian Harry Elmer Barnes and specializing in Holocaust denial, antisemitism and studies of the occult: https://barnesreview.org/

139. Hugh Thomas, *Hess: A Tale of Two Murders* (London, revised edn, 1988), pp. 150, 158–9, 163, 292. The first edition of this book was published under the title *The Murder of Rudolf Hess* (London, 1979).

140. Hess, *Rudolf Hess*, p. 171.

141. Kilzer's thesis of a conspiracy orchestrated by Churchill, to deceive Hess into his flight, as discussed above, was compromised by his acceptance of Hugh Thomas's theory of Hess's murder just before the flight, and his substitution by a double.

142. Le Tissier, *Farewell to Spandau*, pp. 107–8, citing investigations by Christopher Andrew for the BBC television programme *Timewatch*, broadcast on 17 January 1990.

143. Nesbit and Van Acker, *The Flight*, pp. 137–9.

144. Ibid, pp. 139–61.

145. Le Tissier, *Farewell to Spandau*, pp. 99–100.

146. 'Exclusive: DNA Solves Rudolf Hess Doppelgänger Conspiracy The-ory', *New Scientist*, 22 January 2019 (online at https://www.new scientist.com/article/2191462-exclusive-dna-solves-rudolf-hess-doppel ganger-conspiracy-theory/).

147. For instance, the theory that Hess was lured to Scotland by the British Secret Service is shared by Gabriel Gorodetsky, *The Maisky Diaries*, p. 355, though in this case he is misled by the fact that Maisky, usually a discerning commentator, believed in the theory, perhaps covering his back with Stalin.

148. Joseph P. Farrell, *Hess and the Penguins: The Holocaust, Antarctica, and the Strange Case of Rudolf Hess* (Kempton, IL, 2017), p. 6.

149. Ibid, pp. 229–32, 253. The alleged 'Nazi-Zionist complicity' refers to a controversial agreement signed between a faction of the Zionist move-ment and the Nazi government in 1933, at a time when Hitler's main aim with Germany's Jews was to remove them from the country, to assist Jewish emigration from Germany to Palestine: see Yehuda Bauer, *Jews for Sale? Nazi–Jewish Negotiations, 1933–1945* (New Haven, CT, 1996).

150. https://crashrecovery.org/OMEGA-FILE/omega20.htm

151. Farrell, *Hess*, pp. 247–8.

5. DID HITLER ESCAPE THE BUNKER?

1. Donald M. McKale, *Hitler: The Survival Myth* (New York, 1981), p. 45; see also Christian Goeschel, *Suicide in Nazi Germany* (Oxford, 2009).

2. Adam Sisman, *Hugh Trevor-Roper: The Biography* (London, 2010), pp. 131–42.

3. McKale, *Hitler*, pp. 49–64. There is no evidence for the claim by Daly-Groves, *Hitler's Death*, p. 93, that it was not political factors but embarrassment about the poor quality of the Soviet investigation that informed Stalin's announcement that Hitler was alive.

4. Sisman, *Hugh Trevor-Roper*, pp. 132–3.

5. For Stalin's disinformation campaign, see Jean-Christophe Brisard and Lana Parshina, *The Death of Hitler: The Final Word on the Ultimate Cold Case: The Search for Hitler's Body* (London, 2018), pp. 149–99.

6. McKale, *Hitler*, pp. 133–4.

7. Daly-Groves, *Hitler's Death*, pp. 33, 88.

8. Ibid, pp. 133–42; see also Richard Davenport-Hines (ed.), *Hugh Trevor-Roper: The Wartime Journals* (London, 2012), p. 263.

9. Sisman, *Hugh Trevor-Roper*, pp. 155–63; Richard Overy, ' "The Chap with the Closest Tabs": Hugh Trevor-Roper and the Hunt for Hitler' (unpublished paper, 2014; I am grateful to Professor Overy for making this article available); Sara Douglas, 'The Search for Hitler: Hugh Trevor-Roper, Humphrey Searle, and the Last Days of Adolf Hitler', *Journal of Military History* 78 (2014), pp. 165–92; Edward Harrison, 'Hugh Trevor-Roper und "Hitlers letzte Tage" ', *Vierteljahrshefte für Zeitgeschichte* 57 (2009), pp. 33–60.

10. Hugh Trevor-Roper, *The Last Days of Hitler* (London, 1952 [1947]). Among many other detailed narratives, see in particular Brisard and Parshina, *The Death of Hitler*, pp. 51–117.

11. See the list, with statements, in Anton Joachimsthaler, *Hitlers Ende. Legenden und Dokumente* (Munich, 1995), pp. 410–14 (published in an abridged English edition as *The Last Days of Hitler: The Legends, the Evidence, the Truth* (London, 1998)); also Wolfdieter Bihl, *Der Tod Adolf Hitlers. Fakten und Uberlebenslegenden* (Vienna, 2000), pp. 11–16. The criticisms levelled at the Trevor-Roper report by the former US intelligence officer in Berlin, W. F. Heimlich, who resented being side-lined in favour of Trevor-Roper's investigation, were ill informed, and his claim that Hitler was murdered on Himmler's orders has never been taken seriously by historians: see Herbert Moore and James W. Barrett (eds.), *Who Killed Hitler?* (New York, 1947, repr. 2011), and for a cogent critique, Daly-Groves, *Hitler's Death*, pp. 14–37.

12. Catherine Sharples, ' "Proof of Death": West German Investigations into the Fate of Adolf Hitler, 1952–1956', Institute of Historical Research, 11 December 2019.

13. Hugh Trevor-Roper, 'Hitler's Last Minutes', *New York Review of Books*, 26 September 1968; Brisard and Parshina, *The Death of Hitler*, pp. 160–62.

14. Ulrich Völklein (ed.), *Hitlers Tod. Die letzten Tage im Führerbunker* (Göttingen, 1998).

15. Joachim C. Fest, *Inside Hitler's Bunker: The Last Days of the Third Reich* (London, 2004 [2002]); *Downfall* (2004, director Oliver Hirsch-biegel).

16. Henrik Eberle and Matthias Uhl (eds.), *The Hitler Book: The Secret Dossies prepared for Stalin (London, 2005)*. Relevant documents were also published in English: see V. K. Vinogradov *et al.* (eds.), *Hitler's Death: Russia's Last Great Secret from the Files of the KGB* (London, 2005); Ada Petrova and Peter Watson (eds.), *The Death of*

Hitler: The Final Words from Russia's Secret Archives (London, 1995).

17. See also Heinz Linge, *With Hitler to the End: The Memoir of Hitler's Valet* (London, 2009 [1980]); Erich Kempka, *I was Hitler's Chauffeur* (London, 2012); *idem, Ich habe Adolf Hitler verbrannt* (Munich, 1950); Christa Schroeder, *He was My Chief: The Memoirs of Adolf Hitler's Secretary* (London, 2012 [1998]); and Traudl Junge, *Until the Final Hour: Hitler's Last Secretary* (London, 2004 [2003]). For Linge's evidence, see Brisard and Parshina, *The Death of Hitler*, esp. pp. 55–72, 248–62, 290–300.

18. Kershaw, *Hitler: Nemesis*, pp. 799–83.

19. Imre Karacs, 'DNA Test Closes Book on Mystery of Martin Bormann', *Independent*, 4 May 1998. The supposed survival of Bormann is the subject of Ladislas Farago, *Aftermath: Martin Bormann and the Fourth Reich* (London, 1975), and is also discussed in Hugh Thomas, *Doppelgängers: The Truth about the Bodies in the Berlin Bunker* (London, 1995), pp. 208–56. See Daly-Groves, *Hitler's Death*, pp. 97–120, for Bormann, citing K. Anslinger et al., 'Identification of the Skeletal Remains of Martin Bormann by mtDNA Analysis', *International Journal of Legal Medicine* 114/3 (2001), pp. 194–6; also Tony Halpin and Roger Boyes, 'Battle of Hitler's Skull Prompts Russia to Reveal All', *The Times*, 9 December 2009; Bihl, *Der Tod*, pp. 103–35, and Joachimsthaler, *Hitlers Ende*, pp. 358–83. The skull is a central focus of the survivalists' arguments claiming that the bodies outside the bunker were not those of Hitler and Eva Braun. Even mainstream newspapers leapt to this conclusion: see Uki Goñi, 'Tests on Skull Fragment Cast Doubt on Adolf Hitler Suicide Story', *Guardian*, 27 September 2009.

20. Thomas, *Doppelgängers*, implausibly claimed that those present were all lying, but (p. 166) he also alleges that Hitler was strangled by Linge when he proved unable to make up his mind about what to do when the doubles were installed. These fantastical inventions make it impossible to take his book seriously.

21. Heinz Schaeffer, *U-977 – 66 Tage unter Wasser* (Wiesbaden, n.d.).

22. Ladislas Szabó, *Je sais que Hitler est vivant* (Paris, 1947).

23. McKale, *Hitler*, p. 129.

24. Ibid, *passim*.

25. Ibid, p. 198.

26. Daly-Groves, *Hitler's Death*, pp. 9, 35, 48–52.

27. Gerald Steinacher, *Nazis on the Run: How Hitler's Henchmen Fled Justice* (New York, 2011); Uki Goñi, *The Real Odessa: How Perón Brought the Nazi War Criminals to Argentina* (London, 2001).

28. Bettina Stangneth, *Eichmann before Jerusalem: The Unexamined Life of a Mass Murderer* (London, 2014).

29. McKale, *Hitler*, pp. 199–200.

30. Ben Knight, 'Pegida Head Lutz Bachmann Reinstated after Furore over Hitler Moustache Photo', *Guardian*, 23 February 2015.

31. Daly-Groves, *Hitler's Death*, p. 23.

32. Hans D. Baumann and Ron T. Hansig, *Hitler's Escape* (revised and expanded edition, Portsmouth, NH, 2014), p. iii.

33. Ibid, p. 30.

34. Ibid, p. v.

35. Ibid, pp. vii, 215.

36. Ibid, pp. 7, 11. There are many inaccuracies in the book's account of German history in the 1930s and 1940s.

37. Ibid, p. vii.

38. http://cryptome.org/douglas.htm, accessed 21 February 2015, and *The Spotlight*, 6 January 1997, pp. 12–14. See also Peter Hoffmann, the world's leading expert on Stauffenberg and the July 1944 bomb plot, on Stahl's attempt to offer him documents, on the website *h-net*, at http://h-net.msu.edu/cgi-bin/logbrowse.pl?trx=vx&list=hgerman& month=9609&week=b&msg=hMUenrd3JoS57/meddq8MA&user=&pw, accessed 21 February 2015, and Gitta Sereny, *The German Trauma: Experiences and Reflections 1938–2000* (London, 2000), pp. 194–215, recounting her dealings with Stahl. The Holocaust deniers of the self-styled Institute for Historical Review were particularly hostile to Stahl because of the support lent to him by Willis Carto, a wealthy Holocaust denier whom they accused of defrauding them of a large sum of money. See http://www.ihr.org/jhr/v20/v20n2p40_Douglas.html, accessed 21 February 2015. For Willis Carto and his relations with Holocaust Denial organizations, see Evans, *Telling Lies About Hitler*, pp. 150–51. For a defence of Stahl by another self-styled Holocaust 'revisionist', Germar Rudolf, who has convictions for inciting racial hatred and defaming the dead, see http://www.vho.org/GB/c/GR/StahlDouglas.html, accessed 21 February 2015. All through this, Douglas continued to assert he was not the same person as Stahl.

39. http://www.reuters.com/article/2013/10/31/us-germany-gestapo-idUS BRE99U0XY20131031, accessed 21 February 2015; see also Daly-Groves, *Hitler's Death*, pp. 121–4.

40. Harry Cooper, *Hitler in Argentina: The Documented Truth of Hitler's Escape from Berlin* (Hernando, FL, 2014 [2006]), p. 121.

41. Kurt Hutton, *Speaking Likeness* (London, 1947), photo 'Forty Winks'. For Cooper's claim, see *Hitler in Argentina*, p. 115, and back cover, and https:// youtube.com/watch?v=Tu_mXmS-3ns. See Roger Clark, http://thepipeline. info/blog/2016/12/22/the-big-read-a-neo-nazi-actually-im-a-republican-hitler-harry-cooper-and-the-pseudohistory-industry-part-two/, posted 22 December 2016, accessed 3 February 2020; and idem, Part One, posted 21 December 2016, accessed 3 February 2020, at http://thepipeline.info/ blog/2016/12/21/the-big-read-a-neo-nazi-actually-im-a-republican-hitler-harry-cooper-and-the-pseudohistory-industry-part-one/

42. http://www.tomatobubble.com/hitler_argentina.html, accessed 21 February 2015.

43. http://www.splcenter.org/get-informed/intelligence-report/browse-all-issues/2013/fall/Touring-the-Third-Reich, accessed 1 March 2015. This is a post from the history section of the Southern Poverty Law Center, which monitors extremism. For Cooper's response to these criticisms, see http://www.hitlerinargentina.com/Clark.htm, and http://www.hitlerinargentina.com/Interesting.htm

44. http://www.adl.org/combating-hate/domestic-extremism-terrorism/c/ rense-web-site-promotes.html

45. McKale, *Hitler*, pp. 202–4; Werner Brockdorff, *Flucht vor Nürnberg. Pläne und Organization der Fluchtwege der NS-Prominenz im 'Römischen Weg'* (Wels, 1969).

46. Simon Dunstan and Gerrard Williams, *Grey Wolf: The Escape of Adolf Hitler: The Case Presented* (New York, 2011), p. 156. For a cogent demolition of the claims advanced by Dunstan and Williams, see the long review by Roger Clark, 'Buyer Beware – Fantasy History' (https://www. amazon.com/review/R3FNO7NT5G2VA3), posted 16 October 2011, accessed 3 February 2020.

47. Dunstan and Williams, *Grey Wolf*, p. xxiii.

48. Ibid, p. xxi.

49. Ibid, pp. xx, 308.

50. Roger Clark, 'The Big Read: Carry on Hunting Hitler', *The Pipeline*, posted 30 April 2016 (http://thepipeline.info/blog/2016/04/30/ the-big-read-carry-on-hunting-hitler/, accessed 3 February 2020), 'The Mystery of the Vanishing Professor'.

51. Dunstan and Williams, *Grey Wolf*, p. 155. It first surfaced in Kenneth D. Alford and Theodore P. Savas, *Nazi Millionaires: The Allied Search for Hidden SS Gold* (Havertown, PA, 2002).

52. http://falkeeins.blogspot.co.uk/2011/11/grey-wolf-escape-of-adolf-hitler-distan.html, accessed 21 February 2015.

53. Dunstan and Williams, *Grey Wolf*, pp. 164–5, 309; Günther Gellermann, *Moskau ruft Heeresgruppe Mitte … Was nicht im Wehrmachtbericht stand – Die Einsätze des geheimen Kampfgeschwaders 200 im Zweiten Weltkrieg* (Bonn, 1988); https://www.dailymail.co.uk/news/article-2478100/Theory-Adolf-Hitler-fled-Argentina-lived-age-73.html, accessed 23 February 2015.

54. Dunstan and Williams, *Grey Wolf*, p. 166.

55. Ibid, pp. 166–9; Werner Baumbach, *Broken Swastika: The Defeat of the Luftwaffe* (London, 1960).

56. Dunstan and Williams, *Grey Wolf*, pp. 168–70, 186–7.

57. For details on their specifications and missions, see http://uboat.net/boats/u1235.htm; http://www.uboat.net/boats/u518.htm; http://uboat.net/boats/u880.htm; all accessed 1 March 2015.

58. Dunstan and Williams, *Grey Wolf*, p. 182.

59. Ibid, pp. 188–92.

60. Milan Hauner, *Hitler: A Chronology of his Life and Times* (2nd edn, London, 2008), pp. 200–204. All the reliable evidence about Eva Braun is gathered together and analysed in Heike Görtemaker, *Eva Braun: Life with Hitler* (London, 2011). Braun was indeed in Italy in 1938 as part of Hitler's entourage but her home-movie films of the visit show no indication that she was either pregnant or had given birth: see the extract http://www.criticalpast.com/video/65675077851_Eva-Brauns-family_Evas-mother_Fanny-Braun_milling-about-on-street, accessed 1 March 2015.

61. *Grey Wolf* movie, at 12–14 minutes; the copy on the film sleeve mentions two.

62. Dunstan and Williams, *Grey Wolf*, p. 278.

63. *Grey Wolf* movie, at 27 minutes 30 seconds.

64. Quoted in Dunstan and Williams, *Grey Wolf*, p. 270. See also Clark, 'The Big Read', 'Did This Woman See Hitler – Yes or No?'

65. For Hitler's diet, see Hans-Joachim Neumann and Henrik Eberle, *Was Hitler Ill? A Final Diagnosis* (Cambridge, 2013), pp. 121–6.

66. Dunstan and Williams, *Grey Wolf*, pp. 251–2; Stangneth, *Eichmann*, pp. 285–91; for the realities of the colony in Bariloche, ibid, p. 252, and Esteban Buch, *El pintor de la Suiza Argentina* (Buenos Aires, 1991).

67. Dunstan and Williams, *Grey Wolf*, pp. 271–3. The movie repeatedly cites evidence from an unnamed 'SS man' who, it claims, was Hitler's bodyguard.

68. *Grey Wolf* movie, at 42 minutes.

69. Dunstan and Williams, *Grey Wolf*, p. 323.

70. Ibid, p. 290.

71. Ibid, pp. xxiii, 286–8; http://manuelmonasterio.blogspot.co.uk/, accessed 1 March 2015.

72. https://pizzagatesite.wordpress.com/2016/12/08/shocking-evidence-that-angela-merkel-is-hitlers-daughter/; https://blogfactory.co.uk/2017/11/26/angela-merkel-is-the-daughter-of-hitler-and-hitler-was-a-rothschild/; both accessed 30 March 2020.

73. See n. 42 above.; Raedar Sognnaes and Ferdinand Ström were dentists who separately identified the teeth of Hitler and Bormann from their remains. See http://www.nl-aid.org/wp-content/uploads/2012/09/Sognnaes-2.pdf, accessed 10 March 2015. Johann Rattenhuber was Hitler's bodyguard from the SS Security Service and under interrogation by the Soviets described watching Hitler's body being burned. The SS doctor Ernst-Günther Schenck also recorded his experiences in the bunker. Traudl Junge was Hitler's secretary. Rochus Misch, the last survivor of the bunker, also interrogated by the Soviets, died in 2013.

74. *Grey Wolf* movie, at 1 hour 27 minutes.

75. See the lengthy critique by Roger Clark, along with numerous positive reviews on amazon.co.uk: http://www.amazon.com/Grey-Wolf-Escape-Adolf-Hitler/product-reviews/145490304X/ref=cm_cr_pr_btm_link_8?ie=UTF8&pageNumber=8&showViewpoints=0&sortBy=byRank Descending, accessed 5 March 2015.

76. http://gallopingfilms.com/gf/2DocSoc2.html, accessed 5 March 2015.

77. https://www.amazon.co.uk/Grey-Wolf-Escape-Adolf-Hitler/dp/B00CL DQC8I, accessed 3 February 2020; also https://en.wikipedia.org/wiki/Grey_Wolf:_The_Escape_of_Adolf_Hitler, accessed 5 June 2015.

78. http://www.thesun.co.uk/sol/homepage/features/4170977/Did-Nazi-Adolf-Hitler-live-to-old-age-in-Bariloche-Argentina.html, and http://www.dailymail.co.uk/news/article-2478100/Theory-Adolf-Hitler-fled-Argentina-lived-age-73.html, both accessed 23 February 2015.

79. See McKale's review on amazon.co.uk on 7 June 2012. Also the cogent demolition by Guy Walters, 'Did Hitler Flee Bunker with Eva to Argentina and Live to 73? The Bizarre Theory that Landed Two British Authors in a Bitter War', *Daily Mail*, 28 October 2013.

80. *Grey Wolf* movie, at 15 and 22 minutes.

81. http://www.walesonline.co.uk/news/local-news/death-threats-hitler-book-author-1806731, accessed 4 March 2015.

82. Clark, 'The Big Read', 'Enter a Millionaire Fraudster', also for the following.

83. http://www.telegraph.co.uk/finance/financial-crime/11365885/
Weavering-hedge-fund-founder-Magnus-Peterson-jailed-for-13-years-
over-fraud.html, accessed 3 March 2015; Dunstan and Williams, *Grey
Wolf*, p. 293.

84. Clark, 'The Big Read' 'Enter a Millionaire Fraudster'; see also the inform-
ative Wikipedia article on *Grey Wolf*.

85. http://www.amazon.co.uk/Jan-van-Helsing/e/B0043BV6MS, accessed 1
March 2015. See Bundesamt für Verfassungsschutz, *Argumentations-
muster im rechtsextremistischen Antisemitismus* (Cologne, 2005), p. 10.

86. Abel Basti and Jan van Helsing, *Hitler überlebte in Argentinien* (Fichtenau,
2012), p. 29.

87. Ibid, p. 33.

88. Ibid, p. 407.

89. Vanessa Thorpe, 'Hitler Lived until 1962? That's My Story, Claims
Argentinian Writer', *Guardian*, 27 October 2013. See also Annette
Reiz, solicitor, from the British Association to Bradley A. Feuer et al.,
7 May 2013, at http://www.barilochenazi.com.ar/documentos/nuevos/
24junio2013.pdf, accessed 1 March 2015. For virtually identical interview material with Ancín, see Dunstan and Williams, *Grey Wolf*,
pp. 274–6, and Basti and van Helsing, *Hitler überlebte*, pp. 337–41; or
with Batinic, *Grey Wolf*, pp. 271–3, and *Hitler überlebte*, pp. 285–91.
The interviews were adapted and edited for the movie: for Gomero, for
example, see *Grey Wolf* movie, at 27 minutes 30 seconds; for Monastero,
1 hour 23 minutes.

90. Clark, 'The Big Read', 'Why It Matters'.

91. Brian Lowry, 'TV Review: Hunting Hitler', *Variety*, 5 November 2015.
Baer is also a conspiracy theorist – though he denies being one – who
has appeared in a video being interviewed by Alex Jones, on 9/11, which
Baer appears to believe was orchestrated by Israeli agents. He also has a
television programme spreading conspiracy theories about the assassination of US President John F. Lambert, 'Hunting
Hitler', 2 February 2017, accessed 3 February 2020: https://jamesklam
bertblog.wordpress.com/2017/02/02/hunting-hitler/

92. Clark, 'The Big Read', 'The Biggest Cover-Up in History?'

93. https://en.wikipedia.org/wiki/Hunting_Hitler; https://www.renewcan
celtv.com/hunting-hitler-cancelled-history-no-season-4/

94. Clark, 'The Big Read', 'Unreliable Evidence' and ' "This is Better Evidence than we Have from the Bunker" [Not]'.

95. Ibid, 'Hitler's Secret Hideout?'

96. Ibid, 'They Seek Him Here, They Seek Him There'.

97. Fritz Hahn, *Waffen und Geheimwaffen des deutschen Heeres, 1933–1945* (2 vols., Koblenz, 1986–7), Vol. I, pp. 191–4; Mark Walker, *German National Socialism and the Quest for Nuclear Power, 1939–1945* (Cambridge, 1989). Further critiques of *Hunting Hitler* in Steven Woodbridge, on the website of Kingston University, who notes that 'If people do not co-operate with the team's inquiries, there are dark hints that such individuals may be part of the "cover-up" of the real story': see his article 'History as Hoax: Why the TV Series "Hunting Hitler" is Fiction not Fact', *History@Kingston*, posted on 8 February 2018, https://historyatkingston.wordpress.com/2018/02/08/history-as-hoax-why-the-tv-series-hunting-hitler-is-fiction-not-fact/, accessed 3 February 2020. For a further critique of the nuclear idea, see https://jkkelley.org/2018/02/06/scumbag-studies-whats-wrong-with-hunting-hitler/

98. Clark, 'The Big Read', 'Questions Hitler Conspiracy Theorists Must Answer'.

99. Jon Austin, 'Is This Hitler's Secret Argentine Bolt-Hole? Führer's Loot Found behind Hidden Doorway', *Express on Sunday*, 9 July 2017. In fact, there is nothing to show that this collection of Nazi memorabilia actually belonged to Hitler personally at all. The discovery is more accurately reported by Deborah Rey, 'Behind a Secret Door in Argentina: A Huge Nazi Treasure Trove with Connections to Hitler', *USA Today*, 20 June 2017, claiming that the 'treasure trove' probably belonged to 'high-ranking Nazis'.

100. Gerald Conzens, (Hitler "lived and died in Brazil" – author makes SENSATIONAL claims', *Daily Star*, 24 January 2014).

101. Peter Levenda, *Ratline: Soviet Spies, Nazi Priests, and the Disappearance of Adolf Hitler* (Lake Worth, FL, 2012), p. 196. Nicolas Hays, the publisher, specializes in astrology, the occult and similar themes.

102. http://nexusilluminati.blogspot.co.uk/2013/11/fabricating-hitlers-death.html, accessed 7 March 2015.

103. Uwe Backes and Patrick Moreau (eds.), *The Extreme Right in Europe: Current Trends and Perspectives* (Göttingen, 2011), pp. 403–4.

104. Jerome R. Corsi, *Hunting Hitler: New Scientific Evidence that Hitler Escaped Nazi Germany* (New York, 2014), p. 95. Farrago was characterized by intelligence historian Stephen Dorril as 'the most successful disinformer or dupe' in relation to rumours of Nazis in postwar Latin America (Stephen Dorril, *MI6: Inside the Covert World of Her Majesty's Secret Intelligence Service* (London, 2002), p. 95.

105. Corsi, *Hunting Hitler*, p. 110. A few helicopters were indeed used by the Nazis during the war. The first production model was developed by Igor Sikorski in 1942.

106. Ibid, p. 124.

107. Ibid, p. 129.

108. Ibid, pp. 131–3. The WTO was founded in 1995.

109. 'Participants in Mission, Documents, Support Kerry's War Claim', *Seattle Times*, 22 August 2004.

110. Sin Rutenberg and Julie Bosman, 'Book on Obama Hopes to Repeat '04 Anti-Kerry Feat', *The New York Times*, 12 August 2008.

111. Sarah Wheaten, 'Anti-Obama Author on 9/11 Conspiracy', *The New York Times*, 14 August 2008.

112. http://www.teaparty.org/corsibio/, accessed 20 February 2015.

113. https://www.youtube.com/watch?v=UyrncbZtZzM, accessed 20 February 2015. The OSS (Office of Strategic Services) was the wartime forerunner of the CIA (Central Intelligence Agency); 'the Bushes' are US Republican Presidents George H. W. Bush and George W. Bush, regarded by the Tea Party as 'liberals'.

114. https://en.wikipedia.org/wiki/Pizzagate_conspiracy_theory

115. https://theoutline.com/post/3831/jerome-corsi-killing-the-deep-state-infowars?zd=1&zi=lzkb7zem

116. See also the lengthy, rambling discussion, posted in 2016 by 'firestarter', on a website associated with the conspiracy theorist David Icke, *The Lawful Path Forum*: https://www.lawfulpath.com/forum/viewtopic.php?f=30&t=1082, accessed 3 February 2020. Among other things, the blogposts describe Reuters as a source of 'propaganda' fake news. Icke has also personally endorsed the view that Hitler escaped to Colombia: see for example https://www.davidicke.com/article/435069/cia-found-hitler-alive-colombia-1954-agency-told-man-familiar-face-lived-ex-ss-community-called-fuhrer-given-nazi-salutes-declass, reprinting an article by Andrew Cheetham, 1 November 2017, and the same author's article, also on David Icke's website: https://www.davidicke.com/article/532930/fbi-searched-hitler-supposed-death-declassified-documents-reveal

117. Nicholas Goodrick-Clarke, *Black Sun: Aryan Cults, Esoteric Nazism and the Politics of Identity* (New York, 2002); see also the relatively recent posting, reasserting his theories about UFOs, by Ernst Zündel, http://www.csicop.org/si/show/hitlers_south_pole_hideaway, accessed 23 February 2015. Zündel died in August 2017.

118. Arguments to the contrary by Eric Kurlander fail to convince: see Richard J. Evans, 'Nuts about the Occult', Review of Eric Kurlander, *Hitler's Monsters: A Supernatural History of the Third Reich* (New Heaven, CT, 2017), in *London Review of Books* 40 15 (2 August 2018), pp. 37–8.

119. https://rationalwiki.org/wiki/Maximillien_de_Lafayette, accessed 3 February 2020; http://maximilliendelafayettebibliography.org/biblio/, accessed 3 February 2020.

120. http://www.nizkor.org/hweb/people/z/zundel-ernst/flying-saucers/, accessed 23 February 2015.

121. Robert Ressler, with Thomas Schachtmann, *Whoever Fights Monsters: My Twenty Years Tracking Serial Killers for the FBI* (New York, 1992). For a different connection between antisemitism and the UFO subculture, see Michael Barkun, 'Anti-Semitism from Outer Space: The *Protocols* in the UFO Subculture', in Landes and Katz (eds.), *The Paranoid Apocalypse*: pp. 163–71.

122. http://www.bibliotecapleyades.net/luna/esp_luna_46.htm, accessed 24 February 2015.

123. Gavriel D. Rosenfeld, *Hi Hitler! How the Nazi Past is being Normalized in Contemporary Culture* (Cambridge, 2014), pp. 198–203.

124. Clark, 'The Big Read', 'Rubbishing the Truth'.

125. Butter, *'Nichts ist, wie es scheint'*, p. 17.

126. Michael Saler: *As If: Modern Enchantment and the Literary Prehistory of Virtual Reality* (New York, 2012).

127. Nicholas Carr, *The Shallows: What the Internet is Doing to Our Brains* (New York, 2011), p. 16, cited in Rosenfeld, *Hi Hitler!*, p. 295.

128. For Baumgart, see Daly-Groves, *Hitler's Death*, pp. 39–41, 56, noting that Baumgart was a notorious liar.

129. McKale, *Hitler*, p. 128.

130. http://www.zeit.de/1966/33/gisela-kein-hitlerkind, accessed 1 March 2015.

131. See for example https://en.mediamass.net/people/napoleon/alive.html, accessed 30 January 2020; https://forums.spacebattles.com/threads/what-if-fredrick-barbarossa-survives.652812/, accessed 30 January 2020.

132. Clark, 'The Big Read', 'Why It Matters'.

CONCLUSION

1. Butter, '*Nichts ist, wie es scheint*', p. 57; Mark Fenster, *Conspiracy Theories; Secrecy and Power in American Culture* (Minneapolis, MN, 2008), p. 119.
2. Evans, *Altered Pasts*, pp. 3–43.
3. Evans, *The Feminist Movement in Germany*, pp. 180–81.
4. These features of conspiracist techniques are outlined in Butter, '*Nichts ist, wie es scheint*', pp. 57–79.

Index